Business

Hodder INTERMEDIATE GNVQ

Business

■ NEIL DENBY   ■ PETER THOMAS

Hodder & Stoughton
A MEMBER OF THE HODDER HEADLINE GROUP

Orders: please contact Bookpoint Ltd, 78 Milton Park, Abingdon, Oxon OX14 4TD. Telephone: (44) 01235 827720, Fax: (44) 01235 400454. Lines are open from 9.00–6.00, Monday to Saturday, with a 24 hour message answering service. Email address: orders@bookpoint.co.uk

British Library Cataloguing in Publication Data
A catalogue record for this title is available from The British Library

ISBN 0 340 753153

First published 2000
Impression number   10 9 8 7 6 5 4 3 2 1
Year   2005 2004 2003 2002 2001 2000

Copyright © 2000 Neil Denby and Peter Thomas

All rights reserved. No part of this publication may be reproduced or transmitted in any form or by any means, electronic or mechanical, including photocopy, recording, or any information storage and retrieval system, without permission in writing from the publisher or under licence from the Copyright Licensing Agency Limited. Further details of such licences (for reprographic reproduction) may be obtained from the Copyright Licensing Agency Limited, of 90 Tottenham Court Road, London W1P 9HE.

Typeset by Fakenham Photosetting Ltd, Fakenham, Norfolk
Printed in Great Britain for Hodder & Stoughton Educational, a division of Hodder Headline Plc, 338 Euston Road, London NW1 3BH by
J. W. Arrowsmith, Bristol.

Aknowledgements

The authors and publisher would like to thank Julie and Chris Stephenson of Cookswell Garage, for permission to use coursework in this book.

The author and publisher would like to acknowledge the following for use of copyright material:

Corbis, pp. 29, 78, 138.
Help the Aged, p. 16.
Life File, pp. 5, 22, 35, 36, 45, 78, 79, 98.
PA News, pp. 18, 50.
Scottish Widows, p. 159.

Every effort has been made to trace copyright holders but this has not always been possible in all cases; any omissions brought to our attention will be corrected in future printings.

Contents

Unit 1 Investigating how businesses work — 1

Section A Introduction — 1

Section B Business aims and objectives — 5

1. Satisficing aims and maximising aims — 5
2. Business aims and objectives – profit — 10
3. Business aims and objectives – non-profit-making organisations — 16
4. Business aims and objectives – getting bigger — 22
5. Reviewing business objectives — 29

Section C Functional areas of business — 35

6. Marketing 1 – marketing department — 35
7. Marketing 2 – advertising and promotion — 42
8. Human resources 1 – recruitment and selection — 49
9. Human resources 2 – rights and responsibilities — 59
10. Human resources 3 – equal opportunities — 66
11. Finance department — 71
12. Administration department — 77
13. Production department — 81
14. Customer services department — 86

Section D Business communications — 90

15. Organisational structures — 90
16. Internal communication — 98
17. External communication — 104
18. Information and communications technology (ICT) — 110

Section E Case Studies — 117

Case study I Libran Music — 117
Case study II ICI — 120

Unit 2 Investigating how businesses develop — 124

Section A Introduction — 124

Section B Types of business organisation — 127

19. Sole traders — 127

20 Partnerships	133
21 Limited liability companies	138
22 The public sector	145
23 Franchises	152
24 Cooperatives	158

Section C Business context and influences   163

25 Industrial sectors	163
26 Business activity	167
27 Stakeholders	173
28 Location	178

Section D Case studies   185

Case study III Sole trader – Set yourself up!	185
Case study IV Growth of a firm – Cookswell Garage	188

Unit 3 Business finance   193

Section A Introduction   193

Section B Financial accounts   196

29 Costs and revenue	196
30 Break-even	203
31 Cash flow forecasts	209
32 Profit and loss	215
33 Financial documents used for buying goods and services	221
34 Financial documents used to sell goods and services	233

Section C Case studies   240

Case study V Hardings Ltd	240
Case study VI Nugardens Ltd	243

Key skills consolidation – Case studies   245

Case study VII Communication – The National Stadium	245
Case study VIII Application of number – Garden centres	249
Case study IX Information technology – Masterspeak and JET	256

Index   **259**

Unit 1 Investigating how businesses work

SECTION A

Introduction

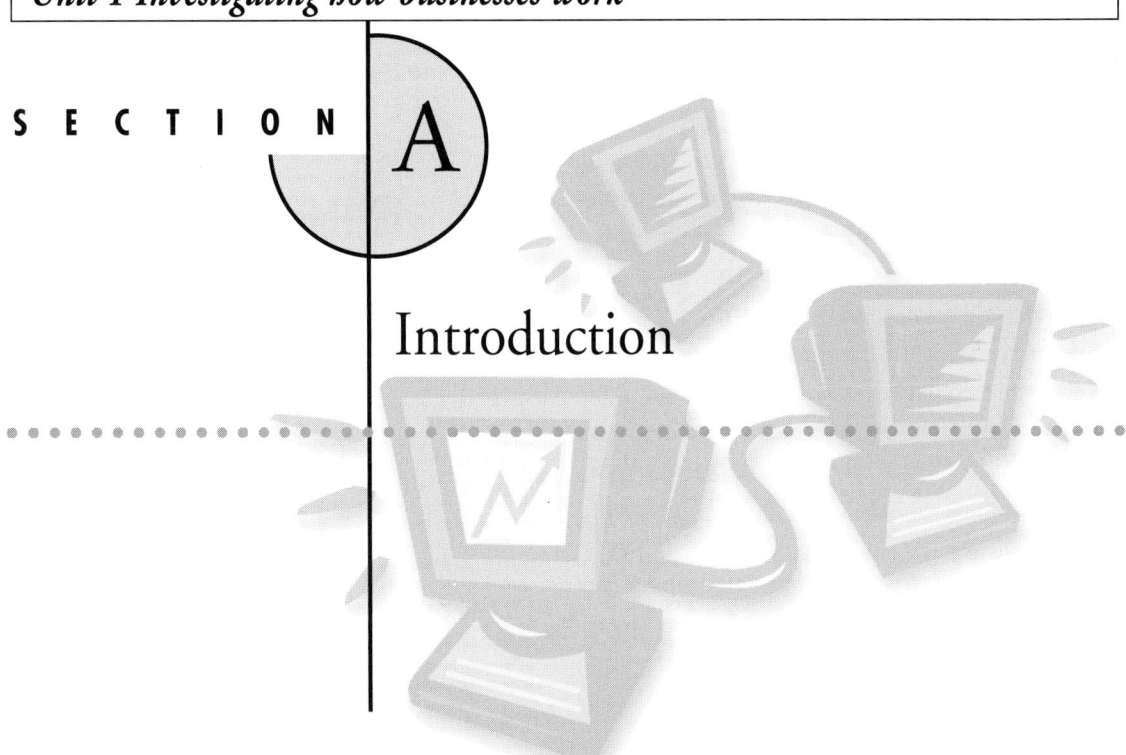

This unit requires you to investigate how businesses organise themselves to successfully meet their aims and objectives. As this unit is assessed internally within your educational institution, you will be required to collect evidence towards a portfolio. You need to present your evidence in the form of a case study. Your case study will be graded and this grade will then become your grade for the whole of Unit 1.

In your case study you are expected to investigate a large or medium-sized firm and show you understand how it works using a number of broad headings. The first five are shown below:

1. The activity, aims and objectives of a medium to large-sized firm.

2. The main functional areas (or departments) of the firm, their purposes and activities.

3. The effectiveness of the departments' communications.

4. The organisational structure of the firm.

5. A record of your sources of information.

You will have to prepare your case study using at least four methods of presentation, eg text, charts, pictures and diagrams. It is not compulsory to use IT methods of presentation but it is advisable to do so.

Finally, you are also expected to:

6. Give an oral, illustrated presentation comparing the customer service in your chosen business with best practice.

What do you have to do?

The main part of the written case study requires you to show that you understand how your chosen firm works, starting with its main activities and setting out its aims. You then need to show how the firm sets objectives to help achieve its aims, with the objectives linked to the purposes and activities of the departments within the firm. You must describe the human resources department and any three other departments, but not including customer service. In your description of the human resources department, you also need to explain the impact on both employer and employee of four employment laws. For all departments you need to give brief descriptions of typical job roles in each.

As part of your case study you will need to describe and illustrate the organisational structure of the firm, and this then needs to be compared with other structural models and, if possible, you need to evaluate the strengths and weaknesses of the firm's structure. Finally, in this written part of the case study you need to describe at least six different types of communication being used within the firm, covering both paper-based and ICT methods. Within this description you need to show why the types are appropriate, how they help the firm meet its objectives, and you need to evaluate the strengths and weaknesses of the different types.

Your oral presentation needs to be illustrated with images to help make your key points. You need to describe the ways in which the firm attempts to meet customer expectations. Try to compare this with 'best practice' so that you are able to evaluate the customer care and service being offered and, if it is relevant, suggest some realistic improvements that the firm might make.

How will this textbook help your preparations for the case study?

Each chapter for this unit will give you all the knowledge you need to help build up your understanding of how a firm works. The first chapters look at the aims and objectives in some detail so you will be able to understand the mixture of aims and objectives that your chosen firm has set itself. The next chapters describe the main departments or functional areas of a wide variety of firms so you should be able to read the descriptions of the typical functions and activities of all the departments together with some general job roles. This should then enable you to apply the information to those departments in your chosen firm. The final chapters describe the variety of organisational structures used by firms and the extensive forms of both internal and external communications used by firms and their departments.

All chapters have progress checks and some have key skill activities to take you through the unit in a logical way building up your knowledge and understanding and helping you to begin your collection of evidence. Early on in each chapter, there are descriptions of what you need to do to achieve pass, merit- or distinction-level work. These descriptions will help to guide you as you start to undertake the work on the unit and the student checklists at the end of each chapter will act as reminders. Chevrons are used with the progress checks to indicate ▶ pass, ▶▶ merit and ▶▶▶ distinction levels. Each chapter also has a list of key terms, which may be used as a reference tool at any time.

The textbook is packed with real-world illustrations of the content you need to cover for this unit. These may be used either as a starting point for the collection of information on a specific firm mentioned in the text or as a guideline on the information that might be available from other firms not included. Remember – you have to describe just one firm in your case study although comparisons may need to be made with others, and this is where the text in the chapters will particularly help you.

A checklist of evidence for your case study

You need to:

- Describe the activity, aims and objectives of your chosen business.
- Describe the human resources department – what it does, why and how; how it contributes to the business and a brief description of at least four job roles in this department.
- Describe three other departments (not including customer service) – what they do, why and how; how they contribute to the business and brief descriptions of at least four job roles for each department.
- Show how the departments interact with each other to achieve the firm's aims and objectives.
- Describe the purposes and impact of four employment and equal opportunities laws on both employer and employees.
- Explain one issue, using an example of a situation, relating to each of the four acts – The Employment Rights Act 1996, The Sex Discrimination Act 1975, The Race Relations Act 1976 and The Disability Discrimination Act 1995.
- Describe how the departments in the firm communicate with each other and with people and organisations outside the firm, using at least six different types, covering both paper-based and ICT, explaining the nature and content of the form of communication and why its use is appropriate.
- Explain how effective communication helps the firm achieve its aims and objectives and evaluate the forms of communication being used by your chosen firm.
- Describe the organisational structure of the firm and compare the basic features with a different structure for another firm.
- Evaluate the structure of your chosen firm explaining how it might affect its success in achieving its aims and objectives.
- Give an oral description of the firm's consumer service, showing how it meets customer requirements, and suggesting improvements when you compare it with best practice.
- Use illustrations in your oral presentation that help explain key features.
- Keep a record of all the sources of information you use for the preparation of the case study and oral presentation.
- Try to show an overall, coherent understanding of how your chosen business works.

What about the key skills?

The key skills that are signposted in the unit specifications (Communication, Information Technology and Application of Number) are set out in key skill activities in the relevant chapters for this unit. They may be integrated with your portfolio evidence for the case study quite easily. For example, the illustrated talk on customer service will cover the Communication key skill listed, while your inclusion of organisational charts, tables and diagrams will be evidence for the IT key skill if you create them using appropriate computer software. Finally, you might collect information on your firm from IT sources using CD-ROMs such as the Times 100 or from the Internet; and so in this way cover another IT key skill involving you collecting information from a computer-based source.

Remember to combine all this advice and guidance with the specifications provided by your awarding body and your teacher/lecturer. Plan your work and check that you are attempting all the items so that you maximise your chances of achieving a distinction.

Section B Business aims and objectives

CHAPTER 1

Satisficing aims and maximising aims.

Tesco expands its Internet business

Tesco, Britain's leading supermarket chain, has announced a strategy intended to speed up the introduction of Internet shopping to its 100 UK stores. The scheme has been tried out in 30 supermarkets and is already responsible for 7% of Tesco's turnover in the trial areas. Tesco has taken the Internet initiative as one of the ways to combat the increased competition from its main rivals, in particular Asda. As well as the Internet strategy, Tesco is expanding its non-food lines – selling goods such as clothes and luggage bought from the Far East. It has also been at the forefront of trying to lower the prices of branded goods like Levi jeans and Adidas trainers by buying stocks of these outside Europe and then selling them cheaply in its stores.

Tesco's main rivals are Sainsbury's and Asda. Sainsbury's is the second largest supermarket chain, having lost its market leader's position to Tesco in 1995. They are currently suffering a downturn in profits as they feel the

FIGURE 1.1 *Asda: a major rival for Tesco*
Source: Emma Lee/Life File

effect of an unsuccessful advertising campaign and the failure of some of their experiments in expansion. Shares in Sainsbury's have lost a third of their value in the previous twelve months and this has wiped over £3 billion off the market value of the company.

The third major player, Asda, has recently been taken over by the American giant Walmart and has set out on a programme of across-the-board price cuts, following Walmart's philosophy of low prices and high turnover. Tesco is responding with price cuts of their own and some new strategies.

Micromagic

Micromagic is a very small firm. It has one employee – its owner and founder Jenny Church. Jenny has two small children at primary school. Jenny used to work for a supermarket as an IT specialist but, although the pay and conditions were excellent, she found that her home life was suffering and that child care costs were wiping out much of what she earned.

Jenny left her job three months ago and established her own business, providing IT advice and solutions to small firms. She advertised her services on the Internet and built up a small group of clients. This week she removed her advertisement. 'I don't want any more clients', she said. 'I have enough to work from 9 till 3 and can then go and pick up the children. My quality of life has greatly improved.'

What you need to do

- **To gain a pass** you need to be able to show that you can describe clearly the aims and objectives of a business.
- **To gain a merit** you need to be able to explain clearly how the different functional areas of a business interact to achieve aims and objectives.
- **To gain a distinction** you need to evaluate the strengths and weaknesses of a business and explain how these may affect its success in reaching aims and objectives.

What are business objectives?

A business will exist in order to provide goods or services to consumers. Such goods or services must be what consumers want and what they are willing to pay for; they must be supplied at a time and place that is convenient to the consumer and at a price that the consumer is willing to pay. They must be produced at a cost that the business can afford. If a firm succeeds in providing such goods and services, is it likely to have fulfilled its aims? In most cases, the answer is no. A firm will have other objectives that it aims to reach.

Setting objectives

Business organisations need to know where they are, where they want to be and how they intend to get there.

An organisation needs to take measurements of where it is now – to do this it can use its own internal information, external market analysis, market research or 'benchmark' its performance against other organisations in similar businesses.

It must then decide where it wants to be – and when. The long-term objective may be to gain the largest market share, or maximise profit, or to be the best in a particular field. Short-term targets may also involve profit, or providing a service or, in some cases, just surviving.

> **GET IT RIGHT!** ✓
>
> The long-term objective of a firm may be stated in fairly vague terms – 'to be the best in the world'; 'to seek to find new processes'; 'to be as environmentally friendly as possible'. More short-term objectives are likely to be measurable so that the firm will know when it has achieved them. These could be aims such as 'to increase market share by 10%'; 'to improve sales to reach a turnover of £1 million'. These aims can be seen as intermediate targets which need to be reached if the firm is to keep on track in meeting its main objective.

Reaching objectives

Strategies are the ways and means that businesses devise to reach their objectives – what might be called the methods that they use. The two firms at the start of this chapter are trying for two very different types of objective. Jenny Church is seeking a satisficing objective – this means that she is not aiming for the 'most' of anything, but for a level of income that is enough to satisfy her needs. Typically, a small trader will be looking for satisficing objectives. Tesco is seeking a maximising objective – in other words, making the most of something. It is trying to maximise its market share in the supermarket sector – and achieved this when it became the largest supermarket chain in Britain. It is trying to penetrate the Internet market – being the first into a new market often allows a company to maximise its market share and to maximise its profits.

It could also be looking at minimising objectives – trying to make the impact of a negative factor as small as possible. In the case of the example it could be trying to minimise the effect of the price reductions brought about by Walmart after it took over Asda. It is doing this by following with its own price cuts and by extending into areas where it does not have as much competition, in particular non-food goods such as clothes.

> **GET IT RIGHT!** ✓
>
> Businesses may have mission statements, stated aims, vision statements, trading charters, corporate goals etc. They are basically all the same thing, stating the objectives of the firm and the corporate culture in which it operates.
>
> Corporate culture is the 'atmosphere' in which a firm operates. It may be a company that relies on aggressive sales techniques – the 'hard sell'; it may be a company that relies on its technological reputation 'being at the cutting edge'; it may be a company that promotes an image of caring and support for issues such as the environment.

Stating objectives

A small business, for example a corner shop, butcher's, baker's or service provider such as a plumber or electrician, may not state their targets in writing. They will, however, know why they are in business. Their reasons are likely to be satisficing reasons such as independence (being your own boss), wanting to provide a service, earning enough money. They are not likely to have maximising targets, like having the biggest market share. An electrician is unlikely to be looking to put all the other electricians in his town out of business, for example.

Bigger firms are likely to have bigger objectives. The major one is likely to be the maximisation of profit. This is covered in detail in the next chapter. Other objectives may be formally written down in a 'mission statement' which outlines the general long-term aim of the business or in a 'trading charter' or 'code of practice'.

Kodak, the leading camera company, has a Corporate Vision Statement that says 'Our heritage has been and our future is to be the world leader in imaging' – saying that they have always been the best in the world and always will be. Their mission statement ends with the promise that 'In this way we will achieve our fundamental objective of Total Customer Satisfaction and our consequent goals of Increased Global Market Share and Superior Financial Performance.' It is obvious that their major targets include increasing market share and increasing returns to shareholders.

Other businesses may have different goals, such as social or ethical ones.

COMMUNICATIONS *activity*

Look at the list of objectives shown in the checklist and at the information on Micromagic, above. Write a set of 10 interview questions for a local business and interview the businessperson to find out what his or her objectives are. You could tape-record the interview (with the interviewee's permission) to play back to your tutor. In a group, discuss the different types of objective that you have found. Whose chosen organisation had the clearest objectives? Whose was the most ambitious? What was the main type of objective? You should keep a neat record of the questions (and your reasons for asking them) and the answers (and your interpretation of them) as this could be used in your case study.

(C1.1)

IT *activity*

Use a selection of company reports to see what the stated objectives of a number of limited companies are. How do they differ from the objectives of small traders?

Using on-line or CD-ROM-based resources find an image that a company uses to reinforce its corporate culture – for example, a company with an environmentally friendly culture might show a picture of a whale or a dolphin or a rain forest. A company with a reputation for technology might picture a new machine.

Using the same sources, find images that you think best show the corporate culture of a number of different firms. You could display the information under three headings – image, company, objective – as a table or as a wall display.

(IT1.1)

SATISFICING AIMS AND MAXIMISING AIMS

PROGRESS CHECK

1. ▶ Write an introductory paragraph which outlines the following:
   - the main objectives of a business such as Tesco
   - the main objectives of a business such as Micromagic
   - the main objectives of a business that you have chosen for yourself.

   What is the main difference between satisficing aims and maximising aims?

2. ▶▶ Write a paragraph to explain how the main activities of the business are affected by its objectives.

3. ▶▶▶ Explain what is meant by the term 'corporate culture'. Why do you think that particular businesses have particular types of corporate culture?

Key terms

OBJECTIVE – an organisation's target or aim.

STRATEGY – the ways and means that businesses devise to reach their objectives.

SATISFICING – being satisfied with a certain outcome.

MAXIMISING – making or wanting to make the most of something.

MISSION STATEMENT – sets out the general objectives of an organisation and how it might reach them.

CORPORATE CULTURE – the way in which an organisation operates.

STUDENT CHECKLIST

The main objectives that businesses will try to achieve are:

1. **Satisficing objectives** – these are when a business reaches a point where it is happy with what it is achieving. They are targets such as:
   - independence
   - survival
   - breaking even
   - providing a good service.

2. **Maximising objectives** – these are when a firm tries to make the most of something, for example:
   - sales of a product or service
   - market share
   - profit.

3. **Challenging objectives** – these are when a firm sets itself targets as challenges, such as:
   - maintaining the best possible quality of goods or services
   - providing a better service than a competitor
   - providing a cheaper service than a competitor
   - being an environmentally friendly firm
   - being a socially aware firm.

CHAPTER 2

Business aims and objectives – profit

Restaurants and radios don't mix

Capital Radio, the London-based independent radio station, made a decision in 1996 to expand into the restaurant business. It bought a chain of restaurants (called 'My Kinda Town') for £55 million. The idea was that the restaurant would provide music (from Capital's entertainment business) and would allow customers to see its DJs at work. However, investors were not impressed by the move and Capital's share price fell.

In 1999, Capital Radio sold off almost all of its restaurants in order to 'cut its losses'. It sold its six restaurants selling Latin-American-style food in London, Manchester, Liverpool and Glasgow to the SFI Group – a business which specialises in the licensed trade – for a total of £9.45 million. A further two restaurants in Paris – The Chicago Pizza Pie Factory and Chicago Meatpackers – were sold to a French restaurant business, Groupe Bertrand, for £1.6 million. This has meant that the restaurant division of Capital is now closed, although it has kept its four radio cafés, in London, Birmingham and Southampton so that they can be used to help market the radio station and host appearances by Capital's DJs.

The Chief Executive of Capital Radio said that the company had been concentrating on building strong brands but would now be focusing its attention solely on its radio business.

Capital has been intending to sell the business for some time after having to decrease its value on paper twice in the previous two

FIGURE 2.1

years. Overall, the company's shareholders will have lost around £35 million on the experiment.

What you need to do

- **To gain a pass** you need to be able to show that you can describe clearly the aims and objectives of a business; these aims include profit.
- **To gain a merit** you also need to be able to explain clearly how the different functional areas of a business interact to achieve its aims and objectives.
- **To gain a distinction** you also need to evaluate the strengths and weaknesses of a business and explain how these may affect its success in reaching its aims and objectives.

What is profit?

A business organisation has to pay for certain things such as its supplies, its premises, its rents, its taxes and its staff. These are the costs to the business. It will be selling a good or service and receiving amounts of money for so doing; this is the revenue of the business. If revenue is greater than cost, then the firm is making a profit. If revenue equals cost, the firm may be said to be breaking even; if revenue is less than cost then the firm is making a loss.

GET IT RIGHT! ✓

Don't get confused over the definition of profit. Think of it as if you were in business. If you bought ten chocolate bars at 10p each and then sold them at 12p each you would have costs of £1 and revenues of £1.20. You would have made a profit of 20p. If you sold them at 8p each you would still have revenue (80p), although you would have no profit but a loss of 20p. It is quite usual for firms making a loss to still have revenue coming in.

Profit or loss?

Look at the figures relating to Capital Radio's attempt to enter the restaurant business. They paid £55 million for the chain and sold it for approximately £11 million – a loss of £44 million. Yet the figures quoted say that they have only lost £35 million on the experiment. How can this be so?

It is because the group has received some revenue from the restaurants. The restaurants are open for business, they have been selling food which customers have been paying for. They have been taking money. Therefore, in business terms, there has been a stream of revenue.

This revenue was not, however, enough to offset all the costs of the group. Some costs have nothing to do with the operation of the restaurants – such as the cost of buying the businesses in the first place or the rents on the properties where the restaurants are situated. So, while a restaurant may be making a profit, the group could be making a loss.

COMMUNICATIONS
activity

Write two different accounts of Capital Radio's sell-off of its restaurant businesses. One account should be in the form of a letter to shareholders, explaining why Capital has decided to sell. The other should be in the form of a press release. The press release would be upbeat about the sale, as Capital would want the newspapers to treat it as a positive move on their behalf.

(C1.3)

The profit motive

Did you manage to avoid the mention of profit when completing the exercises in Chapter 1? It is unlikely that you did, as profit is seen as one of the major reasons for firms to be in business and as one of the major objectives of some organisations. It is, however, not the only objective, as you have seen, and was deliberately given a chapter of its own so that you could concentrate on the other important objectives that a firm may have.

The profit motive is often given as the single most important reason for a firm to be in business, with profit maximisation being the ultimate goal of many organisations. Many of the other objectives – efficiency, quality, market share, market domination – will help to contribute to profits if they are reached. However, while some organisations are undoubtedly in business for profit, not even all of these are necessarily trying to maximise profit. Many will be happy with reaching a certain level of profit.

Who benefits?

Profit is seen as the reward for enterprise. The person who takes the risk – introducing a new product, a new type of market, a new process – is called the entrepreneur; profit is the reward for (successful) risk-taking.

Risk-takers tend to be the owners of a business. Shareholders are the people who own shares in a business and who have risked their money by buying shares. Profit is therefore a reward to shareholders and much of it will be paid to them in the form of dividends.

'Dividend' just means that the profit is divided into equal amounts according to the number of shares there are in the company. Each shareholder then gets a part of the profit for each share that they hold. The more shares, the more risk has been taken, the greater the amount of dividend paid.

IT activity

Using the two documents that you prepared for the Communication exercise on page 12, prepare the same two documents using Information Technology. You should include text, at least one image and the use of numbers.

(IT1.2)

Gross and net profit

Profit is shown on a business balance sheet as follows:

- Gross profit minus Expenses equals Net Profit.
- Gross profit is revenue from sales minus the cost of sales (the cost of ingredients, parts etc.).
- Expenses include fixed costs or overheads.
- Net Profit is, therefore, revenue minus all operating costs (cost of sales and overheads) and is sometimes called Operating Profit.

GET IT RIGHT!

Even though a firm may be looking like it has made a profit, it is the net or operating profit that is important. In the example shown before, you started with 10 chocolate bars bought at 10p each and sold at 12p. This looks like a profit of 2p per bar or 20p. However, if it took you half an hour to sell them and your labour is worth £2 an hour, you are actually making a loss of (£1 – 20p) 80p. If you also had to rent somewhere to sell them from, had to travel to a supplier to buy them, had to provide advertising and promotion, you can see that very quickly you are not making a profit but a loss. Operating profit takes all costs into account.

Retained profit

Some profit will not be distributed to the owners of a business but will be kept or 'retained' for use within the business. Such retained profit may be used for buying new machinery, research and development or as a source of finance so that the firm does not have to borrow money and pay interest. Companies need to make sure that the level of dividend payment is enough to keep their shareholders happy but also not too much so that some profit can be retained for internal investment.

COMMUNICATIONS activity

'Profit is the main reason why any business is in business'. Use this statement as the basis for a class discussion about profit. You should be able to take a point of view on the

question, clearly express it and listen and respond to what other people in your group say.

Write down what you think the general feeling of the group was – did members of the group tend to agree or disagree with the statement?

(C2.1a)

Profit as a signal

If a business is making a lot of profit, this is often taken as a sign by other businesses that they should be entering that particular market. In theory, when they do enter the market, competition will force prices down so that only normal profits will be made. However, many businesses try to protect their market either by law, through patents and copyrights, or by ensuring that they control supplies of raw materials, the necessary technology and/or the consumers themselves (this is one reason why businesses try to establish strong brands). Profit can therefore be seen as a kind of traffic light – a lot of profit being made is a signal for firms to enter the market, losses are a signal for firms to leave it. The losses being made by Capital's restaurant operation meant that it had to leave that particular market.

PROGRESS CHECK

1. ▶ List the reasons that Capital Radio may have had for buying a chain of restaurants. (Capital's core business is music broadcasting and entertainment promotion.)

2. ▶▶ Explain which of the reasons do you think was most important to them, and why? Which do you think was least important, and why?

3. ▶▶ Outline the groups of people who you think will benefit most from Capital Radio's decision to sell the restaurants. Who do you think will suffer the most? Give reasons for your answer.

4. ▶▶▶ Compare Capital Radio's reasons and objectives with another firm of your own choosing. What are the similarities? What are the differences?

5. ▶▶▶ 'The profit motive is the main reason why most firms are in business, all other reasons are secondary.' Discuss this statement with regard to at least two firms that you are familiar with.

Key terms

REVENUE – money received from sales.

PROFIT – when total revenue is greater than total cost, the firm is making a profit.

GROSS PROFIT – total revenue minus cost of sales.

NET (OPERATING) PROFIT – gross profit minus overheads.

ENTREPRENEUR – the person who provides the ideas or 'enterprise'.

DIVIDEND – the portion of profit given to each share after it has been divided up.

 **STUDENT CHECKLIST**

1. Profit is a major motive for organisations to stay in business.

2. Profit maximisation may not always be the goal.

3. There are objectives other than profit.

4. Operating profit (net profit) is more important than gross profit.

5. It is good practice for a firm to retain some profit if possible, to provide an internal source of finance.

6. Profit can act as a signal for other firms to enter a competitive market. A lack of profit can act as a signal for firms to leave.

CHAPTER 3

Business aims and objectives – non-profit-making organisations

Help the Aged

The leaflet shown (Figure 3.1) is typical of many that will be delivered to households up and down the UK almost every day. It is issued by an organisation called Help the Aged and is part of their 'Adopt a Granny' campaign. The aim of Help the Aged is stated as to 'provide practical support to help older people live independent lives, particularly those who are frail, isolated or poor'. The particular campaign shown says that sponsor's donations will be used to improve the lives of over 25,000 people who are elderly and needy. The money is needed to pay for food, clean clothes and proper medical care for individuals as well as helping to raise the standard of living for the whole community.

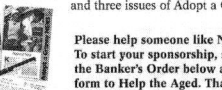

FIGURE 3.1 *Help the Aged leaflet*

What you need to do

- **To gain a pass** you need to be able to show that you can describe clearly the aims and objectives of businesses, including the special aims and objectives of non-profit-making organisations.
- **To gain a merit** you also need to be able to explain clearly how the different functional areas of a non-profit-making organisation can interact to achieve its aims and objectives.
- **To gain a distinction** you also need to evaluate the strengths and weaknesses of a non-profit-making organisation and explain how these may affect its success in reaching its aims and objectives.

Not a business?

Help the Aged is a registered charity – meaning that its name and aims are recorded with a government-appointed group called the Charity Commissioners. It is not in business to make a profit. In fact, it may be said that it is not 'in business' at all. However, it is an organisation that has employees, an income, expenditure, aims and objectives, organisation, communication, marketing (of which Figure 3.1 is an example), products and services. It is run on business lines seeking efficiency, value for money and business objectives. Objectives may be stated in a way that make them unachievable ('to bring justice to all victims of injustice, wherever they may be in the world' is an example), but this does not stop the organisation from seeking to reach the objective, from working towards it.

Non-profit-making bodies in the private

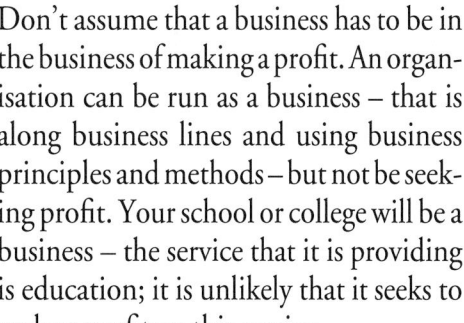

GET IT RIGHT! ✓

Don't assume that a business has to be in the business of making a profit. An organisation can be run as a business – that is along business lines and using business principles and methods – but not be seeking profit. Your school or college will be a business – the service that it is providing is education; it is unlikely that it seeks to make a profit on this service.

sector include both charity and voluntary organisations.

Charities

Charities are usually involved with a particular issue or type of issue (Help the Aged obviously targets its support at old people). Sometimes an organisation is a charity because of the service it provides; some schools, for example, have charitable status – their aim will be to produce a good-quality education but not to make a profit. Surprisingly, some public schools (where parents have to pay fees, such as Eton) are registered charities. This is because all the income they receive goes into providing the educational service that they offer.

Major charities, such as Oxfam (which began as the Oxford fund for the relief of Famine), Amnesty International, Save the Children Fund and Guide Dogs for the Blind, are household names. They exist to provide services where government or private industry is unable or unwilling to provide them. In the case of government, this is usually on cost or political considerations; in the case of private industry, it is because there are no profits to be made.

Charities will be involved in a mixture of campaigning – for changes in the law, for better deals for certain sections of society (or animals, or birds etc) or on specific issues – or in the collection and redistribution of resources.

Greenpeace International is a good example of a campaigning charity. It operates ships and aeroplanes and conducts its own research into problems. These problems are seen as those that threaten the planet or species (including humans) on the planet – a very wide brief. Campaigns have focused on things such as toxic or nuclear waste, the killing of seals or whales, the use of pesticides, or the dangers of asbestos. Greenpeace believes in a headline-grabbing policy of 'direct action' (for example, its anti-whale-hunting campaign involved getting boats between the whalers and the whales). It is manned, however, by volunteers with only a very small number of paid staff.

Other charities will concentrate on collecting money or goods in order to provide a particular service. The Red Cross, for example, provides medical assistance in war or conflict to either side without bias and collects money through voluntary donations for its mission. The Samaritans provides help for people who are threatening suicide, Childline was established so that children being abused could get help.

Some organisations concentrate on the redistribution of income to the needy – Help the Aged may be seen as one of these, along with organisations like the Salvation Army and Oxfam. The collection of such income may be made in a number of ways – door-to-door collections, collections of bags of clothes, toys etc, flag days or major 'one-off' events such as Live Aid, Red Nose Day or BBC Children in Need.

There are a number of medical charities which can perhaps be classified separately in that objectives may be achievable. The breast cancer awareness charity or the Macmillan Nurses (who tend to cancer patients) would no longer be needed if a cure for cancer were to be found.

COMMUNICATIONS *activity*

Collect some other leaflets or publicity material for various different charitable organisations. Compare them with the leaflet that is shown on page 16. What are the similarities? What are the differences? What sort of things do the writers of the leaflets appeal to? The leaflets could be displayed in your portfolio with an explanation of which you think is most effective and why.

(C1.2)

FIGURE 3.2 *Children in Need*

Source: PA News

Voluntary organisations

Volunteers are people who offer to work for no pay. They may, however, gain longer term benefits from voluntary work, such as experience. VSO (Voluntary Service Overseas) is one such organisation which encourages young and newly qualified volunteers to spend some time in a country where their skills (such as engineering, education and medicine) are needed. The volunteers gain valuable experience. Some volunteers may just want to help. Some volunteer organisations are charities while others may not be. For example, the Lions is an organisation that exists to raise money for causes. Membership is voluntary but it is not a charity. For many volunteers, the experience gained in a voluntary capacity will help them in their ordinary career; for many others, it is the act of helping someone else which is important.

Providing a service

Some organisations concentrate on providing an excellent service. These may include charities (such as the RNLI, providing lifeboat services throughout the British Isles) and voluntary bodies, as well as some business organisations. Organisations such as The Consumers' Association concentrate on providing a service to anyone who is a consumer. Much of their revenue is raised through the sale of their magazine *Which?*. If the objective of the organisation is to provide a service then many organisations may be said to be achieving their objective constantly. This contrasts with those organisations where objectives are too far-reaching to be achievable.

IT *activity*

Look at the leaflets or publicity information that you collected. Now use a word-processing or desk-top-publishing program to write two leaflets of your own. The leaflets should be for the same charity or voluntary organisation but should contain different types of appeal – either to different groups of society or to different emotional 'triggers'.

(IT1.2)

Pressure groups

Pressure groups are single-issue organisations that are formed to try to sway public opinion or government policy on particular issues. Some have a very narrow focus (such as stopping a new motorway from being built, or a piece of woodland from being destroyed); some – like Greenpeace or Amnesty International – have a very wide range ('saving the Earth' is not a very focused objective).

Pressure groups which achieve their objectives are no longer needed and often disband. If your issue was to prevent the building of a road and the road is abandoned, then the need for the pressure group has gone.

IT *activity*

Search on the Internet for factual information regarding your chosen charity or voluntary group. This should include words, figures and images. Select the most suitable information to enhance the two leaflets that you have planned and produce new leaflets using it. Printouts of this work, explaining what you have selected and why, could be included in your portfolio.

(IT2.1)

Public sector businesses

Some organisations are owned or run by government but do not attempt to make a profit. This includes essential services, such as defence, as well as services to various parts of the economy. There are organisations that are set up and funded by government, accountable (in most instances) to government, that have a public duty to provide a particular service. Examples of such organisations include the National Parks Authority, the National Rivers Authority and The Countryside Commission.

Criticisms are made of such bodies because their members are appointed by government – they are not elected, nor do they go through a selection procedure, but are invited to serve by government. Also, there is no incentive for such bodies to be efficient or fair.

GET IT RIGHT! ✓

Don't confuse charitable groups, voluntary groups and campaigning or pressure groups. Charities provide goods or services to help others less fortunate. They may have paid staff and administration and must be registered as charities with the Charity Commissioners. Voluntary groups can be anything from the Women's Institute and the Scout movement to the group which comes together once a year to collect firewood for a sports clubs money-raising bonfire. Campaigning or pressure groups exist in order to try and get things that they don't like or don't want changed.

NHS

The National Health Service is a non-profit-making body that can be considered as a special case. It is funded through National Insurance Contributions paid by all employed workers. The government decides on the allocation of the money but, apart from that, does not interfere in the day-to-day running of the Health Service. Local Health Authorities are expected to manage their own budgets, once allocated, as efficiently as possible.

COMMUNICATIONS
activity

Use the leaflets that you have created and the information that you have collected to give a short talk on your chosen charity or voluntary group to the rest of your group. You could keep a record of this either by tape-recording the talk or by writing up the notes that you use for the talk and putting these in your portfolio.

(C2.1b)

PROGRESS CHECK

1. ▶ List the different types of non-profit-making organisations.

2. ▶ Explain why you think these organisations do not wish to make a profit.

3. ▶▶ Functional departments in a profit-making business involve finance, human resources, marketing, administration, production and customer services. Which of these functions do you think is likely to be most important to a charity?

information necessarily become more complex.

It may also be the case that there are many levels of management in a large firm, this could mean either that no-one is really sure as to who is responsible for what, or that no-one is certain of their own responsibilities and therefore do not have the confidence to take decisions. A firm that diversifies – that is, goes into the production of something that is not really linked to its core business (conglomerate integration, see below) – can find itself pulling in several directions at once, causing inefficiency and uncertainty.

Internal growth

Firms may grow internally; this is called organic growth. It means that a firm will use its own resources (retained profits) and grow in the field where its core business lies. This method of growth does not involve the takeover of other businesses or business mergers.

GET IT RIGHT! ✓

Buying in bulk means buying in large amounts. This means that a business can buy at a lower unit cost. For example, a café selling baked beans could buy the stock it needs for a week in 200 400-gram tins at 20p each – a cost of £40.00. Alternatively, it could buy 20 4000-gram tins at £1.50 each – a cost of £30.00. The unit cost has therefore fallen from 5p per 100 grams to 3.75p. A larger firm might be able to gain even more by going for a bigger size again!

It tends to be a slower method for growth but one which is much less risky.

It could grow through good marketing and sales, through introducing a wider range of products or by being the first to develop or to use new technology.

Being first into a market can give a firm an enormous advantage. Providing the product being sold is successful, being first in a market can give a firm a dominant market position and major market share before any competitors are able to enter the market. The Microsoft corporation, for example, was the first into the field of personal computers with first the Dos and then the Windows operating systems, and the first to introduce a low-cost web browser. These firsts have given it complete dominance over this market. This advantage can sometimes be protected in law through the use of patents or copyrights, preventing other people from stealing or using an invention.

IT *activity*

Find as much information as you can on Japanese spending patterns. Find as much information as you can on Boots, including any reasons that it has given for expanding, particularly into Japan. Arrange the information in such a way that you can easily access it.

(IT2.1)

External growth

This is when an organisation gets larger by combining with other organisations. This could be either through merging with another company (where both businesses are given equal status) or by taking over another company. Take-overs may be agreed (where benefits can be gained by both parties) or hostile (where the 'victim' does not wish to be taken over). In the case of a hostile take-over, where both firms have shareholders, a firm has to declare its intention to buy out the other firm and make a firm offer for its shares. If the shareholders agree (because the offer is high enough) then the take-over can take place. In some cases, with big take-overs, the government body called the Competition Commission (previously the Monopolies and Mergers Commission) will look into the businesses to make sure that a business is not gaining an unfair amount of control over a market.

Integration

The joining together or merging of two firms is called integration.

- Horizontal integration is where a business joins with another at the same level of production. For example, a sweet manufacturer joining with another sweet manufacturer.
- Vertical integration is where a business joins with another that is at a different stage of production. For example, a sweet manufacturer going vertically backwards to a cocoa grower; a sweet manufacturer going vertically forwards to a sweet retailer.
- Lateral integration is when the products are related but not the same. For example, a sweet manufacturer joining with an ice-cream manufacturer. Both could be said to be in the same 'snacks' market, but the products are not really substitutes for each other.

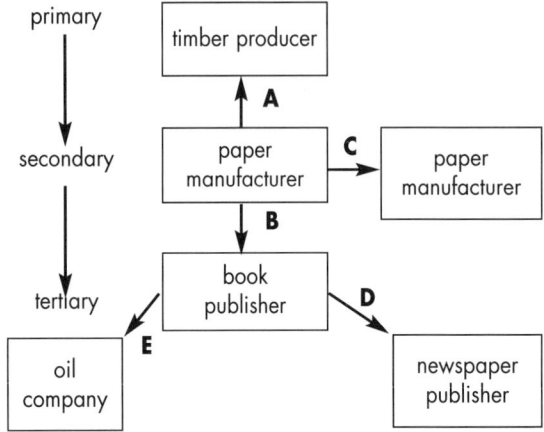

A backward vertical integration
B forward vertical integration
C horizontal integration
D lateral integration
E conglomerate integration

FIGURE 4.3 *Integration diagram*

- Conglomerate integration or diversification is when a company buys into something with which it has no connection. For example, a sweet manufacturer buying a chain of record shops.

Japanese women have much higher salaries than their European counterparts. However, they do not spend these salaries on houses, cars or holidays as many European women would. House prices are so high in Japan, due to the premium prices set on building land, that single women tend to live at home with their families. Car ownership in the already overcrowded roads is discouraged and single women are not encouraged to travel abroad alone. All these factors mean that the Japanese woman has a lot more disposable income to spend on 'luxuries' such as clothes, electrical goods and cosmetics.

How do you think that this information affected Boots' decision to expand into Japan? In a small group discuss the benefits and drawbacks of this pattern of expenditure to a firm like Boots. You may need to collect more information from sources explaining Japanese spending patterns or from Boots' own reports to make the discussion properly informed.

(C1.3a)

Not growing

In some cases, businesses decide that they would rather stay small. There are tens of thousands of small firms in the UK. Most stay small for one or more of the following main reasons:

- They may have only just started up and have every intention of growing larger as soon as they can.
- Their owners may have reached their satisficing targets and not want any more work or responsibility – the bigger a firm is, the harder it is to manage, the more responsibility and worry there is, the more staff are needed and so on. Some owners will be happy with what they have got.
- Small firms may be providing a personal or local service – hairdressing, painting, plumbing, building, motor vehicle maintenance are all examples. They may also be selling to a small or limited market, in many instances because they are selling specialised goods or services. Such small markets are called 'niche' markets.
- Small businesses may be providing component parts or materials for large businesses. The size of the business will therefore be limited by the demands from their customers.

- Sometimes a firm may decide that it has grown too large and decide to cut out some of its activities. In extreme cases a demerger might happen. This means that two companies that have joined together decide to separate. Imperial Chemical Industries grew into what were seen as two distinct businesses, one dealing in paints (including the Dulux brand), plastics and industrial chemicals, one dealing in fertiliser, pesticides, inks and dyes. The giant organisation made a loss in 1993 and management decided that it would cope better if it was split into the two groups linked to the two core businesses. The ICI name remained to deal with the chemical side of the business and a new company, Zeneca, was formed to deal with paints and dyes.

PROGRESS CHECK

1. ▶ List the different reasons why a business might want to grow.

2. ▶▶ Explain what is meant by economies and diseconomies of scale. Give an example.

3. ▶▶ Describe which functional areas in a business are likely to gain the most from scale economies.

4. ▶▶ Explain the difference between external and internal growth. In what ways is internal growth better than external?

5. ▶▶ Draw a diagram to show an example of each type of integration.

6. ▶▶▶ Look at the information on Boots and on the spending patterns of

Japanese women. Explain in what areas a firm like Boots will have strengths and in what areas it is likely to have weaknesses.

7. ▶▶▶ Advise Boots as to what areas it should concentrate on to best compete with Matsumoto.

Key terms

GROWTH – a firm getting bigger (there are many different ways of doing this).

ECONOMIES OF SCALE – lower unit costs achieved by being, borrowing or buying bigger.

DISECONOMIES OF SCALE – higher costs brought about by growth.

INTERNAL (OR ORGANIC) GROWTH – a firm growing from within.

EXTERNAL GROWTH – a firm growing by taking over or merging with other firms.

INTEGRATION – the process of one firm joining with another.

DIVERSIFICATION – a firm entering markets or areas that are not part of its usual business.

NICHE – a small corner i.e. a tiny part of a market.

STUDENT CHECKLIST

1. There are many different ways in which firms can expand, including seeking bigger market share, bigger turnover or bigger geographical spread.

2. Economies of scale (lower costs through being bigger) may often be the reason for expansion.

3. Expansion may be internal – the firm growing from within. This tends to be slower but more certain.

4. Expansion may be external – the firm integrates (joins) with another firm.

5. Such moves may be friendly, with equal partnership (a merger); an unequal partnership (a take-over) which could be unfriendly (a hostile take-over) or friendly (a 'white knight' protecting the smaller firm from hostile take-over).

6. The direction of integration is shown by the chain of production.

7. Many businesses are happy to stay small.

CHAPTER 5

Reviewing business objectives

Trocadero to go!

Observers would have thought that Richard Branson's Virgin group was in its usual expansionist move when it decided to enter the cinema market in 1995. Other markets have been transformed by the arrival of Virgin, and this has often resulted in lower prices or better choice. So it must have come as a bit of a shock to City watchers to see that Virgin has sold off its cinema group – the ABC chain of cinemas – which it bought from MGM in 1995. It had already sold some of the smaller cinemas to a consortium of their own management and has now decided to sell the rest to a French cinema company. This is in spite of having just opened the largest cinema complex in Europe – the giant 22-screen Trocadero in Glasgow. Virgin could see the chain needing huge injections of investment cash over the next few years in order to keep its share of the market as the increase in cinema users has been outstripped by the growth of cinemas.

Management reviewed the objectives of the cinema chain and compared these with the objectives of Virgin as a whole.

FIGURE 5.1 *A multiplex cinema*
Source: © Michael Nicholson/CORBIS

Virgin is not in expansionist mood at the moment, for it to keep its promise to make its railway franchise the best in the country within five years, it needs injections of capital into new rolling stock. Other parts of the business are also becoming cash hungry. ABC needed to expand to meet the surge in demand for cinema seats which has followed the successful blockbuster movies of the 1980s and 1990s. However, other cinema companies, such as UCI, had a head start on Virgin and few other commitments for investment money. Virgin management thus decided that to expand in such a competitive and high-risk market was not the correct objective for the cinema arm of the business. Getting rid of it meant that other, more important objectives, might be reached more easily.

What you need to do

- **To gain a pass** you need to be able to show that you can describe clearly the aims and objectives of businesses and how they might review those aims.
- **To gain a merit** you also need to be able to explain clearly how the different functional areas interact when objectives are being reviewed and which areas are more important in achieving any changes.
- **To gain a distinction** you also need to evaluate the strengths and weaknesses of business and explain how these may affect the success or otherwise of expansion or contraction.

Why review?

The cycle of objectives is a constant one – the reaching of one target is really just a signal to see how easily the target was achieved and then setting a new target. Reviewing targets means that a firm is permanently looking at how near it is to achieving targets, what steps may need to be taken in order to achieve targets and what new targets ought to be set. If a firm is failing to achieve its targets, it needs to know whether to revise methods, timescales or other factors in order to achieve them. The cycle of setting and reviewing objectives can be seen as:

> Set objective → plan how to reach objective (strategy) → communicate strategy to team members → organise resources, teams, feedback etc → coordinate and control → review progress towards objective (monitoring) → act on monitoring information → achieve objective → review → set new objective →

Evaluating objectives

Firms can use various measures to see whether they are reaching objectives or not. These measures will depend on the nature of the objective. Sometimes an objective will be measurable – indeed, many objectives are deliberately set as what are called SMART objectives. SMART objectives are:

- Specific – you should know when an objective has been reached by making it as definite as possible;
- Measurable – you should, where possible, be able to measure whether the objective has been reached, or see how close you are to it;
- Attainable – a target that it is not impossible to achieve;

- Relevant – it should form a sensible part of the organisation's overall strategy and way of working and it should be
- Time-related – organisations should be trying to achieve the objective in a specified time period.

Note that these five aims may be stated slightly differently but still using the word SMART as an aid to remembering them.

Some objectives, especially the objectives of different groups within an organisation, may conflict with each other (see Chapter 27 on stakeholders).

Write a report which explains to Virgin's shareholders why the company has decided to sell off the cinema chain. Using the same information, write a press release for a Glasgow newspaper that puts the sale in as positive a light as possible.

(C1.3)

Measuring objectives

Some objectives will be reasonably easy to measure, some will be more difficult. Some can be measured quantitatively, some must be measured qualitatively. This means that for some objectives a figure (quantitative measurement) can be put on the objective, for others it is the quality that is important and this cannot be measured in figures.

Quantitative objectives
- Profit. The most obvious measurable objective is profit – first, whether a firm is making a profit or not, secondly, how much profit and thirdly, relating that profit to the resources that have been used to make it.
- The level of sales of a product or service can be measured and comparisons made between the actual level of sales, those of previous time periods and forecast levels of sales. Sales figures are thus a major motivational factor in many firms and will be published on a regular basis. Comparisons can be made with competitors' sales, as such information is usually readily available, and objectives such as selling more in a certain market or certain time period than a competitor can be accurately measured.
- The objective of survival may be an objective that can be seen in measurable terms. A businessperson may say that providing they make a certain income (generated by sales and profits) then they will stay in business. However, such targets tend to become flexible in that the businessperson can easily review and alter the target. (For example, they may decide that the target was not reached in March, as they wanted, but will be reached in April, therefore move the objective by a month.)
- Market share. This is not measured as the share of an entire potential market. The potential market for cars, for example, could include everyone in the population over the age of 17 – would a percentage of this market be a realistic objective? A car firm will, instead, look at the percentage it has gained of the actual number of cars sold and gauge its success on this basis.
- Efficiency – this can be measured as productivity (how hard or efficiently workers or machines are working). Productivity measures may be used to compare

efficiency with other producers in the same industry rather than being used as absolute measures.

- Expansion – a firm could measure its expansion in terms of increased sales, increased market share, increased range of products or acquisitions of other firms. The amount of expansion – and how important it is to the firm – can usually only be seen by comparing figures for a previous time period. For example, an increase in sales of £10,000 means very little unless you know that the original sales level was £5,000 (therefore a 100% increase) or £1,000,000 (therefore a 1% increase).

COMMUNICATIONS activity

A major feature of Coca Cola's annual report of 1998 was its celebration of the fact that Coca Cola had sold its one billionth bottle of Coca-Cola. When the target was set, it seemed like an impossible one. This annual report reviews the target and sets an even higher one. Write about what you think is now the target of Coca-Cola? How will they know when they have achieved this target?

GET IT RIGHT! ✓

Many of the objectives which a firm reviews will be aimed for with the intention of increasing profit. Not all objectives, however, are necessarily profit related.

Qualitative objectives

Some objectives cannot be easily measured. These are what are called qualitative objectives. A firm may review these by being able to state how much nearer they are to their target than they were in a previous time period. Such objectives include:

- Customer satisfaction – a satisfied customer will return to make repeat purchases rather than taking business elsewhere. Many businesses will try to build in an amount of customer inertia – meaning that customers will be reluctant to move to a different supplier of the same service. Banking is a good example of this. The most important objective to a bank is to get a customer (preferably a teenager) to open a first account. Rewards and attractive benefits will be offered, as the bank is aware that changing a bank account is not something people tend to do. Banks will further tie in customers with standing orders and direct debits to make it increasingly difficult to transfer business elsewhere. They may also make a point of building up a personal 'manager/customer' relationship to make the person feel 'special'.

Some firms make attempts to measure customer satisfaction. For example 'the phone will always be answered in three rings' could be an objective that a firm could easily measure whether or not they were achieving (and how near they were getting). Some organisations carry out regular surveys of customers in order to collect their views on the firm's service and performance.

- Customer loyalty – this will be strongly linked to customer satisfaction. Customer loyalty may be measured by the number of

REVIEWING BUSINESS OBJECTIVES

times customers return with repeat business and is extremely important for many businesses. Loyalty may override factors such as price – if a customer thinks that they are getting a particularly good service, then they will use that service or supplier again and again. In some businesses keeping customers loyal is attempted through loyalty bonuses or loyalty cards (where customers receive prizes or points that can be converted into cash or prizes). Many schemes have involved collecting 'sets' (the earliest being sets of cigarette cards) while modern schemes rely on electronic technology.

- Being innovative – a company may establish a reputation for itself as being the first with new technology, being at the 'cutting edge'.
- Being competitive – making sure that they match rivals in terms of price, quality and range of products. Even though this may, in some cases, lead to a loss of market share, firms will still aim to achieve this objective. The supermarket group Sainsbury's lost market share and position when they tried to compete with their high-volume/low-price rivals by lowering price.
- Providing a charitable or voluntary service. An organisation may be able to say that they are providing such a service but will continually review the efficiency, availability etc of the service. While their long-term objective may not change, they can review how much nearer they have moved to the objective and, in particular, in what areas they have had success. 'To cancel out Third World debt' may be an aim of an organisation such as Netaid, which in 1999 tried to organise the first Internet-based pop concert. They are unlikely to reach that aim but can say which governments have responded, in what ways they have responded and which countries have benefited from their help. This sort of review can lead organisations to decide where their help is most needed or where pressure will produce the best results.
- Being a socially aware firm. Many firms aim to be socially or environmentally aware – either in their treatment of workers, suppliers or customers. For example, ensuring that they pay a fair price for produce coming from poorer countries or making sure that they do not exploit labour. This can enhance a business's reputation and lead to more sales.
- The firm's reputation – many businesses rely on getting trade by building up a good reputation. This is often true of small businesses providing a personal service – a wedding caterer, a disco operator, a hairdresser. Often such organisations rely on word-of-mouth recommendation rather than on advertising or promotion. They build up a strong customer base which may be considered as part of the assets of a business. If, for example, a catering business was being sold, a value might be put on the firm's good name and on its client list – this would be priced as 'goodwill'.

IT *activity*

Produce a newspaper page which compares Virgin's objectives with those of Coca-Cola. Scan in appropriate images for the two companies. You should find out some of the financial information about the two companies and present this in order to help with your comparison.

(IT1.2)

PROGRESS CHECK

1. ▶ Explain why a firm would want to review its objectives.

2. ▶▶ Describe what is meant by a SMART objective. Why is it important for objectives to be SMART?

3. ▶▶ Describe the main quantitative objectives that a firm might have.

4. ▶▶ Describe the main qualitative objectives that a firm might have.

5. ▶▶▶ Which parts or departments of an organisation would have the biggest role in reviewing objectives?

6. ▶▶▶ How would a firm like Coca-Cola review its objective of wanting to be 'the beverage of choice' or Oxfam 'reducing poverty and hunger'?

Key terms

REVIEW – checking and evaluating objectives.

REVIEW CYCLE – the continuous process which involves reviewing objectives and setting and managing new targets.

SMART OBJECTIVES – Specific, Measurable, Attainable, Relevant and Time-related targets.

QUANTITATIVE OBJECTIVES – those which can be measured, that a figure can be put on.

QUALITATIVE OBJECTIVES – those which cannot be measured as a quantity.

STUDENT CHECKLIST

1. Objective setting and reviewing should be a continuous cycle.

2. It is one of the main functions of management.

3. A major objective is profit; many other objectives will lead to greater profit.

4. Some objectives are measurable – they can be quantified.

5. Often objectives are a matter of quality and cannot be measured.

Section C Functional areas of business

CHAPTER 6

Marketing 1 – Marketing department

Light(s) at the end of the tunnel?

Golden Wonder has once again had to change the direction of the marketing for their 1990s snack 'Golden Lights'. Market conditions change so rapidly that it has been necessary to reposition the product again. Golden Wonder is very much a marketing-oriented firm and was responsible for producing the first ready salted crisps (instead of crisps with a little blue bag of salt) and flavoured crisps (they pioneered Cheese and Onion and Salt and Vinegar flavours).

Market research had shown Golden Wonder that there was a gap in the snack market – people are becoming more reluctant (or too busy) to prepare proper meals and, in many cases, even to pack lunches. However, they are also seeking more healthy lifestyles. This combination of factors led Golden Wonder to develop the low-fat 'Golden Lights' – a snack with the added incentive of being healthy.

However, customer reaction and changing customer tastes have meant that the product has had to be relaunched and repositioned twice since its initial launch in 1991. Golden Wonder is responding to market changes that have been identified by their analysts.

FIGURE 6.1 *Golden Lights*

Source: Emma Lee/Life File

FIGURE 6.2 *The mobile phone user*
Souce: Dave Thompson/Life File

ET – don't phone home; send an e-mail!

The latest generation of mobile phones don't quite sing, dance and play the piano – but it's close! New generation mobiles have a colour screen for Internet access and video-conferencing (the video-phone so beloved of science fiction finally made fact), can send and receive e-mails and attachments, take messages, give reminders, keep diaries and much else besides. All the operators now have to do is persuade us that we need them!

What you need to do

- **To gain a pass** you need to be able to show that you can describe clearly the functional business area of marketing, job roles associated with it and how it contributes to the business.
- **To gain a merit** you also need to be able to explain clearly how the marketing department interacts with other functional areas.
- **To gain a distinction** you also need to evaluate the strengths and weaknesses of the marketing department in its relationships with other departments in the business that you have studied.

What is the role of the marketing department?

The marketing department is central to the success of a business. Its role includes finding out what customers need and want, through market research, analysing and interpreting that information and then producing goods and services to provide for those needs. It also involves using advertising and promotion to create consumer wants.

The decision to change the marketing direction for Golden Lights will have been made as a result of market research, conducted by the marketing department. The department will also have overseen the creation of the new image. In the case of the new mobile phones, it will be a marketing department that convinces us that we must have them.

Jobs in the marketing department

There are a wide variety of jobs involved with promotion and advertising. These can loosely be grouped into three areas.

1. Jobs involving analysis of the market – market researchers, statisticians, analysts.
2. Jobs involving the creative part of advertising – copy writers, graphic artists, editors, creative consultants, producers, directors, actors etc.
3. Jobs involving buying and sales – accountants, salespeople who seek new clients, media buyers etc.

The size of the contribution to the organisation can be seen by the range of jobs and tasks carried out. They include market research, market analysis and market segmentation. These elements are essential before the organisation can move on to the advertising and promotion.

Market research

Market research is the collection of information from and about customers and potential customers. It is important that this distinction is recognised – if a firm is going to expand its market it needs to look at possible (or potential) customers as well as the ones that it already has. Market research involves collecting secondary data – material that has already been published – and primary data – original material and information that has not been collected or published by anyone else. The information that businesses will collect includes:

- who are their customers
- how much are they willing/able to pay for the product
- where and how the product can best reach its maximum sales
- what advertising or promotion will be most effective.

Primary research

This is called 'field' research – researchers cannot collect the information without going out into the market they are researching. Such research gathers data that has not been collected before and can be tailored to the exact needs of the organisation that is collecting it. The main methods of field research are:

- Observation and counting – this can include traffic counts, footfall counts (to see how many people pass a particular shop window, for instance) and such things as observing which way customers turn when they enter a store (generally right).
- Surveys – often done with the aid of a set of questions (a questionnaire), which can be specific to the information that is required.
- Tasting and testing – inviting people to comment on a product after they have had a chance to sample it.
- Panels – groups of people who give in-depth feedback to firms. For example, new television advertisements are often shown to a panel of people (sometimes called a focus group) who will comment on the advertisement and suggest changes to make it more effective.

Secondary research

This is research that has already been completed with its results published, plus information, statistics etc that have been collected for other purposes. It is called desk research because it is information that can be collected while sitting at a desk. The most likely sources of such information are newspapers and magazines, books, business and govern-

FIGURE 6.3 *Field research: surveys*

ment reports (try www.open.gov.uk or www.hmso.gov.uk/acts (for Acts of Parliament)). One of the biggest sources is the annual reports and accounts of limited companies which must, by law, be made available to the public. Information may be written, photographic, statistical, electronic and even presented on video.

One of the most important sources of secondary data is the Census. Every ten years, on the year ending in '1' (1971, 1981, 1991 – next in 2001), the government hold a National Census of Population. This not only counts the population, it also collects a vast quantity of information about family size and structure, shopping habits, incomes, spending patterns and so on. There is a whole government office that collects and publishes this information. It is called the Office of Population Census and Surveys (OPCS). Although such information is very accurate, it is also always out of date by the time it is published as the OPCS is dealing with such huge numbers of respondents that it takes a long time to sort and present the information.

GET IT RIGHT! ✓

Primary school was the first school you went to; followed by secondary school. If you remember this then you should remember that primary is first-hand information – collected directly – and secondary is second-hand information – material that has been published before.

Problems

Secondary data may be out of date; it may not be exactly what you want; it may be incomplete; you may have to pay for it; and it may be in the wrong format for your purposes. Primary data has to be very carefully collected if it is going to be useful; it can provide the wrong results; and it can be expensive and time consuming to carry out.

Analysing the market

Market research information – along with other information that the marketing department can collect (such as competitors company reports) – is used to decide what products to produce and who to target them at.

Producers are generally seeking to either find or create a gap in the market. A gap in the market is a part of the market that has not yet been filled by an appropriate product or service.

- Market-oriented firms (such as Golden Wonder) seek to develop products that are a response to changes in the market; they seek to *find* gaps in the market and produce goods to fill them.

Find two sources of market research information – newspapers may carry such information or it may be found in local council or similar publications. Look at information that has been presented as a diagram, table or chart and write a short piece explaining what the information shows.

(N1.1)

- Product-oriented firms (such as mobile phone companies) tend to be driven by technology and seek to *create* gaps in the market by producing goods and then persuading people that they want/need them.

Consumers are targeted according to which market segment they are in. A segment is like a part or slice of a market and a marketing department will decide which products to aim at which segments (e.g. one market segment is teenage boys; another is young mothers).

COMMUNICATIONS *activity*

The two firms in this chapter take different views on how to bring products to the market. Work with a partner to collect information on as many other firms as you can that share these different views. One of you should choose a product-oriented firm and write a letter to the Chairperson explaining the advantages of being market oriented; the other should choose a market-oriented firm and write a letter to the Chairperson explaining the advantages of being product oriented.

Write a reply to your partner's letter on headed notepaper that you have created for your chosen firm. Use an image like a logo to enhance the quality of the notepaper.

Market segmentation

Markets can be divided in a number of ways. One of the most common ways is through the use of the social and economic groups that people are in. This is shortened to socio-economic groups. Socio-economic groups split the market up into parts based on the occupation, income and education of a person. This means that advertisers can target particular sections or sub-sections of society. Government and statisticians put the population into five classes or groups.

- Class 1, Group A are professional people, for example judges, top civil servants, university professors, etc.
- Class 2, Group B are people in management, technical and executive jobs (even though many have professional qualifications). Examples include bank managers, teachers, company directors, solicitors and accountants.
- Class 3 is usually divided into two groups:
  - Group C1 are people in non-manual occupations such as sales assistants, filing clerks and secretaries in either a supervisory or clerical capacity.
  - Group C2 are skilled manual workers (often self-employed), such as carpenters, electricians and plumbers.
- Class 4, Group D are workers, such as assembly line workers, packers and fitters, who are in semi-skilled manual occupations.
- Class 5, Group E are groups such as the unemployed and other low or fixed income groups. Examples include single parents, state pensioners and students. The group includes unskilled manual workers, and temporary workers.

Other methods of segmenting markets include by geography, by race or religion, by gender, by age or by hobbies and interests. Examples could be:

- geography – the use of a regional television channel or local newspaper
- race or religion – publications aimed at particular groups, products aimed at particular skin tones
- gender – cars tend to be aimed at either men or women; soap powder products are almost always aimed at women
- age – magazines, in particular, may target a very narrow age range
- hobbies and interests – specialist publications for everything ranging from angling to zoology!

GET IT RIGHT! ✓

Socio-economic groups are not always an accurate reflection of society as they are based on the occupation of the head of the household. They also make assumptions, for example, that a tradesperson will not be highly educated or that a student or pensioner will be poor. They do, however, provide a good general indication.

Using information technology

Market research and analysis is one field where the use of information technology has meant that results are both much more accurate and much faster. The use of databases to target particular consumers or types of consumer can mean that marketing is much more effective than it used to be. Spreadsheets can be used to make statistics more presentable, meaningful and easier to cope with and the use of mail merge (where the advertising material appears to be directly addressed to the recipient) to personalise direct mail drops can make both the research itself and its presentation more efficient.

IT
activity

Take a short class survey in your class or group; ask five questions that will reveal what market segment they are in and some of their likes and dislikes. Remember that closed questions are easier to analyse while open questions will give more detailed information. Present the results as a table, chart or graph using information technology and add a short commentary on each image.

(IT1.2)

PROGRESS CHECK

1. ▶ Describe how an organisation could use a) primary research; b) secondary research.

2. ▶ Explain what the drawbacks of primary and secondary research are.

3. ▶▶ 'An organisation should use both primary and secondary research.' Is this statement true? Explain your views.

4. ▶▶ Outline, with examples, what is meant by market segmentation.

5. ▶▶▶ Explain why socio-economic groups may not be an accurate way to divide the population.

6. ▶▶▶ Explain how the other departments in an organisation will interact with the marketing department.

Key terms

PRIMARY RESEARCH – done first-hand.

SECONDARY RESEARCH – already published.

DESK RESEARCH – research that can be done by looking at published materials (while sitting at a desk!).

FIELD RESEARCH – research that is done 'in the field', directly with members of the market or potential market.

MARKET-ORIENTED FIRMS – these find a 'gap in the market' and aim products to fill that gap.

PRODUCT-ORIENTED FIRMS – these develop new products and then persuade consumers to demand them.

MARKET SEGMENTATION – the division of the market into parts, such as by age, gender or income.

 **STUDENT CHECKLIST**

1. **Marketing involves organisations collecting market research information.**

2. **This is collected as either first-hand (primary) or second-hand (secondary) information.**

3. **Markets are analysed and divided into segments.**

4. **An organisation will target a particular market segment or group of segments.**

5. **Organisations can use information technology to make both the collection and the analysis of data easier and faster.**

CHAPTER 7

Marketing 2 – Advertising and promotion

Yorkshire Saddlery straddles the world

The Yorkshire family firm of Fox Saddlers, based in Wetherby, North Yorkshire, is now able to gain customers from anywhere in the world. It has opened a website and, with the aid of some hi-tech software, was able to set up an e-commerce site so that it could accept orders over the Internet. Although the market for its products may appear small, it has now gained entry into world markets for saddlery and horse-related products and this means that every horse owner from Arabia to America can buy from the same outlet. The business has already taken orders from Australia – and you can't get much further from Yorkshire than that!

What you need to do

- **To gain a pass** you need to be able to show that you can describe clearly the functional area of marketing, in particular advertising and promotion, and how it contributes to the business.
- **To gain a merit** you also need to be able to explain clearly how promotional activities affect and interact with the other functional areas of the business.
- **To gain a distinction** you also need to evaluate the strengths and weaknesses of the advertising and promotion in the business that you have studied and show how these strengths or weaknesses affect other departments.

Marketing department

Once the marketing department has analysed the market and identified the target parts of that market, it will then try to sell the organisation's product to that target. It will liaise with the Finance Department to agree a budget to be spent on promotion.

Promotion

Promotion involves the public about a product and persuading them to buy it. Expenditure is divided into above- and below-the-line spending.

- Above-the-line spending is direct expenditure on advertising, such as buying media space or the production costs for television advertising.
- Below-the-line spending is indirect expenditure, such as on promotions, competitions, sponsorship and product placement.

The two parts of promotion are informing the customer or potential customer and persuading them to buy. It is thus a form of communication from the seller to the buyer. As such it requires a sender, a receiver, a medium and a message.

> **GET IT RIGHT!** ✓
>
> Promotion is about sending a message – probably a persuasive one – from a producer or seller to an existing or possible consumer. The effectiveness of the message depends on WHO sends it, HOW it is sent or presented, and WHO receives it, as much as it does on the CONTENT of the message.

Sender

The sender may be the marketing department of the organisation itself or it may use an advertising agency – these are companies which bid for the advertising accounts of the major advertisers. Some accounts are so large that an agency only needs to gain the business of one client in order to be successful. The biggest advertisers in the UK are motor manufacturers and sellers of washing powder and soap products like Lever Brothers and Proctor and Gamble. If an agency is successful at bidding for one of these, it may need no other clients.

Large marketing departments are split into smaller departments:

- An Accounts department which seeks to secure new clients (new 'accounts') and to manage the ones which it has.
- A creative and artistic department, responsible for ideas, images, storyboards etc.
- A production department (although this may often be a separate specialist firm) and a media buying department, responsible for buying advertising space in publications and air time on broadcast media.

Receiver

The idea of advertising and promotion is to reach potential customers and turn them into actual customers. A marketing department will decide, with the help of its market research, which market segments to target and this will affect the nature and timing of promotions. Mothers with young children, for example, tend to be morning television watchers; school-aged children can be targeted in the four to six o'clock television slot;

working people after six. Advertisements can be linked to sporting events or to particular programmes. Guinness, for example, ran a series of advertisements aimed at the audience for the Rugby World Cup.

It is even easier to target segments through magazine advertising as there are so many different magazines catering for many different parts of the market.

> **GET IT RIGHT!** ✓
>
> Media is the word used to mean the main ways of getting messages across. In particular it is used to refer to newspapers, magazines, radio and television. 'A lot of media exposure' usually means in newspapers and on television and radio news. It may therefore mean more public relations than promotion.

The medium

The medium is the way the message is passed on. Media is the plural of medium and refers to all the ways of passing on advertising messages. The more effective the medium is the more expensive it will be. The most effective media are broadcast media – especially television and cinema advertisements which have the advantage of being able to use sound, colour and movement.

- Expenditure on television advertising accounts for almost one third of all expenditure on advertising. Television commercials are generally expensive to make and expensive to show. Even a regional commercial television station (such as Yorkshire TV or Anglia) will charge more than one thousand pounds per second of broadcast time at peak periods.

- Cinema advertisements may not be subject to the same restrictions as television advertisements in terms of what can be advertised and how. If a cinema advertisement has an 18 certificate, it can only be shown to an audience of 18s and over.

- The government has expanded commercial radio by allocating more wave bands to these stations. Radio advertising is a lot cheaper to make and broadcast and, as most commercial radio stations are already aimed at a particular market segment, it is easy to target advertising.

- E-advertising. The 'e' stands for electronic; this means advertising via an Internet address or website and is becoming increasingly popular due to its cheapness and effectiveness. Customers cannot be accurately targeted, but will seek out advertising for particular products as in the case of the Yorkshire saddlery. Some targeting can occur as sites with similar interests host related advertising and weblinks to other related sites. As with all e-commerce, such advertising is fairly unregulated and consumers must be very wary of how they treat it.

- Newspapers and magazines account for well over half of all advertising expenditure. Newspaper advertisements are sold either by the amount of display space (for a display or semi-display type advertisement – generally measured in 'column centimetres') or by the number of lines or number of words in the advertisement. Advertisements may be:
    - display advertisements – a full-page advertisement in a mass circulation tabloid will cost about £30,000.

FIGURE 7.1 *High spenders on advertising*
Source: Emma Lee/Life File

- classified advertisements – where advertisements are paid for by word, line or the amount of space taken up.
- specialised – in trade or special interest publications, which are either 'in-house' magazines produced by a company or industry internally, trade or professional publications or publications (often free) aimed at customers (supermarket in-store magazines, for example).
- Posters, billboards etc. These are used in many different ways; for example, advertising boards around sports grounds, sponsors' logos actually painted on the grass at sports events, teams carrying logos, and poster sites ranging from small sites at places like bus stops and to huge '64-sheet' posters. Messages must be short and direct and the product must have prominence, as such advertising cannot really be targeted. Its appeal lies in the fact that it can reach a large number of people reasonably cheaply – some of whom will be in the target market. Poster advertising accounts for about 5% of advertising expenditure.

The message

The message may be informative or persuasive, but must also be, according to the Advertising Standards Authority, legal, decent, honest and truthful.

COMMUNICATIONS *activity*

One way of selling advertising is through an advertising agency. The agency would bid for the account of a particular client, usually by presenting new ideas for advertising campaigns. Choose a product or service that interests you and prepare a 'bid' of this nature as if from an advertising agency. You should then present your bid to the rest of your group, using whatever images are appropriate. You could judge each other's presentations on a scoring system that included originality of ideas as well as the clarity of the presentation and how well it was delivered.

(C2.16)

The Advertising Standards Authority is a group that is paid for by the advertising industry itself to keep a check on advertisements. The British Code of Advertising Practice describes what is meant by this. They investigate complaints from members of the public if advertising appears to break the code by making false claims, telling lies, breaking the law or being indecent.

GET IT RIGHT!

Advertisements may actually be published or broadcast before the Advertising Standards Authority becomes involved. Often they are acting on behalf of members of the public who have been misled or offended by a particular advertisement.

Public relations

Marketing departments may use public relations specialists who have the job of making sure that the product has a good image in the eyes of the public. PR people may use techniques such as:

- 'making' news around the product (press releases disguised as news, or events linked to the product)
- press conferences and photo opportunities
- endorsements – getting famous people to say that your product is good
- product placement – where a product is provided free for use in a television programme or film
- competitions – prizes involving the product
- gifts and samples – such as free gifts, free posters or items with the name or logo of the firm on (key rings, pens, etc)
- sponsorship – the most common sponsorship deals are with sports companies.

NUMERACY activity

Find out the advertisement rates for a local or national newspaper of which you have a copy. (You may need to look in British Rate and Data or contact the advertising department of the publication.) You are going to find out how much the publication takes in advertising revenue for an average issue. First, work out how much of the publication is devoted to advertising (express this as a percentage – this will give you an idea of how much newspapers rely on advertising revenue). Next, work out how much of the advertising space has been sold as display, semi-display or lineage. Finally, work out the three amounts from the charges that the publication makes for different types of advertisement. You could present the information as pie charts or bar charts, as well as presenting the figures.

(N1.2, N1.3)

Sales promotion

This includes other methods used both to raise awareness of a product and to persuade consumers to buy. For example:

- point-of-sale material – cards, displays etc – used where the goods are displayed in a shop or where they will be paid for (at checkouts, for instance)
- special offers – e.g. 'buy one, get one free'
- price reductions – so much 'knocked off' for a period of time
- discounts – pay cash and get a lower price; pay on time and pay a lower amount
- money-off coupons – published in the press, delivered direct or part of the packaging of goods (to encourage repeat purchases)
- customer loyalty cards – customers collect 'points' electronically every time they make a purchase and are rewarded with money-off or cash coupons
- free gifts – products will sometimes contain such things as small toys, games or other gifts
- joint promotion – where two companies team up to promote each other's products
- banded promotions – goods may be physically 'banded' together – a brand of toothpaste sold with a brand of toothbrush
- direct mail – used to target particular customers; consumers may have filled out questionnaires or guarantee cards or credit agreements and revealed preferences and lifestyle details that can be targeted by advertisers.

Merchandising

This used to be the term used for all aspects of selling products to the consumer – sales promotion, advertising and public relations. It is now more often used to mean the 'spin-off' goods that are sold as the result of a successful product launch. Film companies will produce toys and computer games based on characters in a film; bands will produce T-shirts, posters, etc; cartoon characters will be promoted with clothes, socks and household goods (look at the successful merchandising of, for example, the Wallace and Grommitt characters). Merchandising can often produce more revenue than the actual film, band or character.

Branding

A strong brand image – where a product is linked in the consumer's mind with a particular brand – although expensive to establish, can save money on advertising in the long run, as new product lines will be underpinned by the successful brand name and image. Brand images may become so strong that they are 'generic' – ie used to describe all goods in that particular market, for example, Hoover or Biro. This can lead to an adverse effect on sales (Britvic orange went to court to ensure that if a customer asked for Britvic orange, that was the brand that they actually got).

Advertising – good or bad?

To be good for the firm, advertising needs to be cost effective. This means that the cost of the advertising or promotional campaign should be offset by an increase in sales revenue. Some commentators argue against advertising saying that it can never be cost effective as the resources used in its production are, in effect, 'wasted'. Other arguments against promotion include:

- it increases crime by showing products and lifestyles that can't be afforded by everyone
- it leads to higher prices to pay for the advertising
- it can be used by a large firm as a barrier to market entry for small firms.

Arguments for advertising include:

- competition leads to lower prices
- it reinforces consumer choice by providing information on products available
- it keeps the costs of printed media down (the real cost of producing a newspaper is much higher than its cover price; in some cases, newspapers can be given away free because the advertising has covered the costs).

IT activity

Search for and select information that could be used to support either the case for or the case against advertising. You may be searching in newspaper records held on CD or microfiche for reported cases that support either view. You may also search for crime statistics and reasons given for crimes being committed. To support the case for advertising you could try to find out the number of people employed in the industry and how much it contributes to national income each year.

(IT2.1)

Marketing's links with other functional departments

- Human resources – the number of different

job types in the marketing department mean that human resources will be involved in recruiting the best people and in retaining them. Turnover of staff, particularly creative staff, can be high and human resources should try to minimise this.

- Finance – advertising budgets can be a very large part of a firm's expenditure. The finance department will be looking for value for money and cost effectiveness in advertising and promotion. They may need to be convinced that advertising expenditure is money well spent.
- Production – if an advertising campaign is going to be successful, the production department must be kept informed so that they are ready to meet any increases in demand.
- Customer service – companies can add to their brand image by building a corporate image that shows that they are responsive to customers needs, caring and efficient.

PROGRESS CHECK

1. ▶ Describe how advertising and promotion contributes to the success of a business.
2. ▶ Outline the difference between above- and below-the-line expenditure on advertising. Why do you think that this difference is important?
3. ▶▶ Explain how advertising and promotion interact with other functional areas of the business.
4. ▶▶ Describe the process of advertising, showing how the success or failure of each part of the process affects the success or failure of the process as a whole.
5. ▶▶▶ What are the advantages and disadvantages of e-commerce and e-advertising? How do you think that e-commerce will affect advertising in the future?

Key terms

PROMOTION – this is both informative and persuasive.

MEDIA – the plural of medium – the method by which messages are passed from sender to receiver – usually used to mean publications and broadcast media.

PUBLIC RELATIONS – used to improve the image of a product.

POINT-OF-SALE MATERIAL – promotional material used where the good is actually bought, usually meaning counter displays and advertising.

MERCHANDISING – producing goods linked to a central product or service and used to help promote it.

STUDENT CHECKLIST

1. Promotion involves telling consumers about products and services and trying to persuade them to buy them.
2. Promotion involves a sender, a message, a medium for the message and a receiver. All parts are equally important.
3. Merchandising is an important way of 'hyping' a product. Branding will keep the product in the customer's mind and, in the long run, save on advertising.
4. There are strong arguments both for and against advertising.

CHAPTER 8

Human resources 1 – Recruitment and selection

POWER CONSULTANCY
London Based

Our client, part of a large International group, enjoys a particularly strong reputation with major energy companies in the UK and Continental Europe and is recognised as having real influence in decision-making across investment, fuel procurement and pricing issues. As a result of continued growth we are looking for two quantitatively based individuals; one will concentrate on Downstream Oil and the other European Power. Given the unusually wide range of energy sectors covered these are excellent opportunities to develop a personal reputation as an expert in this dynamic industry.

Three years' experience Is seen as the minimum but the catchment areas for suitable candidates are as flexible as the roles. Energy companies, consultancy. government agencies, academia and financial journalism could all provide intellectually strong, entrepreneurial applicants with a proven track record in modelling and analysis.

The roles will initially focus on statistical analysis, research and report writing but, in due course the emphasis will become more client-facing: we therefore need a combination of characteristics including first class communication skills (written and oral), high computer literacy, attention to detail and, crucially, a strong desire to learn. There are undoubted opportunities for the successful candidates to take early project responsibility.

The salary and benefits package will be as attractive to high calibre candidates as the career development prospects.

Source: Adapted from The Guardian, 18 April 2000

FIGURE 8.1 *New technology: more and more of it*
Source: PA News

What you need to do

- **To gain a pass** you need to be able to show that you can describe clearly the functional business area of human resources and the role of human resource management; the job roles associated with the department and how it contributes to the business. Human resources MUST be one of the functional areas that you study for your portfolio.
- **To gain a merit** you also need to be able to explain clearly how the human resources department interacts with the other functional areas of the business.
- **To gain a distinction** you also need to evaluate the strengths and weaknesses of the human resources department in its relationships with other departments in the business or businesses that you have studied.

Human resources

Human Resources (HR) are not just the people in the organisation, but is the term used to refer to the wider idea of their qualifications, talents and abilities. While many firms have a personnel department that deals with the people in the organisation, forward-looking firms have expanded it to include all aspects of their employees to try and have a workforce that is as happy as possible. The Human Resources Department aims to maximise the contribution of employees to the organisation. This involves not just recruitment and training, but induction, motivation and career planning. Sometimes the department handles its own, direct, recruiting. Sometimes it uses an agency. Either way, the best person for the job will be sought.

Look at the key words in an advertisement, for example:

- three years experience
- flexibility
- intellectually strong
- entrepreneurial
- proven track record.

The consultancy also seeks

- first class communication skills
- high computer literacy
- attention to detail
- a strong desire to learn.

The message is clearly 'we want the best'.

Some agencies act as the 'middle-man', taking and storing details of job-seekers and providing them to employers on request. In this way, the job-seeker is actively selling themselves and the employer can save money on expensive advertising.

> **GET IT RIGHT!** ✓
>
> The personnel department deals with the people employed by an organisation – its human resources. The term 'human resources' has virtually replaced personnel in modern companies. This is because personnel was not seen to be dealing with the welfare of employees but was limited to 'hiring and firing'.

Job roles associated with Human Resources

The contribution of HR to the organisation is in ensuring that the best quality staff are employed. Its further role is to ensure that the business is getting the best from its staff and that the staff are being fairly treated by the business. Major job roles could include:

- The personnel manager was traditionally the head of the department which dealt with all labour matters. Many firms have now replaced this with a human resources manager.
- Trainers may be recruited from either inside or outside the organisation. It may be part of their job to train new recruits or apprentices or training may be their specialist function.
- Recruiter or interviewer. A special type of these are called 'headhunters'. These are people or firms that turn the job seeking role 'on its head'. Instead of advertising for and recruiting applicants, they decide exactly who the person that they want for a particular job is and set about persuading them to leave their current employment and join the firm in question.
- Negotiator/arbitrator. May be needed to settle disputes between workers and management.
- Appraiser. These may be trained 'appraisers' or involve employees appraising each other.

The function of HR is to conduct all stages of the employees connection with the business. From recruitment, selection and training through to discipline, redundancy and retirement.

Agencies

Some organisations are either too small to have a personnel or human resources department or prefer to give the work out to an agency. If, for example, a company wanted to recruit staff from another country, they could use a local agency that knew the job market in that country.

Some agencies act as the 'middle man', taking and storing details of jobseekers and providing them to employers on request. In this way, the jobseeker is actively selling themselves and the employer can save money on expensive advertising.

Recruitment and selection

Recruitment and selection is the process of finding and choosing, from the widest possible selection of applicants, the best people to meet the needs of the organisation. This means that the department must advertise for staff in the right places and at the right time; must ask for the right information from jobseekers and provide good information about the vacancy; must properly and professionally consider applications and be able to assess candidates through interview or other appropriate means in order to make the best appointment.

 COMMUNICATIONS *activity*

Write an advertisement for a job that you feel you would like to do when you have all your qualifications. Use an image such as a logo to make your advertisement look attractive. Now write the job description for that job. Swap your advertisement with that of another person in your class or group and write the application for the job that they have advertised. Now match the application with the job description. Would you give them the job? If so, why? If not, why?

(C1.3)

Where to advertise?

This depends on the nature of the organisation and the type of employee that they are seeking. A small trader might only need a card in a newsagent's window; other outlets include 'situations vacant' in local papers and, for better qualified or experienced staff, national job advertising. This could be through the trade press for a particular industry or through national newspapers. Many newspapers have particular days for particular types of job so if, for example, you were seeking a senior position with the BBC, you would find it advertised in *The Guardian* on a Monday.

Job centres are provided by the Department of Employment and aim to reduce unemployment by providing a free site for employers to advertise. There are also specialist publications that are aimed at people seeking jobs in particular areas of commerce or industry.

Government

The government not only provides job centres, but has set up job clubs, where advice on filling out application forms, writing letters and composing CVs is available and equipment, such as computers, is provided to make job applications with. In certain cases, such things as postage, costs for applications and travel expenses to interviews may be given in the form of a grant.

The Jobseekers' Allowance replaced Unemployment Benefit in 1996; the change was meant to show that someone might be unemployed, but they were actively seeking a job. People claiming benefit must be available for work and must sign a Jobseekers' Agreement saying that they are seeking work. They are obliged to go to regular review meetings to show that they are looking for work and to keep a record of the jobs that they have applied for.

Job analysis

Job analysis is the breaking down of a job into its component parts in order to identify exactly what the job requires. This means that a company can then advertise for staff who exactly match the detailed job requirements. The analysis will be used to draw up a detailed description of the job and of the type of person wanted for the job.

The job description will say what the job entails and what qualifications and experience are wanted. The person specification is written to fit the 'ideal' candidate for a job. It is usually presented in two parts: the essential characteristics that a person applying must have and the desirable characteristics. If, for example, the job says 'good French' is essential, then it is no use a person applying unless they fulfil this requirement. If it says that 'good French' is desirable, then other parts of the job (the 'essential' ones) are more important.

Making an application

Applicants may be able to make informal approaches to employers, for example, by telephoning or calling in to a small organisation's premises. For larger firms, formal applications are generally called for. These could take the form of:

- A letter of application, which could be part of an application form or a separate letter. This is the candidate's opportunity to say, in more detail, what makes him or her the ideal candidate for the post.
- Application forms are designed to give a firm a quick reference to certain details of applicants so that they can easily select the ones that they want to look at in detail. They will ask for personal details such as name, address, national insurance number, education, training and qualifications as well as details of current job and employment history.
- Curriculum vitae or résumé. This is the 'story of your life' and is used to outline personal details, qualifications, education and experience and job histories. To the applicant, it has the advantage of being already prepared for an application. To the employer, it has the disadvantage of not necessarily being specific to the job advertised.

> **GET IT RIGHT!** ✓
>
> You should always make sure that your CV is as up to date as possible. As you get new experiences or qualifications they should be added to it. Earlier ones (baby-sitting, paper round, Saturday job, for example) may no longer be significant once further experiences have been gained.

COMMUNICATIONS *activity*

Each person in your group or class should create a detailed CV for him or herself. The CV should include a passport-sized photograph. They should then exchange it with another member of the class. Their job is to make a summary or précis of the CV so that the members of an interview panel would have the essential information in a format that is easy to understand. Do this again for a second and third class or group member. Now let the person that you have written the summary for see your précis. Do they think that you have included all the vital information? Do they think that you have left anything out?

(C2.2)

Selection

The selection process usually consists of:

- Long listing – when the firm takes a general look at applications and weeds out those that do not appear to fulfil the job specifications; perhaps they do not have the qualifications or, in many cases, they may have produced untidy or illegible applications or may have failed to carry out the instructions on 'how to apply'.

- Short listing – this is those candidates whose applications will be read in detail and from which a list of interviewees will be drawn.
- Interviewing – the candidate will be invited to answer questions put to them by a panel of interviewers or a single person.
- Testing – sometimes simple tests are given to see if a candidate can do the maths involved in the job, or can work at speed, or can speak the languages that they claim to speak.
- Presentations – candidates may be asked to give a presentation on a particular subject, or to say how they would react in a particular situation.

IT activity

Create a CV for yourself on the computer. You should scan in a photograph of yourself and include standard information such as name, age, date of birth, address and National Insurance number; information relating to your employment history, such as jobs held and tasks and skills required for those jobs; and information regarding education and qualifications. Choose two different jobs that you might like to do that are advertised in a newspaper and change your CV so that you produce two different documents, each one specific to the job that you have chosen.

(IT2.3)

FIGURE 8.2

Induction

Induction training is training designed to give a new employee an introduction to the operation of the firm. It should include basic information, for example, the whereabouts of facilities and the usual practices as regards break and lunchtimes. Health and Safety information will also be included as well as introductions to key personnel. Training on the operation of machinery or systems, such as photocopiers, scanners or computer software, filing systems and computer systems, may also be essential in certain types of job. In some organisations it will involve a detailed and lengthy introduction – especially if the job involved is complicated or if it involves interacting with a large number of other people or departments.

Training and career opportunities

Training may be necessary before someone can even begin their employment. People may also need to be trained if there are new processes, new machinery or new regulations to follow. In addition to this, employees may wish to be trained so that they have a greater range of skills and/or expertise. Such training may give them better promotion prospects. The two main types of training are:

- On-the-job training is provided while a person is at work. It is usually carried out by a supervisor or another worker who is qualified to give the training. Such training tends to be both effective and cheap but will only train people in current practices, machinery etc, not new ones.
- Off-the-job training takes place away from the place of work and includes college or university courses. This tends to be more expensive but training is likely to be in greater depth and may well involve gaining a qualification. In many cases employers prefer what is called a 'sandwich' course – part of the working week is spent at college, part is spent at the place of work. In this way the employee will be receiving both sorts of training.

Promotion

This means moving on to a higher position, usually meaning both more money and greater responsibility and workload. The career structure that a firm offers can be an important thing to consider when going for a job. Some organisations provide a highly structured route to management, involving training, education and examinations. Such organisations include banking, accountancy and the legal profession. Some firms are keen to provide a career structure for their staff so that they are motivated to do better and try harder in order to win promotion. Internal promotion may need the employee to put in extra work, come up with new ideas or take on more responsibility without getting more pay (in order to prove that they can do the job).

Retention

Staff turnover (the number of staff leaving a business in any one time period) can be reduced with policies aimed at staff retention – keeping staff. Often this means making sure that staff are being treated properly at work and that they have the opportunities – for example, for training and promotion – that they want. Part of this involves motivating staff; this means getting them to work harder because they want to and can include:

- the provision of a good workplace
- promotion opportunities
- good pay and conditions of service
- good pension arrangements
- 'perks', such as a company car or staff discounts.

If staff can be persuaded to stay, this cuts down on the costs of advertising and recruiting new staff and also on the training of staff. A low staff turnover indicates that the staff are happy where they are and that the firm is happy with its staff.

Appraisal

Staff appraisal is where one member of staff looks at the way that another is doing their job and, probably in a formal interview, finds out what it is that they like about the job, what they dislike, what they think they are doing particularly well, what they think may need improving. In 360 degree staff appraisal, each person in an organisation is appraised by another, including managers, directors, supervisors and workers. In this way, a picture of how well the whole operation is working should appear. This picture is particularly important in the management of change. For example, management could decide that the introduction of new technology would be a good idea, go ahead with it and then discover that staff morale has fallen, staff turnover increased and productivity decreased. The appraisal process could have shown that staff were unhappy about the introduction of new technology and frightened that it would adversely affect their jobs. Management could then have introduced a training programme to alleviate such fears.

Releasing staff

The main ways of leaving employment are through:

- Retirement – statutory retirement ages for most workers are currently 65 for men and 60 for women, although European legislation will change a woman's retirement age to 65. In many industries, retirement will be earlier than this for various reasons; fighter pilots, for example, retire much younger as their reactions slow down. In some cases, workers will have built up enough years of service to allow them to retire early, say at 50 instead of 65.
- Redundancy – when a job is no longer needed, then the person who did that job is said to be redundant. Many industries have suffered massive redundancies in fairly recent years, including coal, steel, shipbuilding and motor manufacture. Some of this will be through the introduction of new technology, some through international competition, some through the inevitable decline of old industries. For example, there is now no place for steam engineers on the railways – the job no longer exists.
- Resignation – a person may resign from their job at any time by giving the agreed notice period. Resignation may be due to a change of circumstances (a worker may decide to spend time at home looking after children; a worker may have a change of career; a worker may move to a different part of the country) or just a desire not to work for that organisation any more.
- Change of career – most young people entering today's job market can expect their job to change during their lifetime, probably between three and four times. They may need to retrain for new employment as their chosen job area shrinks or disappears, or they may feel, as they get more expertise or education, that they can take on a more demanding job. Whereas in the past, a person might have expected a 'job for life', this is no longer the case.
- Promotion – workers may leave because they have applied for, and been appointed to, a promoted position at another firm.
- Dismissal – workers can be dismissed from a job if they are not carrying it out properly or abusing their position. Minor offences will be dealt with by a disciplinary procedure – which must be outlined at the time of appointment. For example, if a worker was persistently late, they would receive first an informal verbal warning; next (if the offence persists), a formal verbal warning; then, a written warning of dismissal if the offence continues and, finally, a notice of dismissal. Workers can be sacked on the spot (a summary dismissal) for serious offences, such as stealing

or being drunk. A driver found guilty of drink driving, for example, could be summarily dismissed.

Job roles associated with human resources

- The personnel manager was traditionally the head of the department that dealt with all labour matters. Many firms have now replaced this with a human resources department and human resources management.
- Trainers may be recruited from either inside or outside the organisation. It may be part of your job to train new recruits or apprentices or training may be your specialist function. If the latter, you will have been through specific courses and gained specific qualifications in whatever field that you train.
- Recruiter or interviewer. Some firms and people specialise in the psychology of the interview and would be brought in by a firm to deal with all recruitment and appointment issues. A special type of these is called 'headhunters'. These are people or firms that turn the job-seeking role 'on its head'. Instead of advertising for and recruiting applicants, they decide exactly who the person that they want for a particular job is and set about persuading them to leave their current employment and join the firm in question.
- Negotiator/arbitrator. Sometimes people are brought in from outside the firm to settle disputes between workers and management.
- Appraiser. While some appraisal may take place within the firm, there are also professional appraisers who can be brought in to do the job.

PROGRESS CHECK

1. ▶ Describe the difference between personnel and human resources.
2. ▶ Outline what is meant by 360 degree appraisal. Why do you think such a system might have problems in a small business?
3. ▶▶ Explain how human resources management might interact with other functional areas of the business.
4. ▶▶ Describe the process of recruitment, selection and training. What do you see as the essential parts of this process? What could be discarded to make the process more streamlined?
5. ▶▶ Describe the methods that a business could use to try and retain staff and keep down rates of staff turnover.
6. ▶▶▶ What are the advantages and disadvantages of using an agency to deal with human resources compared with having your own human resources department.

Key terms

HUMAN RESOURCES – includes both the people in the organisation and their ideas and welfare.

RECRUITMENT – advertising for new staff.

JOB ANALYSIS – a breakdown of the job role to identify exactly what is required.

JOB DESCRIPTION – the tasks and responsibilities of a job.

PERSON SPECIFICATION – the description of the type of person that will fit the job analysis.

CURRICULUM VITAE – the CV or résumé, this is the story of your life and job experience so far.

INDUCTION – initial training into the operation of a business.

RETENTION – the ways in which a business keeps its staff.

STUDENT CHECKLIST

1. Human resources is different to personnel. It is concerned with the 'whole' employee and not just with the process of recruitment, selection and dismissal.

2. When recruiting, organisations must make sure that they are advertising in the right places at the right times.

3. There are certain parts of a CV that are essential; a good CV will help you get an interview.

4. Types of training include induction, on-the-job and off-the-job training.

5. Strategies for retention are important to keep staff turnover down.

CHAPTER 9

Human resources 2 – Rights and responsibilities

Unison stands firm on tickets

Employees of Glasgow City Council were adamant that they were not about to hand back the tickets that they had been allocated for the Scotland–England football match at Hampden Park. Tickets were sold via a telephone 'hotline' system set up specially for the occasion. The fact that Council employees were effectively able to 'jump the queue' once the telephone hotline opened by using the internal telephone system was the reason given by the Council for asking them to return the tickets. One employee stated that 'we are encouraged to use the internal telephones to order tickets for concerts and festivals, why not football matches?'

The union representing the workers is Unison (the union for local government employees). It has said that it is prepared to take the council to court on behalf of its members. The legal advice received has been that the contract is between the Scottish Football Association and the ticket buyers and the way that contract was made – through the use of internal telephones – has nothing to do with the matter. 'The council has no say in this,' said a Unison spokesperson, 'the tickets have been bought and allocated legally and there is no reason for people to give them up; my members had every right to do as they did.' Non-employees of Glasgow City Council found that the 'hotline' system for obtaining tickets had jammed within minutes of its opening, making it impossible to get through on external telephone lines.

What you need to do

- **To gain a pass** you need to be able to show that you can describe clearly the functional business area of human resources and the role of human resource management. You will need to know the basic legislation which applies to employment. In particular, you will need to be able to explain the rights and responsibilities of employers and employees.
- To gain a merit you also need to be able to explain clearly how the human resources department interacts with the other functional areas of the business and give reasons why certain laws and regulations are thought necessary. You will need to show an understanding of why employers and employees have certain rights and responsibilities and how these are protected in law.
- **To gain a distinction** you also need to evaluate the strengths and weaknesses of the human resources department in its relationships with other departments in the business or businesses that you have studied. You should be able to evaluate the effectiveness of legislation affecting the workplace.

Acts of Parliament

There are a number of Acts of Parliament that govern the rights and responsibilities of both employer and employees. These include protection for employees from employers and for employers from employees. They include the rights and obligations of employees and the responsibilities and obligations of employers. Employment law is often changed as new situations arise but the core idea of fair treatment has always been at the centre of it.

Acts of Parliament are only the first step in the management of a law. Once cases come to court, judges make decisions on how the law should actually be interpreted. These rulings are important and are called precedents. Judgements in court will be based on precedents more often than on the legislation. One of the reasons why laws may change is because a judge's interpretation sets a precedent that does not agree with what the government intended.

Contract of Employment

Once the employer formally offers the job and the candidate accepts it, then a Contract of Employment needs to be drawn up. This is the legal agreement between the employer and the employee and is designed to protect both. It contains details of the job title and place of work and the employee's starting date plus the rate of pay and how often payment will be made (this could be a weekly or monthly wage, or an annual salary – usually paid in twelve monthly parts – paid on a certain day of the week or date of the month).

Other details include the normal hours of work, entitlement to holidays and holiday pay and sickness benefits. Any Trade Union agreements will be outlined in the contract (the firm may have, for example, a single union agreement, where they have agreed that one union should represent all their workers) as well as agreed disciplinary procedures and the period of notice that needs to be given by either the employer or the employee to end the employment. Finally, the employee's rights to pensions will be explained as well as the level of contribution expected by them and by the employer.

COMMUNICATIONS activity

Using the information above, draw up two documents for a firm. One should be a contract of employment with blanks left for the employee details to be filled in. It should be written and presented in a formal style and using legal language. The second should use the same information to produce a leaflet that could be given to a new employee to explain what their rights and responsibilities in contract law are. This should be written in much more accessible language. Use the logo of the firm on both documents.

(C1.3)

Health and safety at work

Both employers and employees have a duty to work in as safe and healthy a way as possible. Part of this is the responsibility of the employer, to provide a safe working environment; part is the responsibility of the employee, not to act in any way that will endanger him or herself or any other worker.

The main piece of legislation is the 1974 Health and Safety at Work Act. Many of the other regulations are based on this legislation or amendments to it. It is itself based on earlier legislation, in particular the 1961 Factories Act, which covered general health and safety issues, such as proper washroom and toilet facilities, adequate ventilation, fire exits, heating and lighting and the fitting of guards on machinery, and the 1963 Offices Shops and Railway Premises Act, which extended much of the Factory Act regulations into other workplaces.

The major requirements of the Health and Safety at Work Act 1974 are to ensure that both employers and employees act in as safe a way as possible in the workplace. Employers have a responsibility to make sure that working conditions are safe and that rules are laid down for safe practices. Employees have a duty to work in as safe a way as possible and to follow safety rules where they are laid down. The main points of the Act are that the working environment must be safe and employers must provide all necessary safety clothing and equipment. All businesses with five or more employees must display a written safety policy and Trades Union appointed inspectors have the right to check that employers are following the rules.

The Act set up the Health and Safety Executive (HSE) with Inspectors who can check that premises are safe. The HSE also investigates accidents at workplaces or similar; for example, an HSE enquiry was set up to look into the cause of a fatal train crash.

The provisions of the Act have been added to from time to time as particular issues are seen as being important. For example:

- 1985 Reporting of Injuries, Diseases and Dangerous Occurrences Regulations – certain listed diseases must be reported as must any accident which causes an employee to take more than three days off work. All accidents are recorded in an 'accident book'.

- 1988 Control of Substances Hazardous to Health Regulations – brought about to make sure that people were aware of the dangers of asbestos but it also applies to other harmful substances.

- 1989 Noise at Work Regulations – employers have a responsibility to keep noise levels down and to provide ear protection where this is not possible.

COMMUNICATIONS activity

Prepare a case for a discussion in your class or group. One group should represent the Glasgow Council workers who have tickets, one should represent Glasgow Council, one should represent the Scottish FA and one should represent the people who telephoned for tickets but failed to get through. Record the conclusions that you reach on the rights and wrongs of the case.

(C3.1a)

GET IT RIGHT!

Use an example with which you are familiar to see how Health and Safety Rules apply – use your school or college and see if they are following the requirements of the Acts.

Trade unions

Employees have the right to join a trade union at their place of work. Trade unions have always worked to improve conditions of work, health and safety, and pay and conditions of employment. Often this has brought them into conflict with employers and various pieces of legislation have been enacted to try to keep this conflict to a minimum. Some practices (such as picketing at other than your own place of work) were seen as unfair to employers; some as unfair to employees (not holding a proper ballot before taking action, for example).

Industrial action

Possible action that could be taken by a union in dispute with an employer included:

- work-to-rule – deliberately following every rule and regulation so that production is slowed down
- go slow – similar to work-to-rule
- selective strikes – striking on key days, at key times or at key plants
- strikes – withdrawal of labour
- picketing – trying to persuade other workers not to work by standing, for example, at a factory gate; those who cross the picket line are referred to as 'blacklegs' or 'scabs', those who do not have shown their 'solidarity'
- secondary picketing – picketing at other than your place of work, for example, at a suppliers
- sympathy strikes – taking action because of a dispute in another firm or industry in order to show 'solidarity'.

Weapons available to the employer include:

- dismissing the striker
- taking court action if they feel they are losing money due to industrial action
- lock-outs – not allowing anyone into a building or workplace.

Industrial action laws

The main legislation which covers industrial action is:

- 1980 Employment Act. This removed the right of automatic trade union recognition at a place of work, meaning that employers could refuse to recognise or negotiate with a union. This Act has led to 'beauty contests' between rival unions who wish to represent a firm or industry when employers have decided to recognise and negotiate with only one union. Single union agreements mean that all workers in a plant or factory are members of one union, which the employer recognises. The Act also stopped the practice of 'flying pickets', limiting picketing action to the employee's 'own place of work'.
- 1982 Employment Act redefined what disputes were lawful. They had to be 'in pursuit of an industrial dispute'. This stopped unions from taking secondary action to support workers in dispute in other parts of their industry. If a dispute was judged unlawful, union funds could be seized and unions could be fined up to £250,000. The Act also weakened the employee's right to strike by making it easier for strikers to be dismissed by an employer.
- 1984 Trades Union Act. This laid down that no strike action could take place without a secret ballot, with various rules and restrictions on how these must be carried out. If action was taken without the ballot, employers could sue the union for damages.
- 1990 Employment Act. This extended the right to sue for losses from unofficial action to firms only indirectly affected by strikes, such as customers and suppliers.
- 1993 Trades Union Reform and Employment Rights Act. Employers must be given seven days notice of official action and a 'citizen's right' to stop unofficial strikes was established. This Act also abolished the remaining wages councils and minimum wage rates. It established a worker's right to a Contract of Employment.
- 1996 Employment Rights Act. This is a major piece of government legislation, much of it linked to EU legislation, designed to ensure that employees have certain rights guaranteed in law. Its main particulars are:

1 All employees are entitled to a statement of their employment details. Where a Contract of Employment may be written or oral, this statement must be written and must contain details such as rates of pay, terms and conditions of employment, pensions, notice periods, disciplinary procedures and so on. If a statement is not issued within two months of the employment starting, then the employee can take the employer to an industrial tribunal who will rule on what the conditions should be – a ruling that is binding on the employer.

2 All employees have the right to an itemised pay statement.

3 All employees and employers have the right to a minimum notice period on either side. This is one week for two years or less continuous employment and an additional week per year once two years is reached up to a maximum of twelve weeks.

4 If dismissed, all employees are entitled to a written statement of the reasons for their dismissal.

5 Employees have the right not to be unfairly dismissed. This particularly

includes paragraphs covering the return to work after childbirth. An employee is regarded as being unfairly dismissed if the reason for the dismissal is any reason associated with the pregnancy or birth of a child.

6 Employees can appeal to an industrial tribunal if they feel they have been unfairly dismissed and the tribunal can, if it finds in their favour, order the employer to reinstate the employee in a position and at a level as if they had never been dismissed.

7 Employees have the right to redundancy payments.

- 1999 Working Time Directive. This is a section of EU legislation that could not be rejected by any members as it comes under the heading of 'social' legislation and is designed to improve working conditions. It limits the working week to 48 hours and the working day to 13 hours; sets down minimum rest periods and limits the amount of overtime in jobs involving special hazards or heavy physical or mental strain. The total cost to industry of monitoring the directive is said to be in the region of £1.7 billion. In November 1999, the prime minister promised business leaders that he would cut down on what he called 'over-the-top' rules from Europe on the 48-hour working week. Mr Blair made clear that he wanted to work in partnership with business to relax some of the new regulations that businesses see as adding heavily to their costs.

IT activity

Find any information that you can that will give you the background to the legislation outlined above. Then write an explanation of how you think the background affected the legislation.

TUC

The organisation which represents almost all trade union members is the Trades Union Congress – usually known just by its initials, the TUC. It holds an annual conference where delegates from all the major unions discuss problems and policy issues. The TUC council then represents those views to the government of the day, acting on behalf of its membership.

Employee Organisations

Employees can also join together and form organisations to provide help and support for each other. These may be trade associations (for example, the Society of Motor Manufacturers), local organisations such as Chambers of Commerce and Chambers of Trade or national organisations. The most prominent national organisation is the Confederation for British Industry, usually known just by its initials as the CBI. It also holds an annual conference and represents the views of employers to the government.

PROGRESS CHECK

1. ▶ Describe what the main rights and responsibilities of employer and employee are.

2. ▶ Outline what you think the function of the HSE is.

3. ▶▶ Look at the series of industrial action laws and explain why you think there are so many of them; what events do you think were happening that might have affected them?

4. ▶▶ Do you think that the Glasgow Council employees are wrong or right? Explain your views.

5. ▶▶▶ Explain what is meant by the term 'precedent'. Why is this important in English law?

Key terms

CONTRACT OF EMPLOYMENT – the agreement between the employer and employee which outlines their roles, rights and responsibilities.

INDUSTRIAL ACTION – taking actions that are meant to stop or slow down production, in support of a grievance.

PICKETING – standing at a place of work and trying to persuade workers not to go in, not to cross the 'picket line'.

TUC – TRADES UNION CONGRESS – the national organisation that represents trade unions.

CBI – CONFEDERATION OF BRITISH INDUSTRY – the national organisation that represents employers.

STUDENT CHECKLIST

1. Both employer and employee have rights and responsibilities; most of these are laid down in law.

2. The main laws cover Health and Safety at Work and industrial disputes.

3. Legislation has been used to try to make disputes between employers and employees both less frequent and less damaging.

CHAPTER 10

Human resources 3 – Equal opportunities

No Ken do!

Kenneth Clark had applied for a job at a well-known high street store in the usual way. He had filled out a detailed application form and enclosed a CV giving his extensive qualifications. His degree in Business Management from Harvard – one of the leading universities in the USA – was way above the qualifications actually required by the store. He was invited to interview on the strength of a good application.

At the interview, Mr Clark noticed, in his own words 'that the interview panel looked uncomfortable'. A middle-aged lady – the store manager – seemed insistent on questioning whether his American qualification was genuine. She also said that Mr Clark 'didn't look like the sort of person that our customers could relate to'.

Mr Clark did not get the job but, concerned by the strangeness of the interview, investigated who had been given it. The job had been given to a young man about the same age as him, but who had no university qualifications at all.

The only real difference that Mr Clark could see was that the customers in the shop were mostly middle-aged and white, all the other staff were white and he himself is black.

His case is still being heard at the Race Relations Commission.

What you need to do

- **To gain a pass** you need to be able to show that you can describe clearly the functional business area of human resources. You will need to know the basic legislation which applies to employment. In particular, you will need to be able to explain the rights and responsibilities of employers and employees with regard to equal opportunities laws.

- **To gain a merit** you also need to be able to explain clearly how the human resources department interacts with the other functional areas of the business and give reasons why certain laws and regulations, particularly those to do with equality of opportunity, are thought necessary.
- **To gain a distinction** you also need to evaluate the strengths and weaknesses of the human resources department in its relationships with other departments in the business or businesses that you have studied. You should be able to evaluate the effectiveness of equal opportunities legislation affecting the workplace.

Equal opportunities legislation

The case of Ken Clark is typical of the way that some employers have always reacted to minority groups. Discrimination is taking a decision against somebody because of a reason that has nothing to do with their ability to do the job. Perhaps it is the colour of their skin, their race, their religion, their sex. Usually it is linked to some form of prejudice. Governments have passed laws which cover three of the four main areas where discrimination has taken place – gender, race and disability. They have not yet legislated to prevent discrimination on grounds of age.

Gender equality

These are a series of laws designed to ensure that men and women are treated the same at work. They are intended to outlaw discriminatory practices, such as paying a woman less than a man even when she is doing the same job.

The main law is the 1970 Equal Pay Act. Men and women should receive equal pay for equal work. If a woman is doing the same work as a man, she should be paid the same wage. This applies even if her job has a different title, but she is doing the same work. She can make a claim by comparing her workload and wages with a man who is being paid more. (Men can also demand the same rates as women but it is rare that discrimination is in this direction.)

The 1975 Sex Discrimination Act extended the law to take account of such things as recruitment and training and promotion opportunities. Employers may not discriminate on grounds of the gender of an employee. The Equal Opportunities Commission was set up to enforce the Act.

The three types of discrimination are direct, indirect and positive:

- direct discrimination – for example, stating that a man would be best for a job that could equally well be done by either sex
- indirect discrimination – for example, not appointing a woman to a job because she might get married and have children
- positive discrimination – where an employer is allowed to discriminate in favour of a minority that has traditionally been discriminated against. For example, employers with more than 20 workers have

been encouraged to have at least 3% of their workforce drawn from the disabled; employers of certain local councils will try to ensure that they have a fair representation of the racial and religious groups within their area.

GET IT RIGHT! ✓

Positive discrimination is not only perfectly legal but actively encouraged in areas where minority groups have traditionally been discriminated against. It is one way in which employers seek to ensure that they have a balanced workforce.

NUMERACY activity

In a recently reported case, a woman manager claimed that she was doing exactly the same job as a man. She had been given the title of 'Supervisor' and paid on that scale, while the man had been given the title of 'Manager' and was paid 40% more. The man earned £30,000 a year. At another plant, the same firm was paying a man with the title of 'Supervisor' £25,000 a year, while the women carrying out the same tasks as him had no title and received 25% less. The firm claimed that both the men had more experience and responsibility but the courts agreed with the women and awarded them compensation amounting to five years worth of the salary they should have received.

1. How much were the women earning in each case?
2. On the basis of these figures, how much less, on average, were the women earning per month than the men?
3. How much compensation should the women have received?
4. Show the disparity between the rates of pay on a suitable chart or charts.

Race equality

The main piece of legislation is the 1976 Race Relations Act. This made discrimination on the grounds of race or colour, marital status, nationality or ethnic group illegal and set up

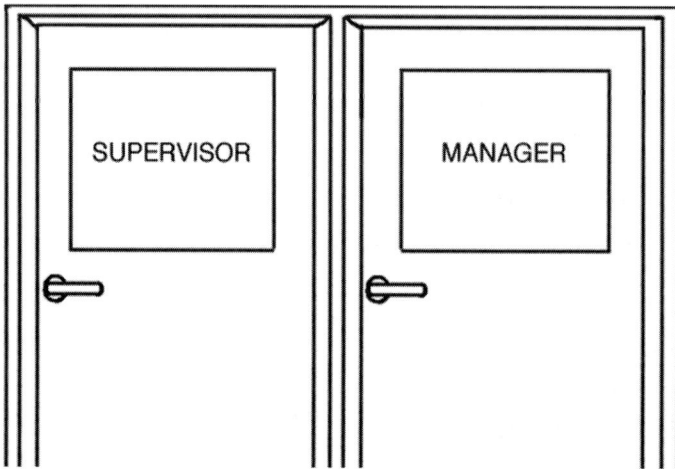

FIGURE 10.1

the Race Relations Board to investigate complaints.

The Act applies to job advertisements, recruitment processes (such as interviews), and training and promotion opportunities, as well as normal employment.

Equality for the disabled

This is covered by the 1995 Disability Discrimination Act. Employers with 20 or more staff cannot discriminate against applicants or employees on grounds of disability, providing that the individual is capable of doing the job. For example, a firm could not refuse to employ someone just because they were in a wheelchair. The employer should employ the person and provide wheelchair access such as ramps.

IT *activity*

List ten public buildings that you can think of. They might be libraries, town halls, museums, even places like the Houses of Parliament and 10 Downing Street. Now use the Internet to find out if they have disabled facilities or not and, if so, what facilities they have. Using the information you have gathered, put the buildings in your list in order of 'disability friendliness'. If you find buildings with poor facilities you could send them a letter asking why their facilities are so poor and what they intend to do about it.

What are the results of your research? Do you think that most public buildings are now disability friendly? Compare your list with two or three other people's and see if you agree.

Equality of opportunity

The government has also enacted legislation to try to make sure that other groups get equal opportunities to work and train. Some of these are meant to protect employees from unscrupulous employers, some are meant to help people back into work and some are a result of European legislation.

Minimum wage

The Labour government which came to power in 1997 has introduced minimum wage legislation. The minimum wage has been set at £3.00 per hour for 18–20 year olds and £3.60 per hour for those over 20. The objective of the legislation is to stop employers from paying very low wages. Employers complained that it would lead to a loss of jobs as they would not be able to afford the new rates, however, over a year into the policy, there is little evidence suggesting this. Unemployment is actually lower than when the minimum wage level was set.

New Deal

In 1998, the new Labour government introduced this scheme to encourage young people who have been unemployed for more than six months back into work. Employers receive a grant of £60 per week for the first six months that they employ an unemployed person between the ages of 18 and 24 who has been unemployed for this length of time. For their part, young unemployed people must 'keep their hand in' by working as a volunteer or entering a course of full-time education that will last at least six months if they cannot find employment.

The Social Chapter

The UK government signed up to the European Union Social Chapter in 1997, after a period of resistance from the previous government. This means that much employment law is now subject to European law. The Social Chapter affects health and safety at work, involvement of workers in the management of firms, and trade union and industrial action rights. For example, the Social Chapter proposes that new parents – of either gender – should be entitled to up to three months leave and that works councils should be set up in larger organisations. The government has asked for time to introduce such changes gradually.

Key terms

EQUAL OPPORTUNITIES – giving people the same chances.

DISCRIMINATION – usually not choosing, promoting etc a worker because of a factor that has nothing to do with their ability to do the job.

POSITIVE DISCRIMINATION – acting in favour of a group who have traditionally been discriminated against.

PROGRESS CHECK

1. ▶ Explain what is meant by the terms discrimination and prejudice.

2. ▶ Describe how the equal opportunities of employees are protected by law.

3. ▶▶ Give examples of how two of the following groups are protected by law: women, the disabled, racial or religious minorities. You should quote the appropriate Act in each case.

4. ▶▶▶ Choose two of the following major Acts – Employment Rights Act 1996, Sex Discrimination Act 1975, Race Relations Act 1976, Disability Discrimination Act 1995 – and say in what ways you think the Act could have been made more effective. Explain why you think that the Government hasn't taken the steps you recommend.

STUDENT CHECKLIST

1. Unfair practices are known as discrimination.

2. It is illegal to discriminate on grounds of sex, colour, race, religion, sexual orientation, or disability.

3. The major UK Acts are Sex Discrimination 1975, Race Relations 1976 and Disability Discrimination 1995.

4. European law is likely to increasingly affect our own laws.

CHAPTER 11

Finance department

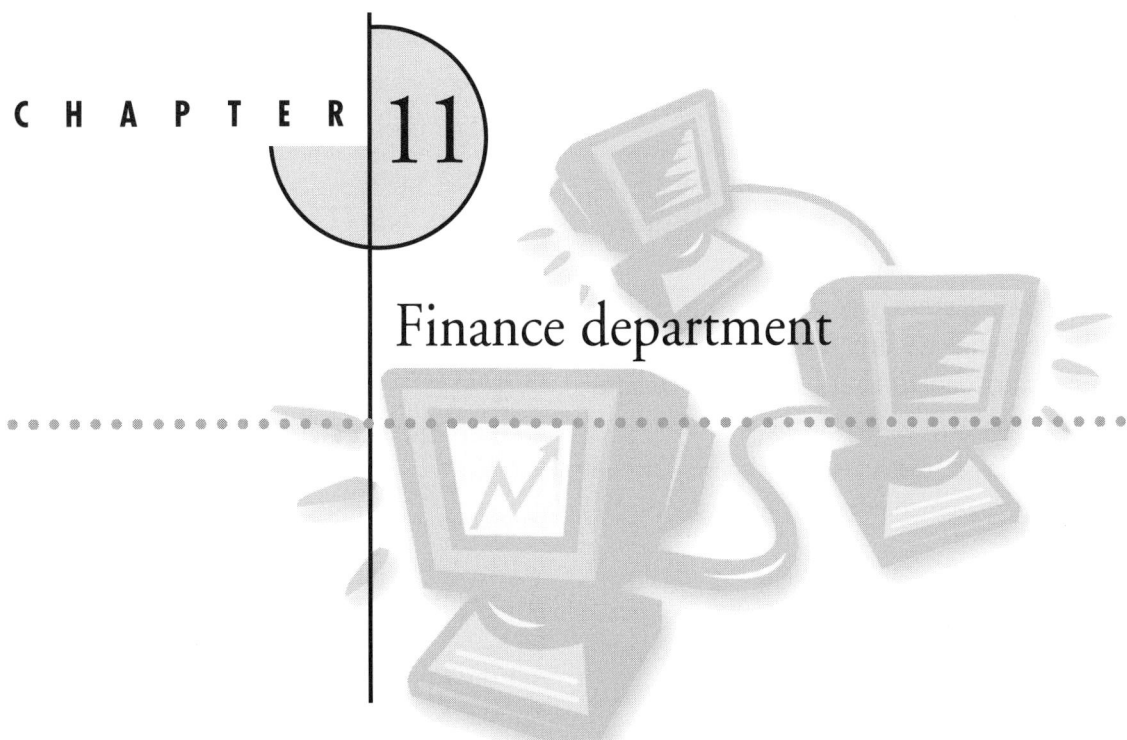

Gloomy headlines for Longbridge

Throughout 1998 and into early 1999, the financial problems of Rover's Longbridge car plant made for frequent gloomy headlines in national newspapers. The financial section of The Mail on Sunday on 7 February 1999 used the headline 'Can anyone beat the Longbridge curse?' as it reported that the two people BMW had put in to reverse Rover's decline had been axed from their jobs.

BMW's decision came after what appeared to be a delayed detailed analysis of Rover's financial situation. After all, the German company had pumped in £2.5 billion worth of investment after it bought Longbridge in 1994 and a range of new models had been promised. In 1998, the Rover workers had agreed to improved flexibility in working practices, which cut costs by £150 million per year. Part of this deal meant the loss of 2,500 jobs in return for a further £2 billion of investment. A series of economic problems hit the worldwide motor industry in 1998 and it is believed that Rover's losses quickly mounted to over £200 million that year. With the help of both the UK government and the EU, Longbridge's future appeared to have been guaranteed with the role of the finance department at Rover crucial in providing future information to the new managers about the health of the car firm. It was a shock then, when BMW announced in March 2000, that Rover was to be put up for sale.

What you need to do

- **To gain a pass** you need to describe the functions of the finance department explaining fully how it contributes to the business activity and give examples of job roles associated with it.
- **To gain a merit** you also need to explain how the finance department interacts with the other departments to achieve the aims and objectives of the business.
- **To gain a distinction** – there are no specific statements for this level.

Finance or accounting?

These are alternative titles for the department that arranges and manages the flows of money into, out of and within a business. The department will be responsible for obtaining the capital required both to start up a business and to finance any expansion, as well as providing enough money to keep all the other departments operating. It will also be responsible for keeping all the firm's financial records, so that checks can be made on all the flows of money, the records can be analysed and accurate accounts kept to inform all the people and organisations with an interest in the financial records.

As with all departments, the exact job titles will vary from firm to firm according to size and type. Typical job titles will, therefore, include the following:

- Chief accountant
- Management Accountant
- Credit Controller
- Cost Clerk
- Cost Accountant
- Chief cashier
- Ledger clerk
- Wages Clerk
- Credit control Clerk

How does the finance department interact with the other departments?

In many ways the finance department is both the servant and the master of all the other departments in a firm. The function of arranging and controlling the supply of capital allows the other departments to then carry out their functions. Without capital, material cannot be bought, goods will not be produced and, therefore, revenue will not be earned because there will be nothing to sell. If, on the other hand, the production department fails to keep costs under control or the marketing department fails to attract sufficient demand for the firm's products, it will be up to the finance department to identify the financial problems and demand that action be taken. In this way the finance department may help the firm to both set and keep its objectives, particularly when these objectives relate to such financial targets as maximising revenue or profits.

Obtaining capital and resources

Some finance will be obtained from the owners – owners' capital. In the case of sole proprietors and partnerships, the owners will use their own personal sources to provide some of the capital to set up, expand and run the business. Most of these owners will have a direct role in helping to run the business. In the case of limited companies, shareholders will use their own personal financial resources to buy a share of the ownership in a company. Most shareholders are unlikely to have a direct role in running the company but may vote on major decisions at the company's annual general meeting. In all cases the capital is permanently invested in the business and the money is not a form of loan.

Additional owners' capital may be suggested by a finance department to pay for an expansion. For a sole proprietor this might mean converting to a partnership, while a partnership might look for additional partners. In the case of limited companies additional sets of shares might be issued for sale. In all cases, the finance department will need to keep a record of the owners and the amount of money they have personally put into the firm. While virtually all owners will expect a share of the profits made by the firm, most owners will use part of their profits to plough back into the firm. These *retained profits* are a major source of finance for all types of business and have the added attraction of no extra cost to the business.

Some capital might be obtained from *grants*. The amounts of money will vary according to the location and circumstances of the firm. For example, new small starters might be able to obtain £50 per week to help with the owners' wages while other multinational firms might obtain many millions of pounds towards building costs by locating in an area of high unemployment.

If the above three sources of capital are insufficient, then a firm might have to borrow money in various ways and this is often known as *debt finance*. This might take the form of an overdraft from a bank to pay for short-term debts; or for larger sums that need to be paid back over several years, term loans might be obtained from banks and other financial institutions. Any form of borrowed funds will involve the business in paying interest and the finance department must take this into account when arranging such financial sources. Trade credit might be used to help buy stock while some items of equipment or even buildings might be leased for a regular payment or rent. Again the finance department must weigh up the 'best' form of finance and keep a record of payments that are required once the financial deal has been made.

Financial and management accounting

Whether the business is small and employs an outside accountancy firm or whether the business is large and operates its own department, yearly accounts must be created. For sole proprietors, partnerships and shareholders in private limited companies these are mainly for the owners to analyse their personal financial interests and for the tax authorities to calculate the amount of tax owed. Public limited companies have to formally publish their annual accounts and may be scrutinised by the general public and by other firms, as well as by the shareholders and the tax authorities.

A firm may produce monthly, weekly or even daily accounts to provide up-to-date financial information for management to use to run the business. This information will help management analyse past and present performance so that it may plan for the future.

There are three main forms of accounts created and used by a firm. A profit and loss account will show a firm its sales revenue, its expenditure on the main items of cost and various measures of profit over a past period of time. Unit 3 Chapter 32 will show you how to present and calculate a simple form of profit and loss account but a fuller version might look something like this.

TABLE 11.1 *Profit and loss account for Glorious Flowers Ltd for the year ending 31.3.2000*

	£
Sales revenue	750,000
Less cost of sales	345,000
Gross profit	405,000
Add other income	5,000
Less expenses	185,000
Net profit	225,000
Less tax	75,000
Profit after tax	150,000
Dividends paid	90,000
Retained profit	60,000

To show the value of the company at this moment in time, a firm will use a balance sheet. This, in effect, gives a snapshot of the company's value but this value will immediately begin to change the next day. The balance sheet will show the main assets that it owns, the liabilities that it owes and the sources and amounts of capital invested in the company. A basic balance sheet is shown in Table 11.2.

To give an analysis of future flows of cash a cash flow forecast may be used and compared with the actual flow of cash. This is explained in detail in Unit 3 Chapter 31, so look there for examples of cash flow forecasts.

Cost accounting

All businesses will want a detailed record of its costs. These records help a firm monitor its day-to-day expenditure. A firm will keep a record of both its direct and indirect costs. Direct costs will include those costs directly paid as a result of manufacturing a good or providing a service, so will include costs of materials and the labour costs incurred in actually making the products. Indirect costs will include costs that are not directly linked to the production process itself, such as heating and lighting, rent, rates and some staff costs. Each firm will need to decide for itself what to include in which category. For example, power costs might easily apply as both direct and indirect since power will be needed to operate manufacturing machinery as well as to heat and light the offices.

Records of direct and indirect costs will be used in conjunction with records of sales and revenue to help feed into the financial and management accounts explained earlier. The records will also help to review such decisions as changes to prices and promotion.

TABLE 11.2 *Balance sheet for Pringles – The Opticians as at 31.3.2000*

	£ '000S	£ '000S	£ '000S
Fixed assets			
Land and buildings	150		
Equipment and vehicles	45		
Furniture and furnishings	12		
			207
Current assets			
Stocks	38		
Debtors	6		
Cash	3		
		47	
Less current liabilities			
Creditors	19		
Bank overdraft	6		
		25	
Net current assets (working capital)			22
Net assets employed			229
Financed by:			
Share capital			104
Retained profit			60
Bank loans			65
Capital employed			229

Key terms

OWNERS' CAPITAL – capital or money put into the business by the owners when they set up or expand their business.

RETAINED PROFIT – part of a firm's profit that is not distributed to the owners but is kept back within the business either to act as a reserve or to purchase new equipment, buildings and vehicles.

DEBT FINANCE – any form of finance that involves a firm borrowing money that has to be repaid and, in most cases, on which interest has to be paid.

GRANTS – amounts of money given by outside organisations such as councils, the government and the EU towards the cost of buildings, equipment and sometimes the training costs of workers.

FINANCIAL ACCOUNTING – the creating of formal accounts to meet the legal requirements on firms and especially on limited companies. Typically this includes the creation of annual profit and loss accounts, balance sheets and cash flow forecasts and records.

MANAGEMENT ACCOUNTING – the production of regular accounts that help managers review the financial position of a firm and then plan and implement changes to the firm.

COST ACCOUNTING – records of the costs involved in making products, providing services and running the business. The records of direct and indirect costs feed into the financial and management accounts along with other records on sales and revenue.

BALANCE SHEETS – an account that acts as a snapshot of the value of a firm at a moment in time. Values for assets (what it owns) and liabilities (what it owes) are balanced by values for the sources of capital that have allowed these assets and liabilities to be obtained.

STUDENT CHECKLIST

1. **The functions of the finance department include:**
   - **obtaining finance or capital**
   - **recording financial transactions**
   - **analysing costs and preparing wages and salaries**
   - **preparing the final annual financial accounts**
   - **producing continuous financial information to enable the managers to effectively run the firm**
   - **managing debt.**

2. **This department will be essential both in providing the money to enable the other departments to operate and in controlling the financial dealings of those same departments.**

CHAPTER 12

Administration department

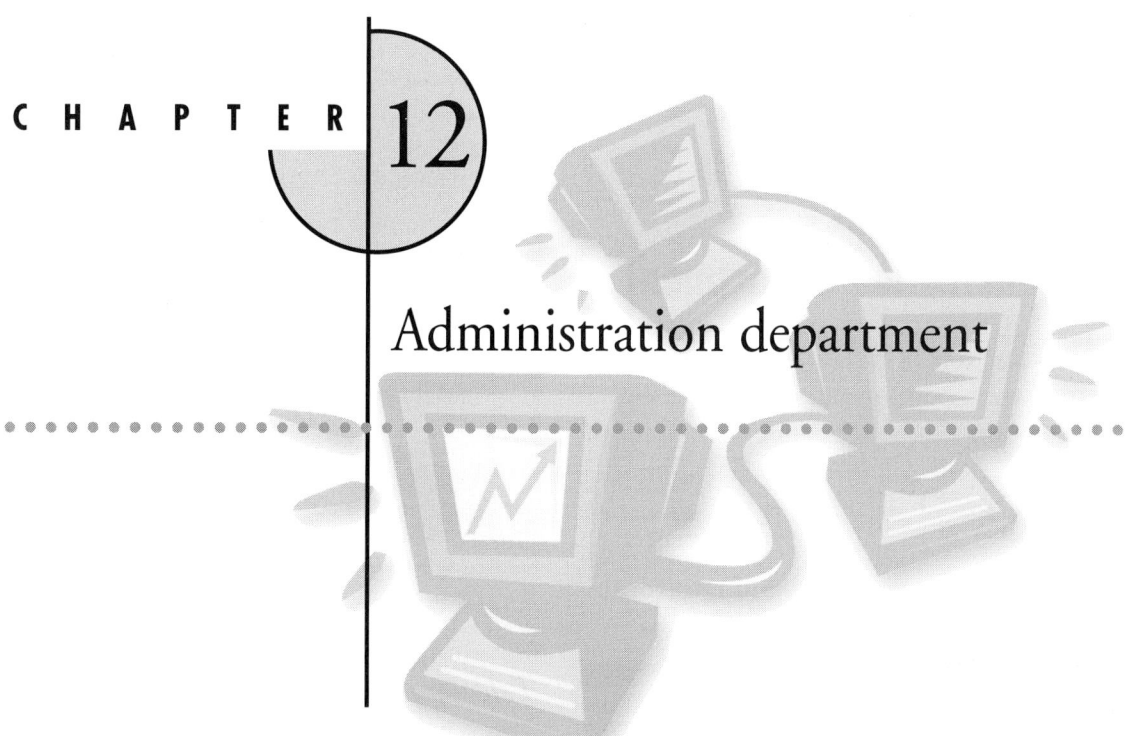

Local councils top for admin

Some of the best examples of an organisation providing an administrative service as its main function are local councils. In many parts of the country, you will have a two-tier system of County Council and District Council with each responsible for quite specific services. For example, the main service of a County Council will be administering the Education service while the District Council will provide a wider number of smaller services including housing and refuse collection. A smaller number of areas will have a unitary council or authority providing and administering all these services. Your own school or college will have its own administration system to support teachers and students and you will be the recipients of much of the output of this provision. For example, consider the forms of administration that are needed to create reports that assess your progress. Alternatively, consider the processes you personally need to adopt to complete your portfolio of work for Units 1 and 2 and for the key skill as you complete this course.

What you need to do

- **To gain a pass** you need to describe the functions and main activities of the administration department; describe the main job roles of the department; and explain how the department contributes to the overall business activity.
- **To gain a merit** you will also have to explain how the administration department interacts with the others to achieve the aims and objectives of a firm.

- **To gain a distinction** – there are no specific statements for this level.

The functions and main activities of the administration department

The overall role of this department is to provide all the service operations required by an organisation. The exact nature and extent of such operations will certainly depend on the type and size of the firm, as well as on its organisational structure. The following breakdown represents a very full range of the typical operations in a large firm.

FIGURE 12.2 *Telephone operator*
Source: © Bill Varie/CORBIS

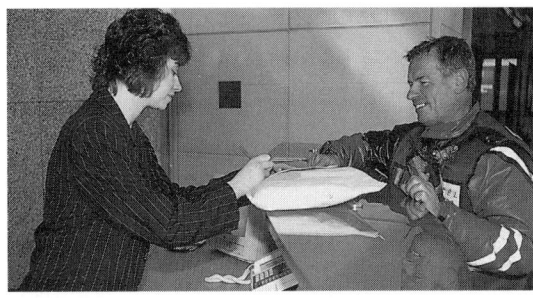

FIGURE 12.1 *A receptionist at work*
Source: Andrew Ward/Life File

Reception

This will deal with all visitors to the firm and will represent the first impression visitors gain of the firm. It may also be responsible for dealing with incoming phone calls in smaller firms.

Mail handling

Incoming mail will need to be sorted and delivered to the right departments; and in some firms the mail may be opened centrally before being delivered to the appropriate sections and personnel. Outgoing mail will be collected and sent via the chosen agency – usually either the post office or private courier firms.

Telecommunications

This is an ever expanding part of any administration department. The more traditional role of managing the telephone system within a firm will have expanded to fax machines and even video-conferencing where that is an important business tool for the firm. It may well include the provision and maintenance of computer facilities with e-mail and access to the Internet becoming increasingly important for all business.

Filing/clerical/word processing/data processing

In most firms a multi-skilled worker is required to handle these sort of jobs, with records being kept both on computers and in hard copy form, and with new technology being introduced to speed up many of the old time-consuming tasks.

FIGURE 12.3 *Using a photocopier*
Source: Emma Lee/Life File

Reprographics

In some firms there will be a small demand to print multiple copies of written materials, while in other firms thousands of copies need to be reproduced each day. In this latter case, a firm will usually find it cheaper to set up a separate reprographics section rather than have each area with its own costly photocopying facilities.

Other services

This could be anything that needs to be provided but has not been provided by another department in the firm. The most obvious examples are the provision of cleaning services and the arrangements of security services.

Legal services

All companies must, by law, have someone to act as 'Company Secretary'. The specific role of this person is to keep a record of the meetings of Board of Directors, to oversee the administration of pensions and insurance, to keep a register of shareholders and to communicate with them, and to keep the company operating within the law. In many firms, the company secretary will also take charge of the administration work of the business.

How does the administration department interact with the other departments?

Some people compare the administration department of a firm with the concept of the importance of oil keeping a car engine from seizing up. Much of the work will lack the glamour of the marketing department or will seem incidental to the production of the good itself. Without the administration department, however, the day-to-day tasks of running a business would not be done and the firm would slowly grind to a halt.

Administration department job titles

The actual number of workers and their actual titles and roles will vary with each firm. The following give an idea of some of the possible jobs in an administration department together with an indication of their relative importance:

- company secretary
- office manager
- secretarial supervisor
- telephonist
- receptionist
- cleaner
- security guard
- reprographics technician
- computer services manager
- mail room supervisor

PROGRESS CHECK

You need to carry out research into the administration department of a business. One of the most obvious organisations to research is your own educational establishment. Attempt to find out:

- the titles of the different sections within the department
- the main job titles within the sections
- the roles and functions of the both the sections and the workers
- how the department helps the other departments to operate.

Key terms

COMPANY SECRETARY – the person required by law to take legal responsibility for the operation of the company.

 ## STUDENT CHECKLIST

1. The administration department will service all the other departments.
2. Main operations might include:
   - reception
   - mail handling
   - telecommunications
   - filing and clerical work, word and data processing
   - reprographics
   - other services such as cleaning and security
   - legal services.

CHAPTER 13

Production department

The making of the 5,000

Nissan opened its car plant in Sunderland in 1984 with the first car being produced in 1986. It now employs about 5,000 people in the North East and is capable of producing over 350,000 vehicles a year. These workers are involved in vehicle assembly, design, and development, vehicle shipment, distribution and component manufacturing. A single car is made up from about 5,000 different components and the Sunderland plant utilises about 200 suppliers in the UK and Europe.

The car plant has three main line shops; body assembly, painting and final assembly. These are supported by five manufacturing areas; the press shop, plastic fuel tank and bumper moulding and painting, engine casting, engine machining and assembly and axle manufacturing. Some areas are highly automated processes. For example, the press shop is linked directly to the body assembly with a family of 250 robots providing an 80% automation level. Other areas are more labour intensive or require specific labour skills. For example, dashboards are pushed into place using the highly skilled feet of a human operative.

FIGURE 13.1

What you need to do

- **To gain a pass** you need to describe the production function of a business, explaining how it contributes to the business activity and giving examples of job roles in the department.
- **To gain a merit** you also need to explain how the production department interacts with the other departments in the business.
- **To gain a distinction** – there are no specific statements for this level.

Role of the production department

Most firms will only have a production department when they are involved in manufacturing or constructing a product. The main tasks or functions of the production department, apart from the possible responsibility for purchasing materials and equipment, will be production planning and production control.

Production planning

Once a produce has been designed, its manufacture or assembly has to be carefully planned. Decisions will have to be made including:

- What raw materials will be needed and in what quantities?
- How will the materials be stored?
- What machinery, equipment and tools will be needed?
- How many workers will be required and what range of skills and experience will they need to offer?
- What production system or method will be used – job, batch or flow? (see key terms)
- How will the product be packaged?
- How many units will be produced and over what time period?
- How will production be controlled?

Production control

Once the production plans have been made and the manufacturing process has started, it will be vital that production controls are in place and are operating to ensure that targets are met. This will involve a number of tasks:

- Maintenance of equipment will be vital to prevent breakdowns and to ensure correct manufacture of each production unit.
- Monitoring and control of stocks of both materials and finished products and perhaps including the use of strategies such as just-in-time.
- Work study of the production processes to measure the output of workers and machines and so check that they are operating in the most efficient way.
- Quality control systems need to be in place to ensure that each unit is produced to the correct standards set by the firm, either through quality control checks or the more modern Total Quality Management (TQM) system.

Structure

The organisation and structure of a production department will very much depend on the type and size of firm and its product. This will also dictate the number of managers or under-managers, and the number of sections that the department is divided into. Broad job titles will include:

- engineers
- supervisors
- production controllers
- storage controllers
- quality controllers
- production operatives

The roles of workers with these titles will vary from firm to firm but typical descriptions of two of them might be:

Production supervisor

- A first line manager for workers to report to.
- An experienced, skilled worker either promoted from within the firm or recruited from outside with the relevant skills, experience and qualifications.
- Will report to production managers.
- Will have control of a number of workers.
- Makes operational decisions about the work being done.

Production operative

- Uses skills to complete the job.
- Works to set targets.
- Works as a member of a production team.
- Makes decisions concerning specific jobs/tasks in hand.

For a manufacturing firm, the production department is often seen as the core department. The other departments exist to enable production to take place. The Human Resources department will be expected to provide suitable workers and look after their general welfare. If there is a separate purchasing department it will be expected to buy in the right materials and equipment at the right price to enable production to take place at the right cost levels. The marketing department will be expected to ensure steady demand for the product being made with the finance department managing and controlling the financial requirements of the firm so that production may take place smoothly and at a profit. Communications between departments and between departments and the outside business world would be helped by the workings of the administration department. All of these would be overseen by the managing director and any additional managers that the firm needed.

Production resources

To make a product or provide a service, businesses need a wide range of resources. One way of grouping these is shown in Unit 3 Chapter 29, but for now we can think of resources under four headings:

1 buildings and land, e.g. offices, factories, shops and farmland

2 equipment, e.g. vehicles, computers and machinery

3 people, e.g. managers, operators, support staff and specialists

4 materials, e.g. raw materials, parts, components and finished products for retailing.

In some large firms, the purchasing and hiring of most resources, with the probable exception of workers, will be the sole responsibility of a purchasing department. This would be run by a purchasing manager together with purchasing assistants and specialist buyers. Buying for the whole organisation, rather than allowing each department to buy its own requirements, usually keeps costs down as items may be bought in bulk at discounted prices. It also allows the buyers to become experts in a particular resource and they can then use this knowledge to approach the best suppliers and obtain the best deals. Specialists might be best in wide range of cases including fashion buyers for the large clothing retailers like BHS and Marks and Spencer, computer experts for firms dependent on the latest computer technology, and tea tasters for the large tea bag manufacturers.

Some firms may prefer to allow the purchasing function to be carried out by a number of departments within the firm. For example, while the hiring of workers will be arranged through the human resources department, the purchase of office equipment is likely to be arranged by the administration department and the purchase or hiring of lorries may be arranged by the warehousing or distribution departments. If this is the case, the production department may be responsible for buying the resources it needs for the manufacturing process, as well as its own equipment requirements.

Most firms will only have a production department when they are involved in manufacturing or constructing a product. In this case, the main tasks or functions of the production department, apart from the possible responsibility for purchasing materials and equipment, will be production planning and control.

FIGURE 13.2 *Car assembly line*

PROGRESS CHECK

1. ▶ You need to carry out research into the production department of a business. This might be a firm like Nissan described at the start of this chapter but it does not have to be. Attempt to find out:

   - what resources are used by the firm
   - how production is planned
   - how production is controlled
   - how the department is structured and organised
   - the main job categories of those working in the department.

2. ▶▶ Also find out and write about:

   - how the department is helping to support the aims and objectives of the firm
   - how the production department interacts with the other departments.

Key terms

JOB PRODUCTION – producing a single, one-off product or service to meet the individual requirements of a customer, e.g. a road bridge, an airplane, an extension to a house, a haircut.

- *Location:* How do I find the shop? Is it convenient for public transport? Is the car parking adequate, free and close to the shop? Is there easy road access to the shop? Are other shops nearby?

- *Information:* Is it clear where the main items are? Do I know what to do to get served at specialist counters? Who do I ask if I need help? What do I do if I have a complaint?

- *Availability:* Are the baskets and trolleys conveniently located? Do the trolleys work? Is there a wide choice of products and brands? Is there adequate stock when I want to buy? Does the store introduce new products regularly?

- *Atmosphere/facilities:* Is the store pleasant to be in? Are the aisles wide enough? Are the staff friendly and helpful? Are there facilities to suit my needs, eg café, children's play area, toilets?

- *Speed:* How easy is it to get around the store? How long do I have to wait at the checkouts or at the specialist counters?

- *Quality and confidence:* Can I return the goods if I am not happy? Do they really listen to my complaints or my suggestions? Are the goods and the service as high as I would like?

2. ▶▶ Find a completely different type of customer to yourself. Ask them the same questions as for task 1 and compare your answers. Give an oral report on both the similarities and the differences of your two types of customer.

Key terms

COMPETITIVE EDGE – a firm is able to offer better products or lower priced goods or better service than its competitors and so has an advantage over its competitors in the eyes of the consumer.

DISTRIBUTION – the services involved in getting the finished good from the producer to the consumer and possibly involving warehousing, stock checks, dispatchers and transport.

PUBLIC RELATIONS – the process of obtaining favourable publicity through providing stories for the media and through the provision of good service for all who come into contact with the firm.

MOMENT OF TRUTH – the points of contact between customer and service provider when judgements may be made about the firm and the quality of its products.

 **STUDENT CHECKLIST**

1. The core issue of customer care is getting the right goods or services to the customer at the right time and place.

2. Customer care involves the distribution of goods, dealing with customer queries and complaints, providing after sales service such as maintenance and repairs, possibly the provision of credit facilities to help purchase expensive goods, and training all staff to treat customers well and to deliver quality goods and service.

3. Different types of customers are likely to require different types of customer care, and firms need to consider this when establishing their standard of provision.

Section D Business communications

CHAPTER 15

Organisational structures

3M's magic 15%

The process of bringing new products and new ideas to the consumer tends to be a difficult one. Someone has to have the idea, someone else has to have the courage to commit the finance to the idea and launch the product into the market. Much of this process depends not on entrepreneurial skill but on having the organisation and communication in place to allow the process to take place. 3M is a giant industrial concern that has operations in over 60 different countries, sales in over 200 different countries and over 70,000 employees. Its turnover is over $15 billion and its product list extends to over 60,000 products – almost one for every employee of the company.

Its organisation and communication is such, however, that it is able to spot new ideas and adapt and adopt them to its own benefit. Its research staff are told to work for only 85% of their time on the company's products. The other 15% is for ideas of their own, which the company organisation may then adopt – rewarding the innovator accordingly.

One product, the now universally used Post-it® note, benefited from the way the organisation's structure lets ideas flow across different parts of the group. Art Fry, the inventor of the concept, was able to draw on expertise from other parts of the organisation to make it work (the important thing is that the note not only sticks first time, but can also be removed without trace and reused several times). Without the organisational structure and the push to innovate, that little piece of paper stuck to your computer to remind you to buy cat food or remember your mother's birthday might never have existed!

What you need to do

- **To gain a pass** you need to be able to describe clearly the different organisational structures that may be found in businesses.
- **To gain a merit** you need to be able to explain clearly how different organisational structures suit the different needs of organisations.
- **To gain a distinction** you need to evaluate the strengths and weaknesses of the organisation of a business that you have studied.

Functions

Organisational structures are the way in which organisations divide their various functions. The larger and more complex the organisation, the more complicated their structure is likely to be. An important part of the way businesses are structured is the way in which the different departments or areas of the business interact and communicate with each other. This is covered in the following chapters, which detail the responsibilities and practices of each functional area and the ways in which they communicate with each other.

Types

Different organisations find that different structures suit them – either because of the size of the operation, or its complexity, or its geographical spread, its history or company philosophy. Structures can usually be shown on an organisation chart and are described in terms of the shape that their chart forms. This will show who is where in the organisation – who is in charge of whom, who people's superiors or managers are and where the power bases in the organisation lie.

Hierarchies

Most organisations have different levels of responsibility, resulting in different layers being shown on the chart. At each layer people will have a certain amount of responsibility – the higher up the organisation, the more responsibility. This is called a hierarchy – each level has more power and responsibility than the level below it. Organisations such as this tend to narrow as you move up the organisation – in other words, there are less people in senior positions than there are in junior ones. The shape of chart formed by this is triangular or a pyramid and it is therefore called a hierarchical pyramid (see Figure 15.1). This, however, may not be sufficient to show the complexity of the different branches of an organisation (imagine trying to show the operations of 3M in its 60 countries on a single chart) so detail can be shown on a family tree or T chart (so called because each junction forms a T) (see Figure 15.2). Large organisations may have extremely complex charts of this nature which can be drawn in different ways. 3M, for example, may have a chart that relates to its products, or to its workforce, or to the organisation of the business in the different countries in which it operates.

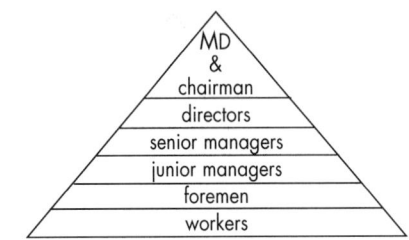

FIGURE 15.1 *Hierarchical pyramid*

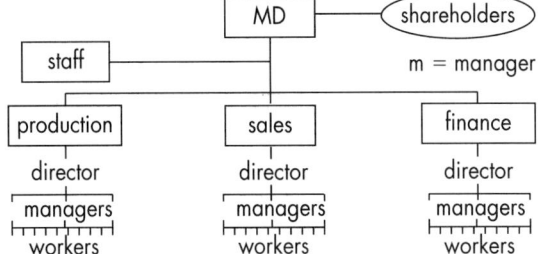

FIGURE 15.2 *Family tree*

GET IT RIGHT! ✓

The word hierarchy is one of the specialist terms that you will be expected to know. If you think of any organisation that has ranks, where one person has authority over and can pass orders down to the level below, then you have a good idea of what a hierarchy is. Think of the number of people at each level in an organisation with ranks. There will always be less admirals, generals and chief constables than sailors, soldiers and policemen or women.

Tall and flat structures

Tall hierarchical structures have many layers of command (a typical tall structure can be shown by the armed forces) with each layer having a narrow span of control – that is, the number of people directly under their authority (see Figure 15.3). Authority means the amount of allowed power (called legitimate power) that a manager or person with power in an organisation actually has; anyone under a manager's authority is called a subordinate. Flat structures have many fewer layers of command and control (see Figure 15.4). A good example of this type of structure may be your own school or college – although there will be a Head or Principal with various deputies and heads of department, the structure of the teaching staff has few levels and all staff share certain central responsibilities.

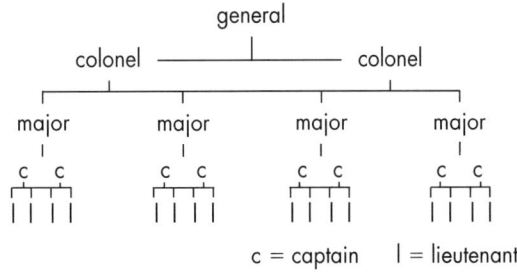

FIGURE 15.3 *Tall structure*

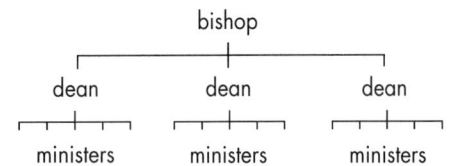

FIGURE 15.4 *Flat structure*

☏ COMMUNICATIONS *activity*

Choose a business with which you are familiar and prepare, either on an overhead slide or on a flipchart, a diagram of its organisational structure, clearly showing chains of command and hierarchies. Explain to the rest of your class or group what the advantages and disadvantages of this particular method of organisation are and how you think they could be improved.

(C3.1b)

Advantages and disadvantages

Each type of hierarchy has its advantages and disadvantages.

The tall structure has very clear lines of command and excellent promotion prospects for those further down the organisation. However, it suffers from a rigid bureaucracy (a set of rules within which decisions have to be taken). This tends to mean there is little initiative or regard for new ideas or new ways of doing something – in an organisation run purely on these lines the Post-it® note would never have been invented. Communication of orders or decisions tends to be very good but communication within the organisation (particularly sideways communication – between people at a similar level of responsibility in the organisation) tends to be poor.

In a flat organisation there are limited chances for promotion and rules may suffer from not being clear enough. On the plus side there will be less bureaucracy, more involvement for people lower down the organisation as decision-making is shared, and good communication within the organisation.

3M has recognised the benefits of both the tall and the flat form of organisation and, while keeping a reasonable amount of control, has also allowed its innovators time to work on their own ideas. Note that this time is carefully limited, however, so that the company suffers no problems from it but only gains the benefits.

Sideways and circular

Sometimes the chart is shown as in Figure 15.5. This may blur the hierarchical nature of the organisation by not showing people 'underneath' their superiors. It is the sort of chart that might be used in an organisation where managers did not want to seem to be 'in charge' – one that might improve the psychology of the organisation by making it seem more democratic.

However, circular charts (see Figure 15.6) which are used to show structure don't really remove the hierarchical nature of an organisation, they just make it look more equal. In circular charts the people with the most power and authority are shown at the centre of the circle with responsibility diminishing as you move away from the centre. In other words, the people at the outside edge of the chart are the same people that are at the bottom of the pyramidical chart.

Matrix charts

In many organisations it has been discovered that teamwork is a more efficient way of working. Teams may be formed according to workers' and managers' expertise and the team or project leader may be the person best fitted to the role in that particular situation or for that particular project. In this case a shop floor worker may be in a better position to lead a team than a senior manager, but the senior manager may be needed for his or her particular skills, experience or expertise. Matrix charts show the two-way

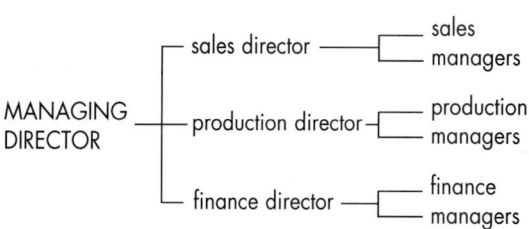

FIGURE 15.5 *Sideways chart*

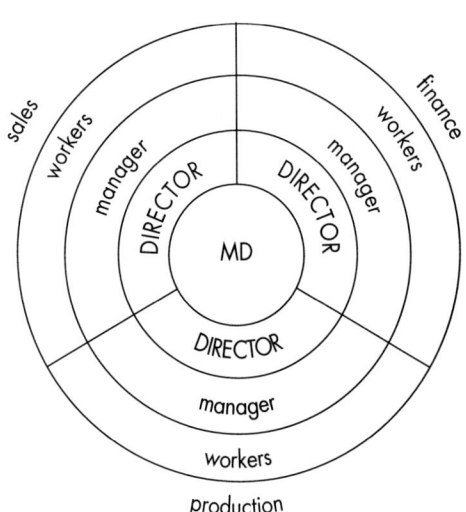

FIGURE 15.6 *Circular chart*

Divisions

There are various different ways in which an organisation might decide to separate its departments. The most common way is a separation by function, that is, by what the parts of the organisation actually do. Thus there may be a sales department, a personnel department, a finance department and so on. The biggest advantage of this type of structure is that anyone dealing with the organisation from the outside will know who to deal with as functions are clearly labelled.

Other organisations may find it more efficient to separate in other ways. Firms may organise on the basis of geography, where it may have regional offices based in different parts of a country or even different parts of the world. Each regional part is still likely to have a hierarchical structure. 3M, for example, will have regional headquarters in those countries where it does a lot of trade, as well as its international corporate headquarters at the top of the entire organisation.

relationships between the various parts of a team as shown at Fig. 15.6. The people within a particular project team will all be working together for the good of that project and the person leading the team may well actually be below other members in terms of the normal hierarchy. This type of organisation is extremely successful at bringing together different skills from different parts and levels of the organisation.

Firms may organise according to the different products that they produce so that a very diverse firm could have different divisions according to what they are making or selling. The Virgin Group of companies, for example, has a records division, holiday division, banking division, airline division and so on. Each division will have its own hierarchical structure, probably ending with a director for that particular product or range of products.

Choose an organisation with which you are familiar. Now choose the appropriate software to demonstrate how the structure of this organisation would look if it were shown on a T chart, a circular chart or a sideways chart. Suggest three projects that the organisation might attempt and list the appropriate members of each project group. Develop the information so that you can show the probable links on a matrix chart for each project.

Firms may also organise according to the different markets or market segments that they are targeting; a firm making cosmetics, for example, might have a division which deals with theatre make-up, one which deals with women's cosmetics and one which deals with those aimed at men. It may also be divided according to the age groups that the cosmetics are targeted at.

Staff

Some roles do not fit into the hierarchical structure because they are staff roles. The personal assistant to a senior manager, for example, may have to report to no-one but the manager. They may not therefore be part of any hierarchy. However, they may have influence out of proportion to their position because of their ease of access to the senior manager. Other staff positions include secretarial staff, accountants and personal assistants. Managers who do have a place in the hierarchy are called line managers and it is the job of staff to advise and assist them in their duties.

Informal structures

Alongside the formal structures there will also be informal ones. Informal structures are not governed by a set of regulations but are sets of people within a firm who form groups. These may be common interest groups based on a shared like for a particular sport, or television programme, or hobby or almost anything! Such groups can actually exert more power and influence than formal groups in certain situations.

Sometimes basic rules have to be drawn up for groups making them 'semi-formal'. This could include financial things, such as pools or lottery syndicates and Christmas clubs, as well as sporting structures, such as squash ladders or five-a-side leagues.

Management functions

The function of a manager is to make decisions and then communicate those decisions to the employees who will have to carry them out. Managers set objectives, organise, distribute work and roles, evaluate progress, report on progress and then set new objectives. All organisations, of whatever size, need good management.

The small firm

Not all organisations are large enough to need a formal structure. In many organisations the management functions are carried out by the owner. Even though the organisation structure may not be in place, all the various functions must still be carried out. One of the businesses you study may well be a sole trader or a partnership in which case you will be able to see that all the functions of management are still necessary, but that it may only be one or two people who carry them out.

Downsizing

Some firms have found it necessary to cut costs by getting smaller. The term that has been coined for this is downsizing. Usually it is a term that is used to mean that a firm or organisation is willing to employ less staff. In many cases this may mean redundancy for some employees, although – as in the case of Rolls Royce – most firms would try to make the cuts by relying on 'natural wastage' (people leaving of their own accord and not being replaced, or retirement).

Delayering

Delayering specifically means the removal of some levels of management. This may be particularly useful in a tall organisation structure where each layer of management may serve to slow down decision-making.

Decentralisation

Decentralisation means taking some of the functions or responsibilities traditionally held at the centre – or top – of an organisation and letting them pass (or devolve) to other parts of the organisation. This gives the parts of an organisation (maybe regions, branches, plants, departments) the ability to make decisions that are more relevant to them. The main disadvantage is that each part of the organisation may not be as effective in isolation as the centralised whole. In terms of buying power, for example, the centre could use its bulk purchasing power to gain lower prices.

PROGRESS CHECK

1. ▶ Describe the most common organisational structures.

2. ▶ Outline why you think the organisation structure of 3M is an effective one.

3. ▶▶ Using a business with which you are familiar, explain why it uses the organisational structure that it does.

4. ▶▶ Outline the different ways of dividing up an organisational structure. Explain why different ways might be appropriate to different firms.

5. ▶▶▶ Using a business with which you are familiar, evaluate the organisation structure that they are using. Suggest changes that would improve it.

6. ▶▶▶ Suggest three projects for 3M or another organisation and show the project teams on matrix charts. Explain why this might be a more efficient way of operating than traditional hierarchies.

Key terms

ORGANISATIONAL STRUCTURE – the way in which organisations are laid out.

AUTHORITY – having lawful or legitimate power over a person at a lower level.

SUBORDINATES – persons over whom someone has authority.

SPAN OF CONTROL – the number of subordinates under a particular person's authority.

DOWNSIZING – reducing the size of an operation, usually by employing less people.

DELAYERING – taking out levels of management to make decision-making easier and more efficient.

DECENTRALISATION – taking some of the functions usually held at the centre of an organisation and letting them be carried out by other parts of the organisation.

STUDENT CHECKLIST

1. Firms have a number of functions and therefore need organisational structures.

2. Structures can be shown on various different types of chart.

3. Most structures are hierarchical with more power and authority and less people at the top of the organisation.

4. Some structures are tall, with many layers of command, some are flat, with wide spans of control and few layers of command.

5. If an organisation sets up project teams, ignoring hierarchies, matrix charts can be used to show the relationships.

6. Organisations can be divided in different ways.

7. Staff roles are not part of the hierarchy.

8. Organisational structures can be altered in a number of ways to make them more effective, e.g. by cutting out levels of management or devolving power from the centre.

CHAPTER 16

Internal communication

Keeping in touch

Treetops is a medium-sized firm based in the North of England. It started as a small nursery business – growing plants and trees from seed and selling them on to garden centres – but has now established two garden centres of its own. It is still, however, a family-owned and mainly family-run enterprise. John Masham, the son of the founder of the business, has been pleased to see the amount of growth that the gardening sector is getting. As a result of a number of successful television gardening programmes and the emergence of several gardening 'personalities', the demand for the sector is increasing.

John has had to take on more staff at the two garden centres, which, although 50 miles apart, are still very much 'of the same firm'.

The smaller of the two has 14 staff at all levels from management down to Saturday part-timers while the larger, older centre has 29 staff. John has always given any decisions to management at a personal level. He has also made a point of being at as many staff interviews as possible and of making sure that he

FIGURE 16.1 *A UK garden centre*
Source: Emma Lee/Life File

has met all the staff. To do this means visits to the two garden centres and the three nursery sites. 'I find I seem to spend more of my time meeting staff and explaining how we are expanding than anything else', Masham is quoted as saying, 'but I've always done it this way, it's the only way I feel I'm keeping in touch with the business.'

As a limited company the firm produces an annual report and statement of accounts, which is made available to all employees.

What you need to do

- **To gain a pass** you need to be able to describe clearly the different methods of communication that may be found in businesses.
- **To gain a merit** you need to be able to explain clearly how different methods of communication are necessary for different purposes.
- **To gain a distinction** you need to evaluate the strengths and weaknesses of different communication channels in organisations that you have studied.

Communication is one of the three key skills that you should also be aiming to achieve.

Keeping in touch

John Masham may still be able to visit all his employees – just – but if the firm continues to grow he will have to find other, less personal but more efficient ways of staying 'in touch' with the various parts of his organisation. Internal communication refers to the various ways that messages are passed around an organisation.

If the organisation is small, then the actual passing of communications should be reasonably easy. But even there, there will be a case for some communication being formal and some being informal. As the organisation grows, there is usually more and more of a case for the establishment of formal communication channels.

Communication channels

Channels may be either formal or informal. Formal channels will take place within a framework that has already been laid down. They will probably also include keeping a record of whatever has taken place. Informal channels can take place at any time and almost anywhere. They are not recorded nor are they limited by any sort of framework.

Choose a point at least three miles away from your school or college. Imagine that you are answering a telephone enquiry from someone at that point who is asking for directions to your school or college. Write out the directions that you would give to them if they were in a car; if they were on foot; if they were arriving using public transport. You could test your directions by giving them to another member of your group and seeing if they can follow them or not. You could help them by drawing a sketch map and faxing it to them.

(C1.3)

Informal oral channels

Informal oral channels mean the spoken word. This may be an instruction, the passing of information or even a reprimand (a telling off). Much informal communication is in the form of conversation, but this can be more powerful than many formal methods. Information may spread within an organisation through 'the grapevine' – in other words, informally, through conversation, faster than any formal channel. Often misinformation and rumour is also passed in this way.

There may also be informal meetings between people within an organisation. For example, John Masham's meetings with his staff are unlikely to be formal ones: he will just go and talk to them while they are working.

Formal oral channels

Information may be communicated in the form of a presentation, lecture or speech. Presentations may include the use of slides, hand-outs, figures, graphs and charts, and are often used to make a sales pitch more effective. They have the benefit to the presenter of being able to address a number of people at the same time and to use various display methods to get and keep their attention.

Conferences may be organised where speakers – making speeches or making presentations – can be listened to by a large number of people. Sales conferences – to share successful sales tactics and pass on information about the organisation are particularly popular.

Choose a subject that you are familiar with and interested in. Imagine that you are the chairperson of the local group involved with this subject. Draw up an official agenda for your next meeting, making sure that you follow the rules and put some items for discussion in the body of the meeting. Conduct the meeting with other members of your class or group.

(C3.1a)

Formal meetings

Business meetings are often held according to a set pattern. This pattern makes sure, importantly, that an accurate record is kept of who attended particular meetings, what decisions were made and whose responsibility it was to carry out the decisions. The business of the meeting will be spoken but the record will be written (see below).

The format for such meetings follows these steps.

- An agenda is issued for the meeting – this is the list of items to be discussed.
- The agenda will start with 'apologies for absence'. This is so that both the membership of the meeting can be recorded and the reasons for people's absence.
- The next item will be the 'minutes' of the last meeting – this is the written record of who took part and what decisions were made. These minutes must be agreed to be a true record by people who were at the meeting.
- Action minutes are a particular form of minutes. The discussions that led to the decisions are not recorded, just the decisions that have been made and, more importantly, who is to carry them out.
- Following the apologies for absence will be the list of agenda items to be discussed. At

What you need to do

- **To gain a pass** you need to be able to describe clearly the different methods of external communication that may be found in businesses.
- **To gain a merit** you need to be able to clearly explain how different methods of external communication may be necessary for different purposes.
- **To gain a distinction** you need to be able to demonstrate that you can evaluate the strengths and weaknesses of different communication channels in organisations that you have studied.

Communication is one of the three key skills that you should also be aiming to achieve.

Interaction

No organisation can exist in isolation. However big or small they may be, they will need to interact with other organisations. This means that they will need to communicate with them. Communication channels need to be two way so that the organisation receives responses or feedback from bodies it has interacted with. Interaction outside the organisation involves external communication.

If we consider the detail of a firm producing a product, we can see how many different types and levels of external communication there are. Look at the diagram (Figure 17.1). It shows the stages in the production, manufacture and sales of a packet of spring bulbs for sale in a garden centre. Along the way the firm has had to communicate with financial institutions of various types, suppliers, transport providers, international bodies (the bulbs are flown in from Amsterdam and subject to regulations), government (both local and national), and customers.

```
seed taken from flower
        ↓
seed potted & germinated
        ↓
   controlled growth
        ↓
    bulb developed
        ↓
     bulb stored
        ↓
 bulbs sorted & packaged
        ↓
   packages boxed
        ↓
boxes transported to port
        ↓
bulbs sail across channel
        ↓
boxes transported to wholesaler
        ↓
wholesaler delivers to garden centre
        ↓
    bulbs on sale
```

FIGURE 17.1

COMMUNICATIONS activity

Research a set of regulations for a business or find some that are appropriate to a business you are studying). Produce a simplified set of regulations, using bullet points. Now try to produce a set that would suit someone of either limited English or limited reading ability – you will have to make use of images wherever possible.

(C2.2)

IT activity

Your simplified sets of regulations could be produced using Information and Communications Technology software. The images you use could be clip art, scanned images or digital photographs. You should choose the most appropriate for effectiveness.

(IT2.2)

Financial institutions

These include traditional financial institutions, such as banks and building societies, that a firm may have to approach for initial finance. They may also include companies who provide or guarantee credit. Other financial institutions will be contacted for insurance, accountancy advice etc. Usually external communication with financial institutions is on a formal level involving written communication. At another level, however, there may be an informal network (such as a golf club) where people from either organisation can meet and make decisions. As with many informal parts of organisational structure, this may be more powerful than the formal structure. Many major deals have been struck over a game of golf and even prime ministers have been accused of over-using the informal (one was said to have a 'kitchen cabinet' – his own personal staff and advisors – who had more power than the real Cabinet).

> **GET IT RIGHT!** ✓
>
> In order to make external communication even more efficient, the government is to introduce legislation in 2000 to make electronic signatures as legally binding as paper ones. At the moment many transactions are slowed down by the need for a written confirmation, with signature, to confirm the transaction. Computer companies have hailed the British proposal as 'a model for the rest of the world'.

Suppliers

Firms need to have information about different possible suppliers so that they can make choices based on quality, reliability and cost. This involves them communicating with different firms by letter, telephone or e-mail and receiving information that may be verbal or written. Written information may be formally produced, such as leaflets or brochures, or could be 'informal', for example, handwritten information or e-mail responses. The use of a website may be one way in which a supplier can compete for business.

Transport suppliers may also be included under this heading as, again, if the firm does not have its own transport arrangements, they will need to communicate their requirements to a supplier.

International bodies

The transport and supply of bulbs will be governed by a strict set of international rules (as will the transport and supply of many products that are organic and may therefore carry diseases) and these will need to be communicated to the people who must carry them out. This will be in the form of notices and reminders or letters sent to bulb exporters and importers. There may be an association to join, which would communicate changes to its members through reports or journals.

Governments

It is governments at a local, national and international level who will have made the laws and be responsible for ensuring that they are carried out. Local regulations may be in force which must be communicated to the firm. This could be done:

- orally, for example through inspectors
- through letters and written notices.

It is likely to be a combination of the two. Firms are obliged to find out what laws and regulations govern their trade – the responsibility is on them to find out, not on governments to tell them.

Local

At a local level there will be regulations that are laid down and overseen by the local council. These will include such things as the correct storage temperature and conditions for organic goods, washing and cleaning facilities, labelling and descriptive accuracy.

National

These will include laws and regulations designed to make sure that the health and security of the country is not put at risk by imports (the import of live animals, weapons, drugs etc are all controlled). Many of these regulations are enforced by Customs and Excise.

International

As a member of the European Union, the UK is subject to European law and regulations. Countries which fail to follow European rulings are taken to the European Court and fined. For example, when the EU reported that British beef was safe, the French still refused to accept it, until threatened with court action. Regulations are designed to ensure the safety of goods, the welfare of animals and the health of consumers.

Departments

Each functional department of a firm will have a particular responsibility for a type of external communication.

External communication with customers is likely to be the job of the marketing department; this could include the production of catalogues, of leaflets, displays and point-of-sale material. Links with financial institutions and lenders will be maintained by the finance department. Advertising for new staff and liaising with the Department of Employment over regulations will be the job of the human resources department, while the production department will deal with suppliers. In a large organisation it is obvious that both internal communication – between the functional departments – and external communication are essential.

Documentation

Much external communication will be carried out using formal documentation: the main examples are:

- a letter of enquiry – a formal letter requesting information, catalogues etc
- an order – a list of requirements signed for authorisation by the appropriate level of staff
- a bill or account – a request for payment, with itemised details
- an invoice – a request for payment for work done or goods delivered, sent by the firm or individual who did the work.

External formal written channels

Some publications have to be produced by

companies (but do not have to be produced by sole traders or partnerships). The main formal external document that must be made available is the Company Report and Accounts. This must be produced at least once a year and contains details of the company's trading, directorial staff, dividends paid to shareholders, and profits and losses throughout the year. The accounts contain a detailed picture of where money has come from and where it has been paid to. These detailed reports will be presented at the Annual General Meeting of the company's shareholders so that they have all the details regarding the company. A public limited company must make these details available to any member of the public on request.

NUMERACY
activity

Send for the company reports and accounts of two public limited companies. When they arrive, compare the way in which the accounts have been laid out and presented. What devices are used to make the figures more accessible? What do you think makes them less accessible or understandable?

Take one of the reports and present the account information in a more user-friendly way, using pie charts, bar charts and pictograms where appropriate.

(N2.3)

Other channels

Firms may communicate with both customers and suppliers through Exhibitions and Trade Shows. Major trade shows for an industry will draw thousands of visitors (for instance, the Motor Show, the Chelsea Flower Show) and are used by manufacturers, wholesalers and retailers to display their latest goods. Smaller trade shows will also take place at various different venues around the country.

Companies may also communicate with customers through the use of catalogues, leaflets and price lists. This will be one of the jobs of the marketing department.

PROGRESS CHECK

1. ▶ Describe the main people that a firm has to communicate with externally.

2. ▶ Outline two situations; one where formal documentation would be necessary and one where an informal approach would be appropriate.

3. ▶▶ Design an exhibition stand for a business that you are studying.

4. ▶▶▶ Look at the documents that a firm you are studying uses for external communication. List the good and bad points for five of them and then give ways in which they might be improved.

Key terms

CHANNELS OF COMMUNICATION – the ways by which messages are passed to and from people and organisations.

EXTERNAL CHANNELS OF COMMUNICATION – these need to be two way.

FORMAL CHANNELS – these usually involve set forms and procedures.

INFORMAL CHANNELS – these may be more effective than formal ones in some cases.

STUDENT CHECKLIST

1. It is important that an organisation chooses the correct channel of communication for the message it wants to carry.

2. Channels may be formal or informal.

3. Formal channels are bound by a set of rules and conventions; external ones tend to involve forms and specific documentation.

4. Other external channels include published materials, such as catalogues, and events open to either the trade or the public, such as trade shows and exhibitions.

CHAPTER 18
Information and communications technology (ICT)

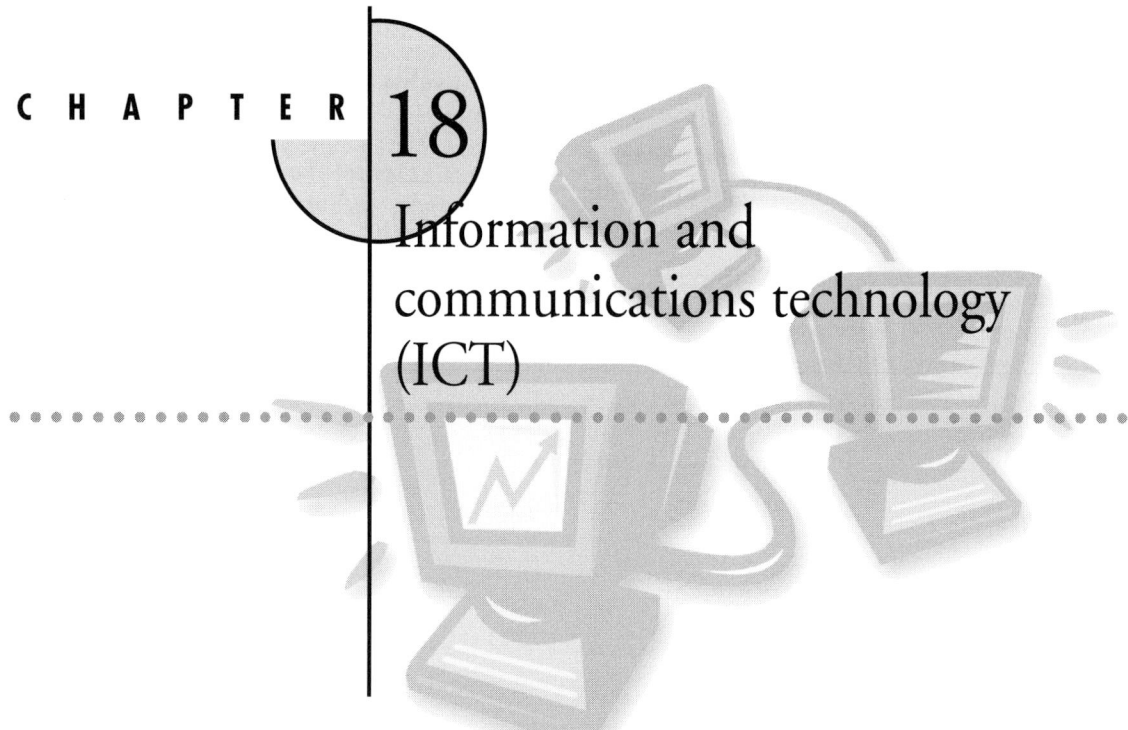

Stay-at-home Steven solves problem

John Masham took on an assistant to help him with his ever increasing task of communicating throughout the company; his idea was that Steven Richard would take some of the work off his hands by travelling to see some of the customers and suppliers who were farthest away, leaving him to concentrate on those nearer to base. However, far from wanting to travel to each of the company's sites, each of their suppliers and to meet all of their staff, Steven Richard was more concerned with setting up electronic systems to make Treetops' communications more efficient. He insisted that Treetops built its own website on the Internet and that communications between the various parts of the company should take place on their own intranet. The newsletter was replaced with a weekly web bulletin and John Masham was stunned (and pleased) to find out that he could maintain the personal touch through video-conferencing without ever having to leave the comfort of his native Yorkshire.

All internal communication is encouraged to be by e-mail so cutting down on the necessity of paper communications. This seems to have motivated the staff and impressed suppliers and customers.

What you need to do

- **To gain a pass** you need to be able to describe clearly the different methods of information and communications technology used in businesses.

- **To gain a merit** you need to be able to explain clearly how different types of ICT application and use may be appropriate for different jobs in different businesses.
- **To gain a distinction** you need to be able to evaluate the strengths and weaknesses of the ICT systems and provision in a business that you have studied.

Information Technology is one of the three key skills that you should also be aiming to achieve.

ICT

Information and communications technology has become increasingly important in business and office environments. It can make communication faster, cheaper and more effective. The government has recognised its importance by building training and education in ICT into both the National Curriculum for pupils and into the training undertaken by all trainee teachers.

Computers

These have become commonplace in all offices and businesses. They range from the large to the very small.

- The biggest are mainframe computers – a large machine, which may be used by an organisation for both storage and control. The mainframe may not be on the same site as the company, who may have to pay to use it.
- Servers are large capacity computers used to store software for other computers to access or to store files (a file server); often they will also run an internal network.
- Desktop computers are the usual office machines, running word processing, spreadsheets, databases and CAD programs where appropriate. They may be 'shell' machines, which are accessing all their information from a server, or they may have their own software.
- Laptop computers perform the same functions as desktops but have the added advantage of being portable. They are usually approximately the size of an A4 pad of paper.
- Palmtops are even smaller, being about the size of a hand, but benefit from their great portability.

Laptops and palmtops will both be able to exchange files and information with desktop computers, either through a linking wire or, with the more up-to-date ones, through an infrared link.

Intranet

An intranet is where a company has linked its computers together and built pages of information – as if they were linked to the Internet – for the machines to access. It is an internal Internet and, of course, the systems manager has complete control over the content – unlike if the computers were linked to the Internet.

COMMUNICATIONS *activity*

Write a description of the ICT system either at your school or college or at a business that you have studied. Compare it with the sytems which you think Treetops has now put in place.

(C2.3)

GET IT RIGHT! ✓

Within a business organisation there may be a network – where computers are linked together and share either files or software – or an intranet. An intranet is where information, similar to web pages, has been placed on the computer. Your school or college may have its own intranet. Remember that the network and the intranet are not the same thing.

Security

Both for individual machines and for the intranet it is important that employees follow a proper system so that machine use can be monitored. Employees should be able to log on with their own password and to further password-protect files or information that they do not want other employees to have access to. When they have finished for a session they should log off. System managers will have higher levels of access for themselves.

These basic levels of security should be common to all businesses using computers. In some cases it is not just computers but other computerised systems where people need to log in or out. For example, an employee might have to log on to an electronic till before recording a transaction.

Video-conferencing

New technology has made video-conferencing an easy way to hold a meeting even if long distances are involved. John Masham is able to video-conference – using his computer, a telephone line and the appropriate software – with people in other countries. The cost of the call will only be a fraction of what the cost of transport might have been and, of course, it is much more convenient.

Even newer technology

The future of the Internet probably lies in an even more varied version of it than the one businesses can currently access. If you do not have a PC to access the Internet, then there are alternatives. A version known as WAP is available to users of the latest mobile phones and providers of cable TV will also provide digital services such as on-line banking, shopping and e-mail via a television set. Even games (the Sega Dreamcast, for example) can provide Internet access.

Websites

These are used to put information – text, pictures, even sound and video – together in a format that is easy and attractive to use. Businesses and other organisations can use websites to advertise their services. A website will also be able, through the host or ISP (Internet Service Provider), to provide e-commerce facilities. The firm can use the site for advertising, demonstrations and to publish catalogues and price lists. Visitors will be able to buy or order goods; competitors can check prices and ranges; businesses can easily 'shop around' for the best suppliers. The biggest advantage is that the advertising is actually global.

COMMUNICATIONS activity

Find two commercial websites for two different businesses. In a presentation to the rest of your class or group describe the features that they share and the features that are unique to each site. Explain which you think is more effective and why.

(C3.1b)

Software

The main software uses in a business are outlined here. Don't forget, however, that computers have uses apart from these – they can send and receive faxes, for example, as long as they are equipped with a modem and the appropriate software.

- Word processing – the advantages of this are that documents can be edited on screen, words and phrases can be 'cut and pasted', layout can be altered, and all communications can be personalised.
- Databases – these are lists of information that can be sorted into different orders and searched very quickly. For example, it could be lists of stock items or it may be customer or client names and addresses (in which case the software can be used along with word processing to personalise communications through the use of 'mail merge').
- Spreadsheets – these are set up to carry out calculations. Spreadsheets can accept numbers, letters or formulae. The use of formulae make them powerful tools for doing such complex figures as a firm's accounts.
- Computer-assisted – this could be CAD, computer-assisted drawing, or CAM, computer-assisted manufacture, or any of a range of specialist jobs that a computer can carry out more accurately than the human hand and eye. In some industries – engineering, for example – the computer has almost totally replaced traditional technical drawing skills.
- E-mail – the ability to send messages from one computer to another via a modem. Such messages tend to be shorter and less formal than traditional methods. They are, however, quicker and cheaper and much documentation can also be sent as an 'attachment'. Virtually anything that can be produced and stored on a computer can be sent via e-mail.

The Internet

The Internet has grown as technology has grown. Originally it was the Arpanet and consisted of American military computers linked by satellite to each other. Now, any computer that can access a telephone line can not only access the Internet for information, but can place its own information there so that other people or organisations can access it. The Internet has grown into a vast store of information – no-one owns it, no-one polices or regulates it. This means that there are dangers in accessing the Internet in that there are little or no controls on what materials people might choose to publish on it; they could be violent, disturbing, pornographic or illegal.

At the same time the Internet has become an enormous positive resource used for example by government and educational establishments. It is, in effect, a giant database – but one that has no indexing system. It is almost like a

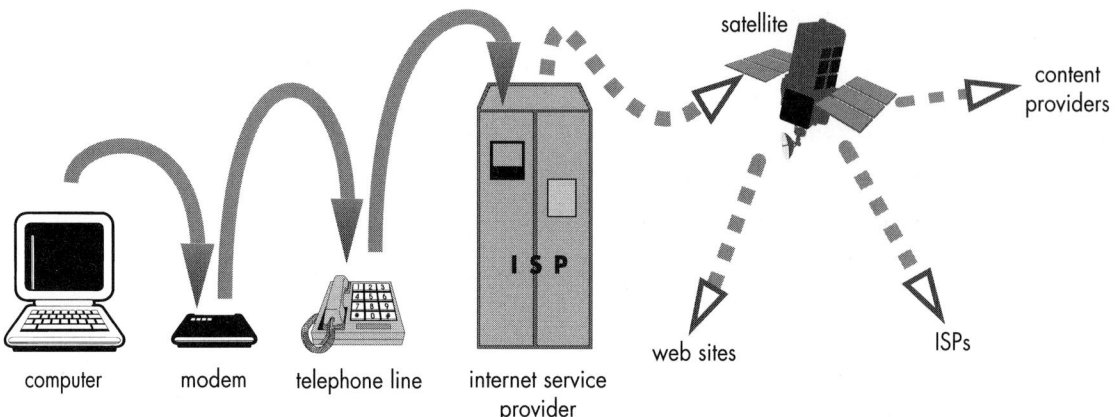

FIGURE 18.1 *How the Internet is accessed*

huge library, containing every book and magazine that you could ever want. The difficulty lies in the hugeness of it – it is not always easy to find what it is that you actually want. Other things will constantly interrupt your Internet search. For example, advertisements will be found on many pages and 'pop-ups' also occur – these are files that will just appear on your screen, again usually used for advertising.

Terms

The Internet is usually abbreviated to the 'net', the 'web' or 'world wide web' (www). Many other abbreviations are used in e-mails and other correspondence to save time typing in commonly used phrases. Some examples are:

- BTW (by the way)
- FAQ (frequently asked questions)
- AAA (any advice appreciated)
- DQM (don't quote me)

E-mail messages may also contain 'emoticons' such as **:)** for happy, **:(** for sad and **;)** for a wink.

To access the Internet you will need to subscribe to an ISP – an Internet Service Provider. Many of these now do not charge for Internet access or for the time that you are on the net. Instead, they make their money by carrying advertising and a tiny percentage from the telephone companies. However, the volume of calls is so large and increasing at such a rate that this is an income worth having. Some ISPs already provide free telephone calls to the Internet at certain off-peak times as well as free access, making the service completely free. Many more operators are considering this, particularly cable firms. The best-known ISPs are probably AOL (America On Line) – one of the early providers, Freeserve – the first free operator, and large commercial operators such as British Telecom and Virgin.

Tools

You will need a web browser to open a web page. The most common ones are Microsoft Internet Explorer and Netscape Navigator although your ISP may provide their own browser and a lot of content specific to their service (Compuserve, for example). When you open a web page there are a number of other tools that will help you navigate around the page. Hot links will take you directly to another page on the web. Generally, they are a different colour to the rest of the text on the page and are usually underlined as well. Sometimes, however, hot links are disguised so that you accidentally visit a page and see the advertising on it. They may be images, headlines or arrows that look like they are taking you to the next page. To discover the hot links on a page, move the mouse pointer around the page – it changes to a hand once a hot link is found. You should also be able to read, at the foot of your web browser, the Internet address of the page being referred to.

Search engines

To find information on a particular subject you will need to search the net with a search engine. This is a device that looks for key words and then lists the websites that are most likely to contain the information that you are looking for in the form of hot links so that you can go directly to the site. Search engines include Yahoo – one of the earliest and biggest, Hotbot, Excite, Lycos and Alta Vista. Each has its good and bad points and you will need to find the one that best suits your purpose.

Building a home page

Businesses that wish to trade over the net need their own home page. Most ISPs will give a certain amount of web space, ranging from 5 to 25 megabytes, which can be used to build a home site. If you were setting up a commercial website for a business then you would need to either buy or register a 'domain' name. The business would choose the name that it wants and then check at www.netnames.co.uk to see if they can have it. Registering a name costs about £50 a year. They would also need to be careful of their choice of ISP – it would need to be reliable and easy for their customers to access. For £150–200 a year a host should provide you with web space, e-mail accounts and the ability to handle on-line transactions and e-commerce.

IT
activity

Build your own web page; then build a commercial web page that a business you are familiar with would be able to use. You should use HTML (HyperText Mark up Language). If you are having difficulty try html.digitalsea.net. Three other sites that you might find useful are www.webreference.com, www.hotwired.com, lycos.com/webmonkey/kids, both of which offer help in using HTML. You could make this exercise into a project for a term's work.

(IT3.1)

PROGRESS CHECK

1. ▶ **Describe the main ways in which a business would use information technology to communicate.**

2. ▶ **Explain the difference between the Internet, a network and an intranet.**

3. ▶▶ **Outline the advantages and disadvantages to a business of videoconferencing.**

4. ▶▶▶ **Look at the software and systems being used by a business. Suggest how they could improve the efficiency and security of their ICT provision.**

Key terms

HARDWARE – the physical machinery (computers, keyboards etc).

SOFTWARE – the programs used by the machines.

PERIPHERALS – 'add-ons' such as scanners, printers, digital cameras.

ISP – Internet Service Provider; provides a 'gateway' to the Internet.

INTERNET – a vast database of information, accessible using a computer and phone line via a modem.

SEARCH ENGINE – a method of finding information on the Internet.

STUDENT CHECKLIST

1. **ICT is so important that the government have built training into the education system.**
2. **Internal systems include networks and intranets.**
3. **The main software used is word processing, spreadsheet and database programs.**
4. **Externally, access to the Internet can be gained.**
5. **Firms can use the Internet to set up their own websites so that they can carry out e-commerce.**

Section E Case Studies

CASE STUDY 1

Libran Music

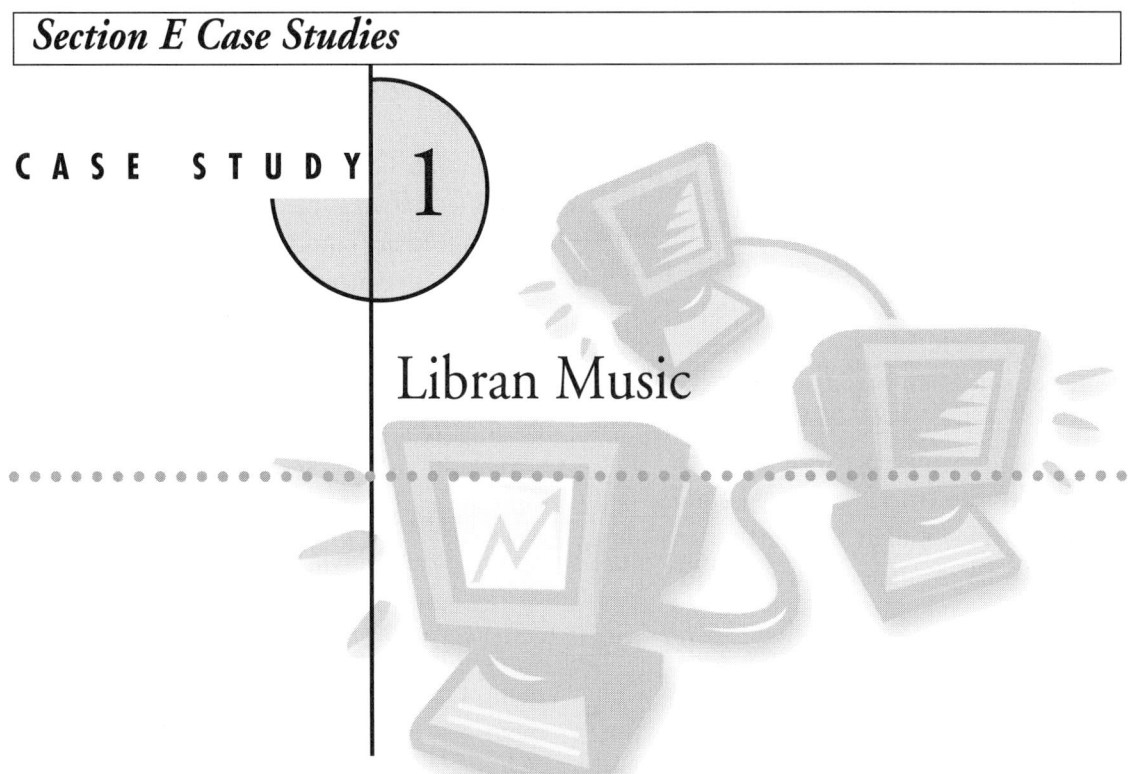

The Libran Group of companies started in the 1960s as a private limited company – Libran Music Ltd – operating mainly in the music industry. At that time, it hoped to increase market share gradually, as it searched for new talent and sounds to challenge its main competitors. It grew steadily throughout the 1970s as it maintained its market share and looked for ways to reinforce sales and profits. Libran Music and its small subsidiaries were changed into a public limited company in 1983 – Libran Group plc. Its main aim was to maximise growth and this has been achieved through diversification into other markets and the creation of larger subsidiary companies. Initially this diversification was directed into the hotel, leisure, and travel industries. More recently growth has been directed into the telecommunications, property, and airline industries as the Libran Group has sought to become a multi-market, multinational company.

Company structure at Libran

Libran Group plc is organised firstly into the seven separate market areas noted above. The Board of Directors for Libran Group plc is chaired by the founder of Libran Music – Clare Smith. The other seven directors each act as managing director for a subsidiary company running each of the market areas. Each subsidiary company also has its own manager who in turn controls department managers. There are separate human resource departments, finance departments and administration departments for each of the seven subsidiary companies. The remaining departments relate to the particular goods or services of each company.

The company running Libran Music Ltd has three additional departments – music production, distribution and marketing. Libran Hotels Ltd has central purchasing and marketing departments for its fifteen major hotels while Libran Leisure Ltd has a marketing department and separate departments managing each of the five major leisure facilities spread throughout the UK. Libran Travel Ltd has a department running the travel agencies together with a separate marketing department. The newly acquired airline business – Libran Airline Ltd – is quite small and has a single department to run all its activities. Libran Property Ltd has three small departments – Property Purchasing, Property Sales and Property Leasing – while Libran Telecommunications Ltd has purchasing, distribution and marketing departments.

1 Identify the main aims that the Libran Group of companies set itself as it developed from the 1960s to the present times.

2 Draw out an organisation chart for the Libran Group plc showing the relationship between the subsidiary companies and their departments to the parent plc.

3 Explain why this is both a functional and a hierarchical organisational structure.

4 One criticism of the organisational structure used by the Libran Group is that there are too many departments across the seven subsidiary companies providing similar functions. Plan and draw out an alternative organisational structure that eliminates some of this duplication of departmental functions.

5 Describe the possible advantages and disadvantages to Libran Group plc of your suggested structure.

The Libran Group currently employs nearly 4,500 employees across all its companies. Each subsidiary company uses its own human resources department to recruit, train and care for staff. For example, Libran Music Ltd has introduced an induction training scheme for all new staff and has asked its existing staff to suggest what might be included in the scheme.

6 Suggest the main types of training that ought to be included in an induction scheme.

In addition to the human resources department, Libran Music Ltd has a finance department to monitor its accounts and financial requirements and an administration department to help carry out the day-to-day communication needs of the company. The production department has two elements to its work. The recording section is responsible for finding and recording music and artists; with the production of cassettes and CDs carried out by the pressing section. The distribution section is responsible for warehousing and transporting the finished albums and singles to retailers around the country; but the promotional aspects are the sole responsibility of the marketing department. It sets prices and special offers, arranges advertising and other promotional activities and sends out sales people to deal direct with retailers. It has close links with the production department to feed back information on current tastes and likely trends in the musical preferences of consumers; and, of course, needs to be kept up to date by the distribution department on stocks. Libran Music Ltd is currently considering adding a customer care department to deal with issues arising from its production, distribution and marketing activities.

7 Describe the likely purposes and activities of each department in Libran Music Ltd.

8 Choose two jobs titles for each department and describe their probable roles in the company.

9 Suggest some of the likely customer care problems that a company like Libran Music might be suffering.

10 How might a customer care department deal with the problems you thought of in the last question?

11 Explain the likely benefits to Libran Music Ltd of having a customer care department.

Libran Group plc wishes to promote equal opportunities throughout its organisation. As part of this policy, it intends to introduce common conditions of employment for all employees in all of its companies. It sets up a small working party to discuss how best to inform and promote these changes to staff across all the companies.

12 Why might the Libran Group plc wish to promote equal opportunities throughout its organisation?

13 What do you understand by common conditions of employment?

14 You are a member of the working party set up by the Libran Group to inform and promote the changes in employment conditions to staff across all its companies. Suggest possible ways that the company might communicate these changes and decide on the best ways, giving reasons to support your choice.

15 Choose one communication method to illustrate how to inform and promote the changes.

CASE STUDY 2

ICI

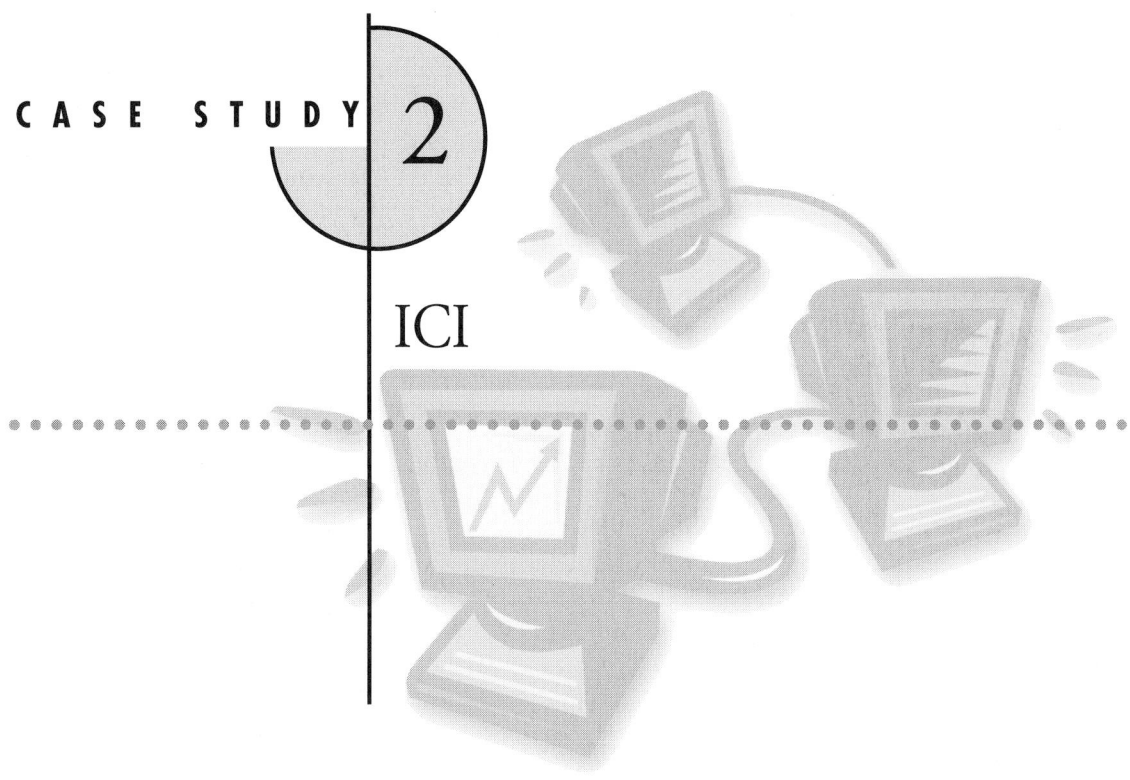

> Businesses have their own ethical character, good, bad or not bothered. We can all recognise them. Sometimes, and dramatically, a business can lose its character and find that to get it back takes a long time.
>
> It happened a decade ago to Guinness – a decent company that went rotten at the top. That is where character is made and maintained. Salomon, the great New York investment bank, went through the same sequence, and was then pulled together by a new chairman, Warren Buffett from Nebraska, the plain man writ large. He gave his crew a simple test of business ethics. 'Ask yourself' he said, 'how you would feel if your actions appeared on the front page of your local paper, for your friends and family to see.'
>
> ICI, by contrast, was given its character by its first chairman. 'We are on trial,' said Alfred Mond, 'before the eyes of the whole world. We are not merely a body of people carrying on industry in order to make dividends, we are much more. British commercialists and British technicians will be judged by the success we make.'
>
> *Rewritten from article in Daily Telegraph, February 1999*

FIGURE CS II.1 *Keeping image on track*

ICI has moved away from its old 'core' business of industrial chemicals. In the late 1990s, it decided that both its image and its more heavy duty plants and products needed to be changed. It therefore began a process of demerging, selling off parts of its chemicals empire and rebuilding by acquiring products that would fit its new image.

The reason for the repositioning of the company lay in three main areas:

1 the volatile nature of traditional chemical markets – whenever there is a recession, sales of chemicals fall

2 the competitive nature of the market – profits were always signals to competitors to move in to the profitable area

3 the small market base for chemicals in the UK.

> **ICI's vision statement**
>
> ICI will become the industry leader in creating value for customers through
> - winning in quality growth markets worldwide
> - providing technology-based solutions for today and tomorrow.

FIGURE CS II.2 *ICI's vision statement*

ICI decided to put together a portfolio of products that would appeal to the senses, while maintaining their reputation for being at the forefront of science. Products were chosen because of their appeal to:

- smell – perfumes, shampoos and soaps

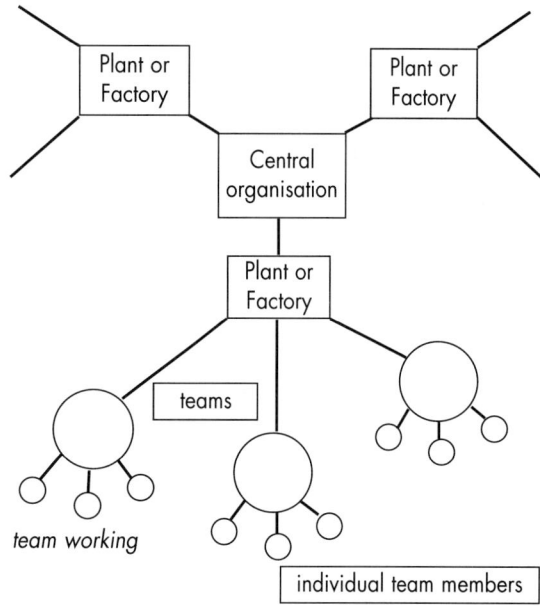

FIGURE CS II.4

- taste – artificial flavourings, food ingredients
- touch – polyurethane, acrylics
- colour – paints, dyes.

ICI also needed to change its organisational structure and the way in which it involved employees in decision-making.

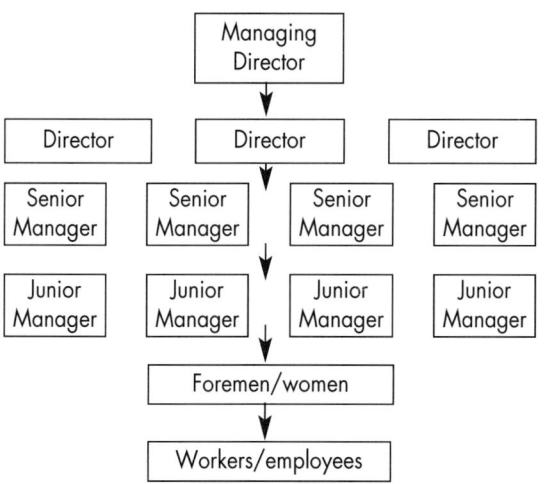

FIGURE CS II.3 *A typical, traditional tall organisation structure*

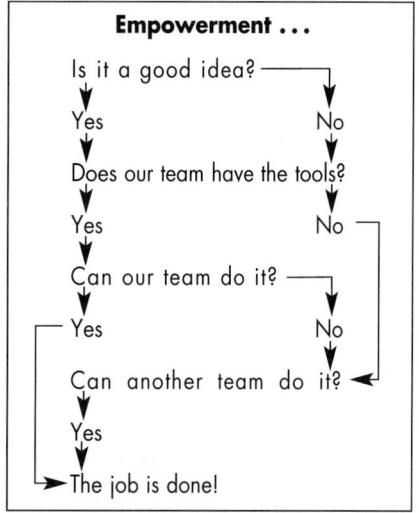

FIGURE CS II.5 *Empowerment flow chart*

Traditionally, it had been a 'top down' company with a tall organisational structure like the one shown in Figure CSII.3. What it wanted to do was to tap into the potential of its employees – to make sure that their ideas and initiatives were not only heard, but acted on by management. This is a concept known as 'empowerment' – workers with power.

The diagram (Figure CSII.5) shows what is meant by an empowered structure. Employees work in teams to meet targets; their targets will be working towards the company's overall objective; they can take their own decisions and will be recognised by the company for decisions and ideas taken.

The success of empowerment lies in each person in a team, each team and the whole organisation itself sharing and understanding common objectives. Traditionally, with a 'top down' approach, employees would be told what was required of them and not be expected to be part of the 'vision' or objective of the company.

In the new structure, all employees are valued and ICI recognises particularly valuable contributions by teams or individuals through its annual Business Excellence Awards.

Successful empowerment programmes mean that employees are more motivated to work for a company, feel more valued and therefore work better. Communication is better, and solutions to company problems are often a great deal more workable thanks to the fact that they come from the people who are having to implement them.

Every part of the company benefits from empowerment, including the employees themselves, managers, customers, suppliers and shareholders as production, productivity and profits all increase.

1. Explain what Alfred Mond meant by his statement and how ICI's new vision compares with that of Mond's.

2. Explain what is meant by 'repositioning'.

3. Outline the reasons why ICI felt the need to reposition?

4. Outline how communication would take place in a 'top down' organisation.

5. Explain what is meant by empowerment.

6. Write a leaflet that could be given to a new employee to explain what the benefits of empowerment are.

7. List the types of skill that you think employees need to be part of a work team.

8. Draw the organisation structure for a company with which you are familiar. Write a report to compare and contrast it with ICI's old approach and with ICI's new approach.

Decide:
- which it is most like
- what direction you think it is moving in (more or less centralised)
- why you think it is moving in this direction.

Assignment

This work should be included in your portfolio.

If you complete these three tasks you are on course for a **pass**.

TASK	COMPLETE (DATE)
1 Describe the human resource area of either ICI or a business that you have investigated.	
2 Explain the roles of five different people within the organisation.	
3 Compare the organisational structure of your firm with that of ICI and explain the different ways in which communication takes place.	

If you complete these two tasks, you are on course for a **merit**.

TASK	COMPLETE (DATE)
1 Look at the different areas of ICI or another business. Explain what the different functional areas are and how they interact with each other.	
2 Look at the objectives of your chosen organisation. Explain how the communications within the business help it to meet these objectives?	

If you complete these two tasks, you are on course for a **distinction**.

TASK	COMPLETE (DATE)
1 Look at the organisational structure of your chosen business. List the strengths and weaknesses of the structure. Advise the organisation as to how it could build on the strengths and diminish the weaknesses.	
2 Study the communications flows in your organisation. How efficient are these flows? Explain how this efficiency contributes towards the objectives of the organisation.	

Unit 2 Investigating how businesses develop

SECTION A

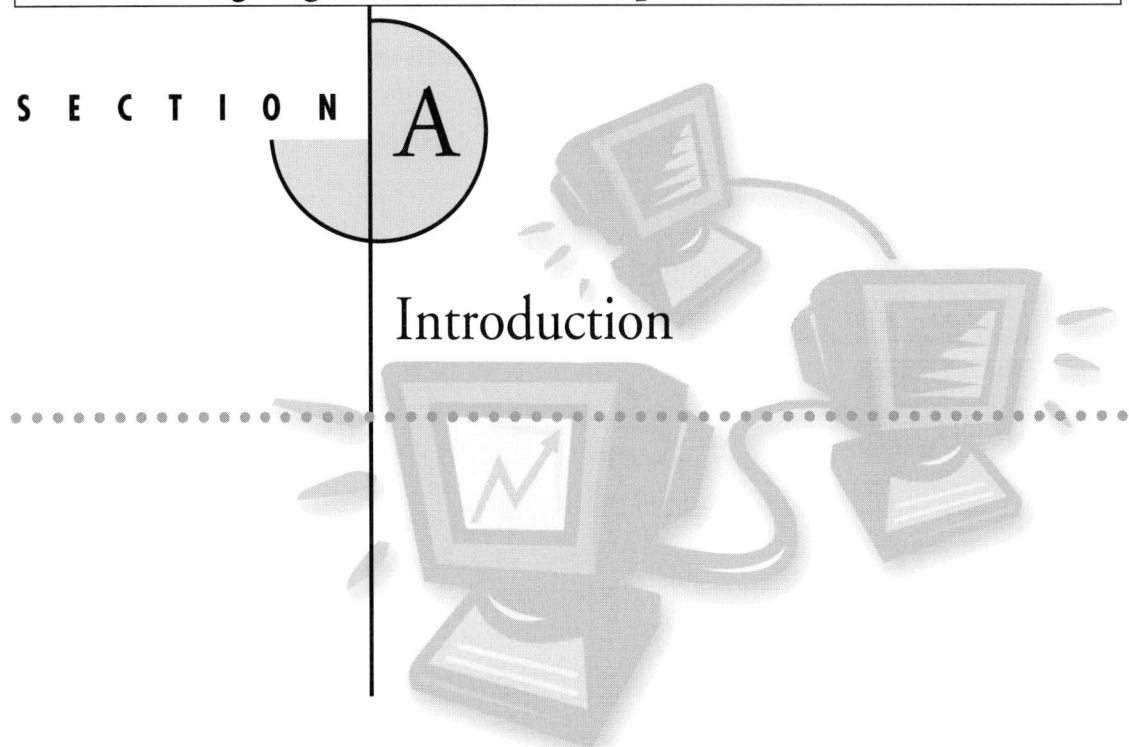

Introduction

In your work for this unit, you need to build up a broad knowledge and understanding of how a range of businesses develop and make this available for your portfolio before you then narrow your investigations to two specific firms. In these investigations, one firm must be either a sole trader or a partnership, and the other must be chosen from a company, a cooperative, a franchise or a publicly owned organisation. In each case you are required to find out their type of ownership, what they do and how they are developing and changing in response to different influences from outside the firm. Your findings on these two firms will then go into a portfolio of evidence, along with the broader information, and all of this will be internally assessed in your educational institution.

The broad features of this unit

There are five broad features that you need to plan for and gather information on for business in general. They are:

1. the main characteristics of the six types of ownership

2. a description of the three industrial sectors; the types of business in each sector, the trends in employment in each sector, and a description of how these trends might affect the businesses

3. a description of the broad activities carried out by business and the regional and national trends in these activities, if this information is available

4 a description of the main possible influences on where a firm locates its business and how these might change over the years

5 a description of the range of influences on a business by different stakeholders and how business might react to them.

What does the portfolio need to include?

1 Information and materials that show your breadth of knowledge and understanding of the five broad features described above.

2 Information and materials on two contrasting businesses that you have investigated:
   - one business a sole trader or partnership
   - one business a company, co-operative, franchise or publicly owned organisation.

Your information and materials on the two firms should include:

- a description of the different types of ownership, the liabilities of the owners and how the type of ownership is suited to the activity of the business
- a description of the industrial sector for each business and the trends of growth or decline in the UK for that sector
- a description of the main activities of each business, how the activities are carried out, and their main competitors
- a description of the UK trends – regional and/or national – in growth or decline of the type of business activities of your two chosen firms
- an explanation of how those trends in both industrial sectors and business activities might be affecting your two chosen businesses and how your businesses are responding to them
- a description of the key features of the location of each business, with an explanation of why each business has chosen its location and how the location might be changing
- a description of the influences of stakeholders on each business
- an explanation of why stakeholders are important and how each business responds to them
- an explanation of how there might be conflicts of interest among different stakeholders within any business organisation.

Note that the best case studies of the two businesses will:

- clearly show an understanding of how and why external influences in the UK affect each business
- be thorough, well organised and select and use a range of information appropriately
- make effective comparisons between the two businesses.

Key skills in Unit 2

There are many opportunities signposted in this unit for you both to achieve key skills assessments and to develop your key skills abilities. Those that should allow you to achieve key skills assessments are:

- Application of number AN2.1 effective and appropriate use of numerical data when handling figures for the employment in industrial sectors and business activities;

and other data from your chosen firms.
- Communication C2.2/3 interpretation of a range of materials on business ownership, activity, location and stakeholders; and preparation of reports, notes, tables and charts etc.

The opportunities that should allow you to develop your key skills abilities include:

- Communication C2.1a discussion in class of your findings from your research
- IT2.1/2 researching data from various IT sources
- IT2.3 presenting data using IT methods
- Application of number N2.3 comparisons of data

Remember, as in unit 1, to combine all of this guidance with that of your teacher or lecturer plus the awarding body's specifications for the unit to produce well-planned portfolios that contain high-quality information that is evaluated at key points.

Section B Types of business organisation

CHAPTER 19

Sole traders

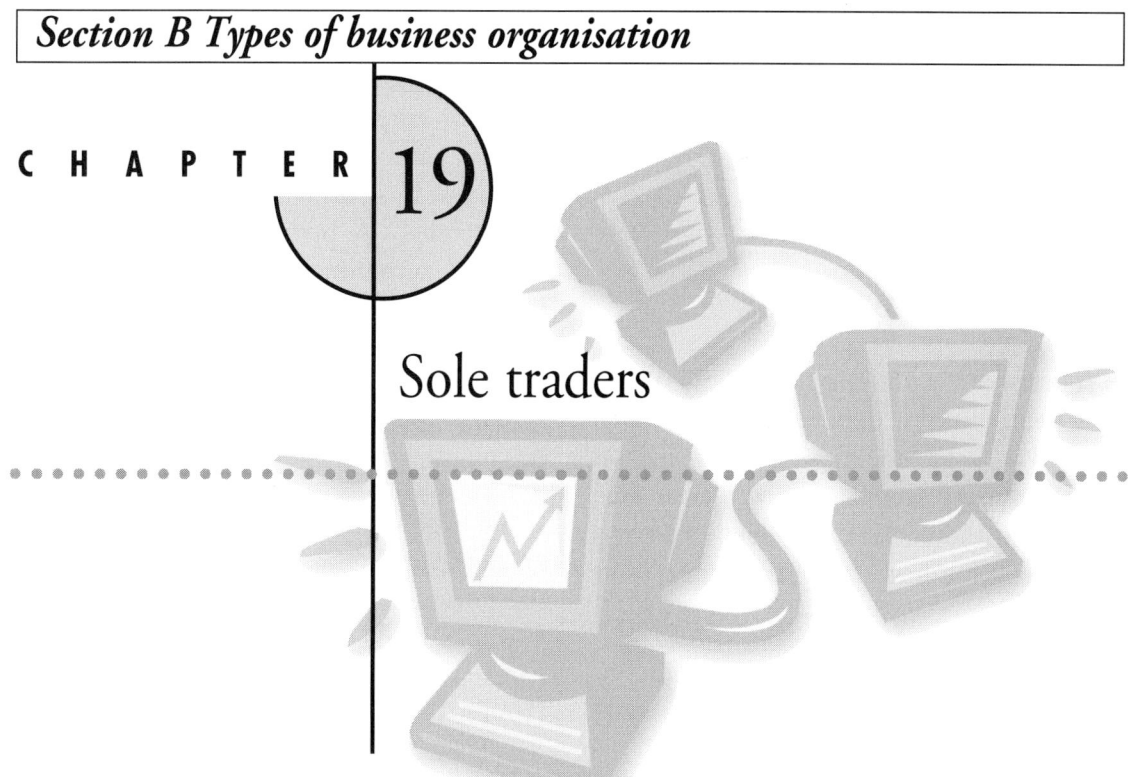

Crash Dummies' unexpected start-up

Jerry Walsh has been working for a firm of computer consultants for the last ten years. He has noticed that his firm has grown to such an extent that some of their smaller clients are no longer important to them. Indeed, a recent directive had said that staff should be winding down their commitment to smaller clients and concentrating on those who have at least ten computers. Jerry decided that in his spare time he would continue to service those clients that his company no longer wanted. He has found that this is taking up more and more of his time and has finally decided to leave his employment and set up on his own. He called his business Crash Dummies as he was dealing with computers that crashed and with people who didn't understand computers.

As he was not sure about what tax he was meant to be paying he hired an accountant and told him that he wanted to set up as a sole trader. 'You already have,' was the accountant's reply, 'you have been operating as a sole trader for the last two years.'

What you need to do

- **To gain a pass** you need an understanding of the main features of ownership and liability. Group 1 businesses are sole traders and partnerships. You must choose an example from this group.
- **To gain a merit** you need to be able to explain clearly how the trends in a particular business sector are affecting your chosen business.

- **To gain a distinction** you need to be able to show how and why external influences affect your business and use your case study work to make comparisons.

One-person business

A sole trader is a business that is both owned and controlled by one person. It is often referred to as a 'one-man business' but, as there are many women who run their own businesses, should better be referred to as a 'one-person business'. Jerry had set up as a sole trader without even realising it, it is so easy.

Interview a sole trader and prepare a report that contrasts the way in which your interviewee set up and the way in which Jerry Walsh started. Explain how easy or difficult your interviewee thought it was to set themselves up in business. What do they think are the biggest advantages of sole tradership? What are the biggest disadvantages?

(C2.2)

Starting up

The sole trader is the easiest form of business to start up. As you can see from the previous example, it is possible to be trading as a sole trader without any formal process of setting up at all. All the sole trader needs to do is to start trading. It is only if certain events happen that they will need to do anything else. For example, if they employ anyone, then they will need a knowledge of health and safety and employment laws and a willingness to make sure that rules are kept, and they will need to ensure that adequate insurance is in place for employees. If they are wishing to trade in particular types of goods, or carry on a business in a particular way, then they may need to apply for permission or licences from the local authority. Restricted goods include fireworks, cigarettes and alcohol; services include music, gambling and entertainment; there are special rules and regulations if food is being offered for sale; permission to trade from a vehicle may be needed, etc.

If the turnover of the business is likely to be greater than a certain amount set each year by the government, then registration with the Customs and Excise department may be necessary for the payment of Value Added Tax (VAT). The business will also have to produce simple profit and loss accounts and a balance sheet so that they can be assessed for Income Tax and National Insurance Contributions.

Aims

It is generally assumed that the major aim of most businesses is to maximise profit. However, this may not always be true and, certainly in the case of the sole trader, isn't always true. There are many reasons for setting up as a sole trader that do not include making the most profit possible. For example, many sole traders may like to be self-employed, to be their own boss. The freedom that this gives can outweigh many disadvantages.

Sole traders may also set satisficing targets rather than maximising ones. Maximisation means making the most of something – the largest amount possible so – in the case of profit for example, it means making as much profit as they possibly can. Satisficing targets

CHAPTER 20

Partnerships

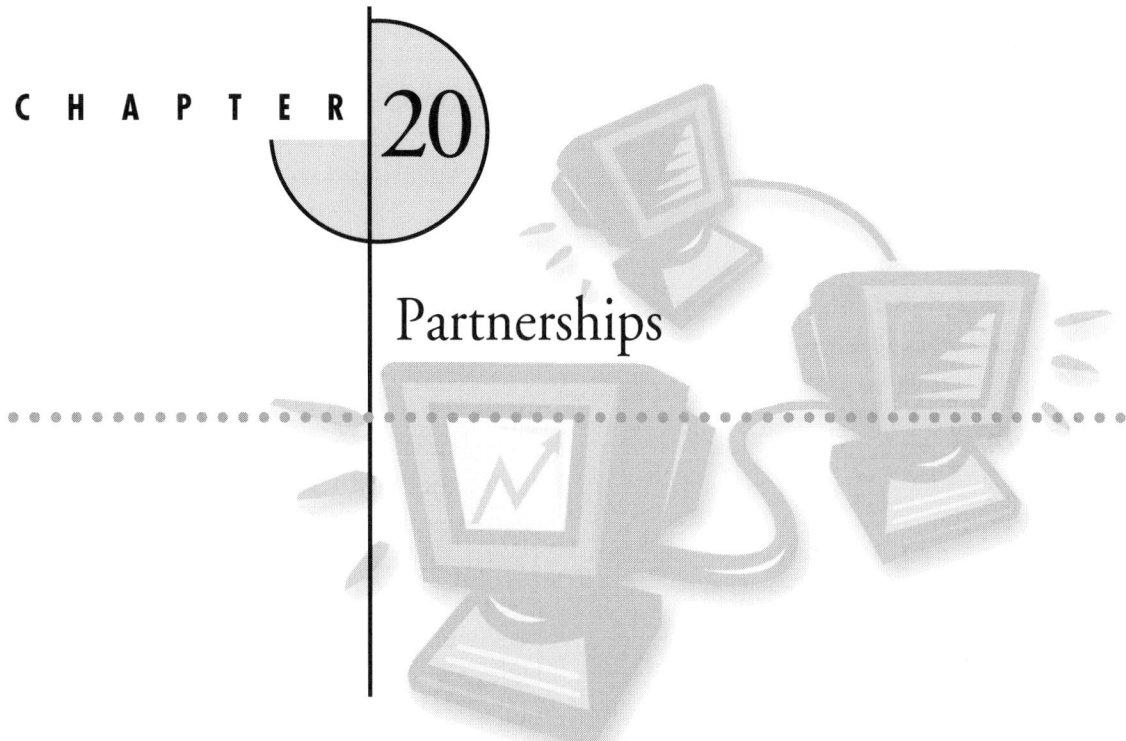

A possible solution

Jerry Walsh found that the computer services that he was offering as a sole trader were actually more needed than he had at first thought and, mostly through recommendation, he soon gained a list of clients. Most were individuals, wanting help in getting computers set up for the first time, installing new software or accessing and using the Internet. Jerry had an eye on the future for Crash Dummies – the name that he had chosen for his business – and always made an appointment to return in three or six months time to check and service machines.

Some clients were small businesses with four or five computers so Jerry helped them with problems such as sharing software and using file servers.

Jerry got some repeat business from these clients but, mostly, they were only interested in 'troubleshooting' and called him in when there was a problem. This meant that it was difficult for him to plan work. As a result, Crash Dummies employed two freelance computer experts who could help out when needed. The growth of the business meant that Jerry needed finance for vans and, rather than raise the money any other way, he offered his two freelancers the chance of sharing in Crash Dummies' success by joining him in a partnership.

What you need to do

- **To gain a pass** you need an understanding of the main features of ownership and liability. Group 1 businesses are partnerships and sole traders. You must choose an

example from this group.
- **To gain a merit** you need to be able to explain clearly how the trends in a particular business sector are affecting your chosen business.
- **To gain a distinction** you need to be able to show how and why external influences affect your chosen business and use your case study work to make comparisons.

Partners

A partnership is where two or more people agree to the joint ownership of a business. This may be an informal agreement or it may be formalised by drawing up a contract – called a Partnership Agreement. If two or more people are working together as joint owners in the same business then they are, legally, a partnership – whether any agreement has been drawn up or not. It is therefore just as easy to set up in partnership as it is to set up as a sole trader. The minimum number of partners is two, the maximum (except in some special cases) is twenty.

COMMUNICATIONS *activity*

Interview a partner and prepare a report that contrasts the way in which your interviewee became involved in a partnership and the way in which Jerry Walsh proposed to start the Crash Dummies partnership. Explain how easy or difficult your interviewee thought it was to become part of a partnership. What do they think are the biggest advantages of a partnership? What are the biggest disadvantages?

(C2.2)

Aims

The partnership is likely to share similar aims to those of the sole trader. Although probably more expansionist than the sole trader – the formation of a partnership tends to signal a larger business looking to expand its client base – the targets are still likely to be satisficing ones. Typically, expansion into a partnership is a way of sharing an increased workload or raising increased amounts of finance, but it is still unlikely that the business is looking to expend any further. Self-employment and independence are going to be two of the main objectives. Partnerships are often found in the service sector of the economy, from professional to personal services. Professionals, such as bankers, lawyers, accountants and medical practitioners, will form partnerships so that they can provide a complete service. Medical practitioners may have different specialisms; lawyers may have qualified in different areas of the law – in each case the partnership enhances the service the business can offer.

For personal services, again, there could be advantages in becoming a partnership. For example, a decorator might go into partnership with a painter and a carpet fitter, in order to provide a comprehensive service.

Advantages

The advantages of forming a partnership rather than operating as a sole trader can be found in the extra help and expertise that a partner would bring to the enterprise. Unlike the sole trader, a partnership can gain the benefits of specialisation. In the case of Crash Dummies, the other two partners may have expertise in areas that Jerry Walsh cannot

> **SUE, GRABBIT AND RUN**
>
> *Specialists in*
> Criminal Law,
> Family Law,
> Consumer Law
> and Company law

FIGURE 20.1

> **GET IT RIGHT!** ✓
>
> Two people working together in business producing goods or providing a service do not have to formally set up as a partnership. The fact that they are in business together makes them partners, with an exactly equal share of the business assets, decision-making etc, each. Only a Deed of Partnership can alter this.

cover. This obviously helps to widen the customer base of the business. Partners may also bring extra money into a business. In the case of Crash Dummies, Jerry would expect the two people joining him to contribute some finance to the business – probably an equal amount to what he himself initially had to put in. Partners will be more motivated than employees as they have a direct concern in the success of the company; they are therefore likely to work harder and be more loyal than if they were just employees. Finally, both the work and the decision-making can be shared, responsibility for decisions is therefore also shared.

Liability

There are no real benefits to a partnership in terms of liability. The partnership still has unlimited liability and now each partner is responsible for the debts of the firm up to the limit of their personal wealth, whether or not they had anything to do with creating the debt. This last is important; partners are said to be 'jointly and severally liable' meaning that they share joint responsibility but, if any one partner cannot pay his or her share of the debt, the others are still responsible for it.

Disadvantages

The biggest disadvantage is the shared unlimited liability. Not only is each partner now responsible for their own debts, they are also responsible for the debts incurred by any member of the partnership.

Other disadvantages include the possible disagreements that may happen now that decision-making is spread between partners and the fact that decisions do not actually have to be shared. One partner can make a decision, acting on behalf of the partnership, with which the other partners disagree but, because the partner was speaking for the partnership, the other partners are then bound by this decision. Obviously, there needs to be a lot of trust in a partnership to ensure that partners are not going to take decisions without consulting the other members.

The partnership suffers from the same problem as the sole trader in that it does not have a separate legal existence to its owners. Should a partner leave the partnership, retire, become bankrupt or die, then the partnership ceases to exist and will need to be reformed.

A further problem is that there can still be a

lack of capital. This is because the partners are still relying on their own sources of finance – what are called 'owner's funds' – and these will not be as substantial as those that could be obtained from a bank or similar form of business loan.

NUMERACY activity

The partnership that you study may have premises or be working from home. List the additional costs of running premises and estimate what they might be for your partnership. What additional costs do you think are involved in working from home? Show a comparison by using charts and graphs as appropriate.

(N1.3)

Control

The control of the business is shared equally between the partners. Usually, in a small partnership like Crash Dummies, decisions will be made in a fairly informal manner. In the case of large partnerships, decision-making may require a formal meeting – making partnerships less flexible than sole traders. While all partners are entitled to an equal say in the decision-making, this does not prevent any one of them from making a decision on behalf of everyone and this can obviously cause problems.

Partnership Act 1890

This is the main Act of Parliament that governs the way in which partnerships are set up, run and dissolved. If a partnership is formed without any formal or written agreement then this Act covers the conduct of the business. It lays down that, without any agreement to the contrary, the assets, profits, decision-making and rights of partners are shared exactly equally, depending on the number of partners involved.

This can be varied by the partners by drawing up their own agreement to share things out differently. This document is called the Deed of Partnership. While it is not essential to draw up a Deed of Partnership, it is a good idea to do so, so that everyone is clear as to what the rights and responsibilities of each partner actually are. If, for example, a partnership wanted to distinguish between 'junior' and 'senior' partners in terms of decision-making and profit-sharing, they would use this Deed to do so. The Deed cannot vary the liability of partners, however. Partners wishing to limit their liability within the partnership can do so with the agreement of the other partners, but at least one partner must always have unlimited liability.

In some cases a partner may be happy to contribute finance to the partnership and share in its profits but have no part in the actual running of it. These are called sleeping partners and are allowed to limit their liability to the amount of money that they have actually put into the partnership.

IT activity

Using appropriate software, devise a template which a partnership could use to draw up a partnership agreement. Present it to the partnership that you are studying and alter and adapt it according to the feedback that they give you.

(IT2.3)

PROGRESS CHECK

1. ▶ Describe the main advantages and disadvantages of setting up a partnership.

2. ▶ What is the main law governing the operation of a partnership? Explain how partners could agree to vary the terms of this law.

3. ▶▶ Explain how you think that the growth of Crash Dummies is linked to a particular market. What are the trends in that market?

4. ▶▶ Describe a sector of the economy that is growing. If you were forming a partnership in that sector, what skills, expertise or experience would you be looking for in your partner or partners?

5. ▶▶▶ What other external influences will affect:
   - the Crash Dummies partnership and its line of business
   - the partnership that you are studying.

Key terms

PARTNERSHIP – wherever two or more people are operating a business as joint owners; a formal agreement is not needed.

PARTNERSHIP ACT 1890 – this lays down that everything in a partnership is shared equally by the partners.

DEED OF PARTNERSHIP – the agreement that can be used to vary the terms of the Partnership Act.

STUDENT CHECKLIST

1. Partnerships are established through people operating a business together.

2. The advantages of the partnership lie in the extra help, expertise or skill that a partner brings.

3. The decisions of one partner are binding on all the rest.

4. Each partner has unlimited liability – this can be a disadvantage.

5. Limited liability for some partners is possible, with the agreement of the others.

CHAPTER 21

Limited liability companies

Taking a risk ...

As Crash Dummies' client list grew, the owners found that the business was not only being asked to fit and service computers and software but also to actually provide them. This meant that the partners were taking more and more risks, paying for stock and systems that customers had asked for but with no guarantees that customers were actually going to buy them.

They felt that their efforts at expansion were being held back by a lack of capital and by the responsibility of unlimited liability. Taking risks on new developments, new hardware, software or systems or trying to enter new markets could have meant bankruptcy for any or all of the partners.

Jerry Walsh decided to meet with the other two partners and propose that they formed a limited liability company. Even though it had certain drawbacks, he was convinced that the benefits would outweigh them.

... and succeeding

Bill and Paul had been friends at High School and later at college. They were interested in

FIGURE 21.1 *Microsoft Place*
Source: © *Wolfgang Kaehler/CORBIS*

the new computer technology that was being developed when they were teenagers in the 1970s. Computers were expensive, large and unwieldy and needed to be given instructions through complex programming languages. At the age of 20, the two friends formed a company which sold kit computers. In 1981, six years later, they won the contract to supply IBM with the operating system for its PCs. At the time, they did not have an operating system but bought one and modified it for IBM's requirements.

The operating system – MS-DOS – became the standard for almost all PCs and the company formed in 1975 – Microsoft – by Bill Gates and Paul Allen became one of the biggest players in the computer market. Its domination of the market has been so great that it has been investigated by the US Justice Department for its restrictive licensing agreements. Gates owns just under a quarter of Microsoft, estimated at a worth of over $25 billion, making him the world's richest man.

What you need to do

- **To gain a pass** you need an understanding of the main features of ownership and liability. Group 2 businesses are companies, cooperatives, franchises and the public sector. You must choose an example from this group.
- **To gain a merit** you need to be able to explain clearly how the trends in a particular business sector are affecting your chosen business.
- **To gain a distinction** you need to be able to show how and why external influences affect your chosen business and use your case study work to make comparisons.

Limited liability

The three parts to the name of a limited liability company give clues as to what its main features are. The 'limited liability' means that the business has limited its responsibility for debt to the assets of the business itself. Creditors can no longer have any claim on the personal wealth of the owners.

The 'company' part of the name shows that the business is an enterprise that is established with a separate legal existence from its owners. As a company, it can be bought and sold and passed from one owner to another like any other commodity. Limited companies are also known as joint stock companies, as shares or stock are held jointly by a number of people. In some parts of the world stocks are known as securities and the fact that companies are 'incorporated' leads to them being called corporations. Bill Gates and Paul Allen's firm is the Microsoft Corporation.

COMMUNICATIONS & IT
activity

Draft a letter to several public limited companies requesting their reports and accounts. You will have to try to find out their registered address (often this can be found on the products they make) and put your request in proper business format. You could use ICT so that you can edit the letter to make it specific to each company. On receipt of the reports, make a summary of three of them that a non-expert would be able to understand. This can be word processed.

(C1.3, C 2.2), (IT 1.1, IT 2.3)

Setting up

Setting up a limited company is a much more complicated process than establishing a sole trader or a partnership. The benefits of having limited liability are so great, however, that there are over half a million private limited companies and many hundreds of public limited companies in the UK. To set up as a company a business needs to follow these steps:

1. Come up with a company name. This must then be registered so that no two companies are using the same name.

2. Register the business with the Registrar of Companies at Companies House in Cardiff.

3. Draw up a Memorandum of Association. This is the document that outlines the information about the company that must be available to the public. It must include the name of the person making the application, the name and address of at least one director, whether shares are to be offered to the public and a statement of limited liability. It must also include the registered address of the company, what the purpose of the company is, what capital it hopes to raise and the name of the company secretary.

4. The company must then draw up the Articles of Association – these are the internal rules of the company and list such things as the other directors' names, voting rights, the rights of shareholders, when and how shareholders and directors are to meet and how profits are to be divided. These articles can later be changed by shareholders as long as the changes do not disagree with the Memorandum.

5. Finally, the company obtains a Certificate of Incorporation from the Companies Registrar. The company has now been formed and can legally begin to trade or operate in business.

GET IT RIGHT!

A company secretary is not a clerk or person who answers the telephone! They are actually an important official who keeps all the company's official records and documentation; they will have a senior position in the company.

Private or public?

A private limited company is different from a public limited company in only one significant way, which is that the shares are not offered on sale to the general public. A public limited company produces an annual report and set of accounts which are made available to anyone who asks for them.

Going public

If it is the intention of the company to raise capital by offering shares to the public – thus making it a public limited company, then there are three further steps which it has to go through. First, the company must issue a prospectus that gives details about the company. These will include its current performance and future prospects, its finances and accounts and the main experience and qualifications of its directors. It will – in the same way that a school or college prospectus tries to sell an educational institution – try to sell the company by showing this information in the best possible light. The offer for sale of shares will be included with the prospectus. The issue of this offer (and people taking it up by buying the shares) is called 'floating' the company or a 'flotation'.

There is a half way house between being a private limited company and a full flotation where share prices are not quoted on the full stock exchange, but on the USM – the Unlisted Securities Market.

When people have bought the shares, the company then issues share certificates to show how many shares have been bought. These will show what is called the 'nominal value' of the shares. For example, a share in Microsoft may today be worth many hundreds of dollars but only have the nominal value, on paper, of the $1 that it was bought for.

Finally, once shares are sold, the Companies' Registrar issues a Certificate of Trading to allow the company to start trading.

Share trading

Once shares in a public limited company have been issued, they are traded on the stock exchange. Much of this trading used to take place on the floor of the stock exchange itself in London, but now trading is almost entirely done electronically. This now takes place 24 hours a day in the main trading centres of the world. To buy shares in a company you would normally approach a bank or a stockbroker who will act as your agent. While many people only buy shares in a company because they want to share in the profits, there are also those who make money out of buying and selling shares.

NUMERACY
activity

Obtain the accounts of a limited company. This could be the company that you have chosen to study or another limited company. (You will already have done this if you have completed the first activity). Look at the figures as presented and simplify them so that a non-expert could understand them. Use appropriate graphs and charts where necessary.

(N2.3)

> **GET IT RIGHT!** ✓
>
> Both public and private limited companies have to warn people of their limited liability. Public limited companies must have 'plc' after their name, private limited companies must have 'Ltd'.

FIGURE 21.2 *Different time zones demonstrate how trading can take place all the time*

Finance

The main sources of finance for a limited company are:

- Owners' funds – this is the money provided by the owners for the initial establishment of the company; this money is not lent, so the owners would not expect it to be repaid, but they would expect to share in the profits of the business.
- Shares – money which comes to the company from the sale of shares never has to be repaid to the shareholders. This is because the company cannot be made to buy back the shares. Shareholders who want to get rid of their shares can sell them on to other people.
- Borrowed funds – loans or overdrafts taken from banks or other financial institutions. Sometimes the amounts of money are so large that the loan will be shared between more than one bank or institution so that they spread the risk. This is called a syndicated loan.
- Debentures – a specific form of borrowing is to issue debentures – long-term loans (the period may be as long as 25 years) issued against a guaranteed return. Some sporting venues, for example, have issued debentures to finance building and the owners of these have a permanent seat in the stadium.
- Retained profits – these are the profits that are not given back to the shareholders, which may be retained for future investment or expansion.
- Factoring – the selling of debt to a third party. If a company buys stock or materials it is common practice for payment not to be due for 90 days, sometimes longer. Factoring works like this. Crash Dummies Ltd buys £10,000 worth of stock from Microsoft Corporation. Payment is due in 90 days and Crash Dummies have no intention of paying before they have to. However, Microsoft Corporation need most of the money now. They therefore sell the debt to a factor. The factor pays them the majority of the debt, £8,000, immediately and 90 days later collects the £10,000 from Crash Dummies Ltd. The factor pays the remaining £2,000, less 90 days interest on £8,000, to Microsoft Corporation. In this way:

- Crash Dummies keeps its 90 days credit.
- Microsoft Corporation has most of the payment immediately.
- Microsoft does not have to worry about collecting the debt, or it not being paid, the factor has taken on that responsibility.
- The factor receives interest and a fee for their services.

Divorce of ownership from control

When a firm decides to issue shares, it is as if it is sharing out everything to do with the business – each share gets an equal slice of ownership and thus an equal slice of the profits and an equal say in the control of the company. There is one vote with each share meaning that the owners of the business share the control equally. However, if there are 10,000 shares, one person may hold a block of shares, which gives them power over the company. For example, if, of the 10,000 shares, 25% is owned by one shareholder and the other 75% by 75 shareholders, the one shareholder is likely to have control of the company. This is because they can always vote their shares as a block, whereas getting agreement among 75 people will be difficult. It must be remembered that while every share has an equal amount of ownership and an equal amount of control – one vote – anyone who holds more than one share therefore has more votes and more control.

The original founders of a company may thus lose control to shareholders with large blocks of shares; this is called the divorce of ownership from control. Shareholders keep the ownership of the company, but directors have day-to-day control. Shareholders elect directors at the AGM and these can also go against the wishes of the owners if they and the shareholders think that their actions are in the best interest of the company.

Controlling interest

Anyone who owns more than half of a company's shares has total control over a company. If the other shares are divided up between a number of people, then even if they all join together, their vote is not big enough to out-vote the major shareholder with a controlling interest. Sometimes, when people float a company, they ensure that they keep hold of at least 50% of the shares themselves, so that they keep control.

In many companies, the shares are spread around so many people that the ownership of just a few per cent of the shares could be enough to give control of a company. This puts control in the hands of the majority shareholder (as organising the other shareholders to all vote in a different direction is extremely difficult). Bill Gates has a 24% stake in Microsoft – a large enough slice for him to keep control.

Directors are elected by shareholders (and are likely to be major shareholders themselves and so will vote for themselves) and take the management decisions for the company on behalf of shareholders. This is called the divorce of ownership from control. If someone manages to buy enough shares in the company from other shareholders then there is always the possibility that the original owners could lose control.

Advantages and disadvantages

The main advantage to the business is the limited liability for debt that it enjoys. Also, because the business has a separate legal existence, there is no problem with continuity. The business can be bought, sold, and passed on like any commodity. There are also advantages in that a limited company may find it easier to borrow money than a sole trader or partnership – although lenders, having no guarantee that their money will be returned, may want a stake in the running of the company, such as a seat on the board of directors for a representative of a bank.

The disadvantages are that the company's affairs have to be made public and there is always the possibility of the divorce of ownership from control. The fact that companies have a separate legal existence also means that they are liable to take-overs by other companies or individuals.

Liquidation

When a limited company ceases trading its assets are sold to turn them into money, money is the most 'liquid' form of an asset (in other words it is easily transferred and easily divided), so the process is called liquidation. The money is then distributed, firstly to pay off any outstanding taxes and wages and then to pay off other debts of the company. Finally, the remaining money is distributed to shareholders in proportion to the shares they own.

The winding up may be called for by a shareholder, by a court-appointed official called the Receiver or by someone that the firm owes money to – a creditor. In this case it would be a compulsory winding up of the business. It is likely to happen because a business hasn't started trading; cannot pay its debts or has failed in its legal duties, for example has produced no report or accounts or has held no shareholders' meetings. The liquidation could also be voluntary by the agreement of the shareholders of the company.

PROGRESS CHECK

1. ▶ Describe the main features of ownership of a limited liability company.

2. ▶ Explain what is meant by limited liability and why firms find it an advantage.

3. ▶▶ Microsoft's phenomenal growth can be at least partly linked to the industry that it operates in.' Explain what this statement means.

4. ▶▶ By referring to current trends in industry, recommend to Crash Dummies the areas where you think they should be expanding.

5. ▶▶ What other external influences will affect: Crash Dummies; the Microsoft Corporation; the business that you are studying?

Key terms

LIMITED LIABILITY – the responsibility for the debts of the business is limited to the amount of money invested.

COMPANY – when a business achieves a separate legal existence from its owners.

LIMITED COMPANY – setting one up is governed by the law.

DIVORCE OF OWNERSHIP FROM CONTROL – the owners of a company may have such a small stake in it that they no longer control it.

STUDENT CHECKLIST

1. Limited liability companies may be public or private.

2. The only major difference is that shares in private companies are not offered to the public.

3. The biggest advantages are limited liability and continuity.

4. The biggest disadvantage is the possibility of the owner losing control.

5. A large minority shareholding may be enough to keep control.

CHAPTER 22

The public sector

Tracking progress in London

Continuing controversy surrounds the race to be London's first elected mayor as the candidates argue over whether the London Underground would best be run by private enterprise or by a public body as it is now. The government has already expressed its doubts over the involvement of Railtrack – the owner of the privatised railway system above ground – in the project to upgrade the capital's underground lines and stations. This is after Railtrack shouldered much of the blame for the rail disaster at Paddington. Railtrack has a £2.5 billion contract to run the below ground stations, a third of the London system. The entire project, including upgrading the deepest lines, was worth £7 billion over 15 years.

Further problems have emerged when other bidders for the public–private partnership have insisted that they must be allowed to close down sections of the Underground while work takes place. A London Underground spokesperson says that this is not possible, as the Underground is relied on by so many people. (November 1999)

What you need to do

- **To gain a pass** you need an understanding of the main features of ownership and liability. Group 2 businesses are the public sector, companies, cooperatives and franchises. You must choose an example from this group.
- **To gain a merit** you need to be able to explain clearly how the trends in a particu-

lar business sector are affecting your chosen business.
- **To gain a distinction** you need to be able to show how and why external influences affect your chosen business and use your case study work to make comparisons.

The public sector

A public sector organisation is any body that is owned or controlled by government. It is called the public sector as it is owned by government on behalf of the public.

There are a number of reasons behind this:

1 Members of the public may not be trusted with some organisations – the armed forces, nuclear power, even the printing of bank notes all need to be controlled by government.
2 Private individuals or private industry may not be able to afford the investment necessary – for example, enormous amounts of investment are needed to initially establish and then upgrade road and rail systems.
3 Government may provide – to the taxpayer – those services that private industry would be reluctant to run due to the difficulty of making a profit from them. This might include street lighting and refuse collection and disposal, as well as leisure areas such as parks and gardens.
4 Government might provide services as a right, so that everyone is able to benefit from them regardless of income – this would include such things as the health service and education.

The public sector is therefore composed of three parts – national government bodies, local government bodies and services that have been 'privatised'.

GET IT RIGHT!

Be careful not to mix up the public sector and public limited companies.

- The public sector is those businesses that are owned or controlled by government on behalf of the public.
- Public limited companies are those where the public can directly buy shares in the company.

National government

The national government is responsible for central essential services, such as the armed forces and the printing of banknotes. The power over such services is still at Westminster, with the UK government and has not been devolved to the parliament in Scotland or the Assembly in Wales (the bodies which deal directly with many affairs in those countries). This perhaps serves to underline the importance of these services to the safety and security of the nation.

Government departments also provide some services – again, ones that the government wishes to keep control over – such as The Stationery Office, which prints and publishes all the proceedings of the Houses of Parliament and all proposals for Acts of Parliament (called green papers for an initial proposal for discussion and white papers for a firm proposal) as well as the actual Acts themselves. Traditionally such government bodies were recognisable by being part of the Queen's government and therefore with the heading 'Her Majesty's' (as in Her Majesty's Inspectors of Schools) but in many cases this has now been dropped in order to give a more modern image.

COMMUNICATIONS activity

Look at the information on the privatisation of the London Underground. Civil servants, when asked to prepare information, have to present ministers with both sides of an argument. Prepare two brief outlines, one for and one against the privatisation of the Underground. Think of graphs, charts or other information that you could use to reinforce your case. Use these outlines to hold a discussion in your class or group. Take a vote at the end to decide whether you agree with privatisation or not in this case.

(C2.3, C3.1a)

Public corporations

Also under national government are organisations that were set up by government in order to carry out a particular service. While some of these have won some independence, they still rely on the government for funding and can be controlled by the government. Examples of these public corporations include the BBC and the Post Office. The BBC is meant to provide a national broadcasting service that has to include educational and religious programmes, which people are entitled to watch by paying the licence fee. The BBC carries no commercial advertising. The Post Office provides a national postal service – even in areas where this is not profitable, such as remote villages or Scottish islands. A commercial firm would be unlikely to continue with non-profit-making services.

Public corporations are created either by being directly set up by government (such as the BBC) or by an industry being nationalised (see below), such as the coal and steel industries.

QUANGOs

These are semi-independent organisations set up by central government, usually with a Board, Council or similar body appointed by government. There are hundreds of these bodies carrying out various different functions and providing different services ranging from the Sports Council and National Park Planning Boards to the Environment Agency, the British Waterways Board (in charge of canals) to the British Tourist Board, the National Rivers Authority (in charge of keeping rivers clean) and Learning and Skills Councils. Because appointments to the boards of such bodies are made by government there is much criticism of the way in which QUANGOs are put together. Equally, because they have to answer to nobody but the government, there is criticism of how they operate.

Local government

Elected locally, your local council is responsible by law for providing certain services. This is usually because they are services that must be available to everyone. In other cases it is because such services would be unprofitable to provide privately. Legally, they must provide education, refuse collection, fire and police services. Most councils also provide other services, such as housing, parks, leisure and recreation facilities.

The council's income comes from business rates, the council tax and the revenue support grant. Business rates are a uniform business rate levied on local businesses, which is linked to the value of the property where the business operates. Council tax is calculated as half linked to the value of a property and half linked to the number of adults living at a property. The revenue support grant is an amount set by central government according to a level called the Standard Spending Assessment. The council can spend more than this up to a certain level but after that the grant is reduced or 'capped'.

Natural monopolies

In the case of some industries, the most efficient way to run them is as a monopoly – a single firm running the entire industry. One example of this could be electricity – no-one can tell where their electricity is coming from – a different supplier does not supply a different quality of electricity, so competition can seem pointless and wasteful. All electricity produced by power stations is fed into the national grid, which distributes it around the country – a system where a monopoly ownership of the grid is the most sensible way to run the industry. The government felt, with many 'natural' monopolies, that keeping control in government hands would be better than letting it fall into private ones. This is especially true of essential services, such as power and water, and government can always take back control of these. The London Underground is also a natural monopoly – while there is competition above ground, from cabs, buses etc – it would be wasteful to provide alternative underground services. If monopolies are sold into the private sector, then government is careful to make sure that there is some control over their activities and appoints 'watchdogs' to oversee them.

NUMERACY *activity*

Look at the Figure 22.1. Roads are still provided and maintained by the public sector, rail is now part of the private sector. Put the figures given in the table below into a bar chart and a line graph. From which one could you best make projections? Why might the government wish to even out the freight market? What policies could the government use? Do you think that they should use such policies or should the market be left to supply and demand?

(N2.1)

Sector size

At its largest, the nationalised industry sector consisted of much of the country's primary industry – coal mining, shipbuilding, the iron and steel industry, the railway network, power in the form of both electricity and gas, and essential services such as water and sewage provision. It also included the Post Office, the BBC, telephone and telecommunications systems (part of the Post Office at the time), British Aerospace and London Transport (buses and the underground), plus many smaller undertakings such as airports, a road transport fleet and air traffic control.

The public sector now consists of only relatively small (but sometimes strategically important) parts of industry. It kept a share, for example, in some of the new technology industries and, although there has been some talk of privatising it, still keeps air traffic control.

What you need to do

- **To gain a pass** you need an understanding of the main features of ownership and liability. Group 2 businesses are franchises, the public sector, companies and cooperatives. You must choose an example from this group.
- **To gain a merit** you need to be able to explain clearly how the trends in a particular business sector are affecting your chosen franchise.
- **To gain a distinction** you need to be able to show how and why external influences affect your chosen franchise and use your case study work to make comparisons between businesses.

Franchises

A franchise is when an established and successful operation decides to expand by selling the right to trade under its name to another person or company. This may involve just the name and products, but in many cases also involves uniforms, training, suppliers and many other details of the parent firm.

The person who takes out the franchise is called the franchisee. The person who sells the franchise is called the franchiser.

A franchise is a way for someone to set themselves up in independent business with less risk than establishing their own firm, due to the use of the established name, format and/or product of the business. They are able to start with a product or service that has already proved itself viable in other markets or at other locations.

The franchise system provides a way for the franchiser to expand their operation with only minimal risk and minimal financial outlay. It has the added advantage of also letting them both retain control of franchisees and share in their success.

Another form of franchising is where a firm buys the right to operate or provide services from an owner. This is the case in independent television where franchises are bought by local independent companies from the IBA (Independent Broadcasting Authority), local radio, and, as outlined in the example, train companies bidding for franchises to run services on Railtrack's rails.

COMMUNICATIONS *activity*

Imagine that you were applying for the franchise for either a McDonald's restaurant or for the right to run commuter trains in the South East of England. Write a list of the sort of promises you think you would have to make and the restrictions which the franchiser is likely to place on you. Now share your thoughts in a group discussion and see if you can compile a definitive list of requirements for each franchise opportunity.

(C3.1a)

Business objectives

The main aim for the franchiser is to expand the business without having to take on the debt that expansion by an alternative route would mean. The franchiser is likely to have profit maximisation or taking a maximum market share as its main objectives and have decided on franchising as a reasonably cheap way of achieving this. They are also guaranteeing themselves an income through the system of royalties.

For the franchisee, the objective will be to set up in independent business by using someone else's successful product or methods – effectively borrowing a tried and tested business idea. Objectives are likely to be those of the small businessperson – independence, the opportunity to 'be your own boss', the opportunity to take some of the rewards for your own efforts. Franchises are extremely safe. The failure rate for franchises is tiny – about 6% – compared with a failure rate for other forms of business of over 50%.

Setting up

If a successful business operation decides that it would like to expand, then it could do so by buying another company or business; by opening another branch or outlet or by selling a franchise.

Franchises may be bought or rented (leased) from the franchiser. The franchiser will set a fee for buying the franchise and will then receive further money by charging a royalty on the franchisee's turnover.

The initial purchase or lease of the franchise could cost from a few hundred pounds to several hundred thousand pounds or, in the case of the railways, a promise to invest several million pounds. The royalty will be charged as a percentage of turnover.

The commercial franchiser will advertise the sale of the franchise in a specialist directory, such as the UK Franchise Directory or Franchise World Directory, and invite people to apply for the franchise. In the case of a successful company, there will be many applicants for the franchises being offered as it provides such a safe and established route into business. The Body Shop, for example, receives over 10,000 applications each year for the few opportunities that are available.

The company will consider applicants in the same way as a company considers applicants for a job. It will initially weed out the unsuitable applicants and may then go to a stage of interview with the short-listed candidates. The franchiser needs to be careful about who is sold the franchise as they will need to make sure that the new franchisee will uphold and not damage their reputation.

Once they have decided on who they are going to appoint and the initial finance is in place, the franchiser will provide some or all of the items needed by the firm. This could include loans, premises, stock, training, insurance, legal advice and design and shopfitting. In many cases the franchiser will also guarantee an exclusive area for the franchisee so that they are not competing with other 'branches' of the same firm. In other cases, the franchiser may provide the point of contact so that franchisees can meet customers. For example, the British School of Motoring has driving instructors who have bought franchises from the parent company. They own their own cars and have obtained their own qualifications, but BSM provides them with its corporate identity and recruits learner drivers through its offices. Franchisees also benefit from the national advertising carried out by many franchisers.

Payments

The franchisee is usually charged a royalty on turnover – this means that a percentage of turnover is the fee demanded by the franchiser. Note that this is a charge based on turnover, not on profits, so that even if the franchisee makes a loss, the royalty payment will still have to be made. In this way the franchiser ensures that there is a return even if the franchisee is not making a profit.

Type of ownership

The franchisee could be a sole trader, a partnership, a limited company or even a cooperative. A franchise is more a way of buying into an established business than a different way of ownership. The franchiser will take on all the rights and types of liability of whatever form of ownership they think is best. The franchiser will need to be satisfied that the franchisee has chosen an appropriate form of ownership.

IT activity

Using electronic means, find as much information as you can about McDonald's and Connex. What are the similarities between the two organisations? What are the differences?

Control

The amount of control that the franchiser has over the business will depend on how much control the franchiser wishes to keep. Some franchisers keep very strict control, demanding, for example, that only certain product lines – as supplied by themselves – are sold. McDonalds provide the exact range of food that can be sold, with specific instructions on how it is to be prepared and cooked, they provide the ingredients, the point of sale material, uniforms and brand image. They provide price lists and determine prices and staff wages.

Not all franchisers keep such a large amount of control and regulation and will allow the franchisee more leeway over what goods and services they can sell. Channel 3 commercial television stations in the UK are franchises – companies who wish to run a station must bid for a franchise that will last for a limited number of years and then rebid if they wish to keep the station. Once the franchise is won, however, it is up to the television companies to decide on exactly what their output will be. Companies such as Thames TV, Central TV, Yorkshire TV, HTV Cymru etc have all bought franchises from the Independent Broadcasting Association – the franchiser. To obtain the franchise they may have had to promise to produce so many hours of religious programming, or of educational material, or of new drama, but apart from this they have a fair amount of independence as to what they broadcast. The prospective rail franchisees will have to promise certain levels of service and investment in order to win the franchise. In their case, if the promises are not kept, heavy fines are a possibility.

The franchiser may also provide national advertising and promotion schemes that the individual franchisee would never be able to afford.

Therefore, in terms of decision-making, in most cases the franchiser makes the strategic and tactical decisions whereas the franchisee makes the operational decisions. In some cases, even these day-to-day decisions may be taken from the franchisee as the franchiser can even decide on details such as opening hours and times.

Finance, risk and liability

All three of these will depend on the type of business ownership which the franchisee has decided on. Sources of finance for the franchisee will be similar to those of other independent business operators – the franchisee's own funds, bank loans and overdrafts or, in the case of a limited company, money raised through the sale of shares.

The low risk involved in franchise operations also brings other advantages. For example, banks tend to look more favourably on this form of business when considering loans since – because the owner will be operating using an established business idea or product – there is much less risk of failure and the owner defaulting on the loan.

Liability, again, depends on the chosen type of business ownership. A franchiser may have unlimited liability as a sole trader or partnership or limit their liability by setting up a limited company. In either case it is the franchisee that is responsible for the debts of the business, not the franchiser.

> **GET IT RIGHT!** ✓
>
> Remember that an employee is employed by an employer; a trainee is trained by a trainer. In the same way a franchisee takes out a franchise from a franchiser.

Profits

The franchisee keeps the profits that they make from their operation of the business. These may not be as high as if the franchisee was completely independent as the franchiser may place price restrictions on them. They may also, for example, be forced to buy their stock from the franchiser – even though it could be available more cheaply from a different source.

Advantages and disadvantages

There are benefits for both the franchiser and the franchisee. The main benefit for the franchisee lies in the low risk attached to a franchise operation and the fact that if it is successful and makes a profit, then the franchisee benefits from that profit. The major disadvantage lies in the amount of control that the franchiser has over the franchisee. In some cases, the restrictions placed on the franchisee may make them feel more like managers than independent owners.

There are few disadvantages for the franchiser – the company keeps control of the operation, expands at a much reduced cost and ensures itself an income through royalties. The major disadvantage is the damage that can be done to the reputation of a company by the failure of even one of its franchisees. Imagine the damage that would be done to McDonald's, for example, if a branch was found to be selling out-of-date and dangerous meat. In this case the damage of bad publicity to the parent company, the franchiser, would be much greater than that to the individual franchiser.

PROGRESS CHECK

1. ▶ Describe the different types of business franchise.

2. ▶ Explain the main aims of both the franchiser and the franchisee.

3. ▶▶ Describe how a franchiser would offer a franchise. What steps would a franchisee have to take to apply for it?

4. ▶▶ Outline the main ways in which a franchise would be organised and financed.

5. ▶▶▶ Why do you think that many franchisers set conditions on how the franchise is to operate? What is your opinion of these conditions?

Key terms

FRANCHISE – the right to trade under an established name.

FRANCHISEE – the person or organisation buying the right.

FRANCHISER – the person or organisation selling the right.

LEASE – to hire or borrow for a fixed amount of time.

ROYALTY – a payment made on earnings, payable as a proportion or percentage of earnings.

STUDENT CHECKLIST

1. Franchises are either the (paid for) right to trade using someone else's successful name or product, or the right to offer services using their equipment.

2. Franchising is the least risky and most successful way to start a small business.

3. Franchisers guarantee an income by charging royalties on turnover.

4. Franchisers can be very restrictive in what they allow a franchisee to do.

CHAPTER 24

Cooperatives

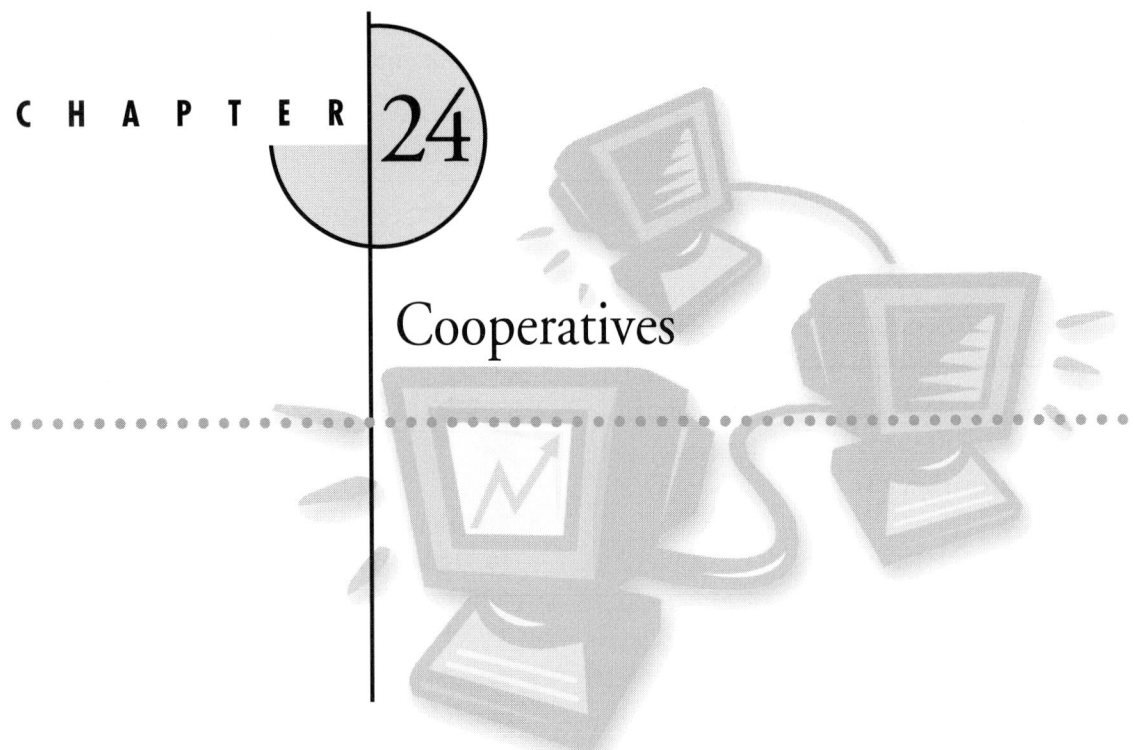

1844 The Rochdale Pioneers

In the nineteenth century, it was the practice of mill owners to have their own shops for their workers to buy from. Often workers were not paid in money, but were paid in tokens that could only be spent in the owner's shop. Often the produce sold was of a substandard quality, or old or impure. Cases are reported of flour being bulked out with chalk, liquid goods being watered down and scales being fixed to give short weight.

In 1844, a group of workers, fed up with such practices, formed the Rochdale Society of Equitable Pioneers and opened their own grocery outlet. Each member contributed just £1 to set up the business. The business sold basic goods at fair prices and did not intend to make a profit. Any surplus was divided up between the members so that everyone benefited – a mutual organisation.

1999 Letter to Scottish Widows members (edited extract)

The Board considered the alternative of continuing as a mutual organisation but concluded that, in the light of the way that firms were growing larger in the financial services sector, Scottish Widows would have to grow considerably to compete in the new mass market products such as stakeholder pensions. Scale allows companies to achieve lower unit costs, which makes them more competitive. The Board believes that, as a mutual organisation, there are too many limits placed for the raising of capital thus making expansion difficult. Having insufficient capital to buy other

FIGURE 24.1 *Scottish Widows*

companies means that the company would not be able to grow large enough to compete effectively. Lloyds TSB made an offer that would mean Scottish Widows joining the Lloyds TSB group but losing its mutual status. The Board unanimously recommended this offer.

What you need to do

- **To gain a pass** you need an understanding of the main features of ownership and liability. Group 2 businesses are cooperatives, the public sector, companies and franchises. You must choose an example from this group.
- **To gain a merit** you need to be able to explain clearly how the trends in a particular business sector are affecting your chosen cooperative or mutual.
- **To gain a distinction** you need to be able to show how and why external influences affect your chosen cooperative or mutual and use your case study work to make comparisons between businesses.

Coming together

A cooperative enterprise is any one where a group of people have come together to work or to buy or sell goods or services for the shared benefit of the group. Another word for this is the 'mutual' benefit of the group and in this class we can also put mutual societies. Many mutual societies started as providers of insurance (particularly fire insurance) and, later, as providers of ways for people with money to invest it in order to maintain an income (hence many of the names of such societies are linked to wealthier professionals or individuals – Legal and General, Clerical and Medical and Scottish Widows, for example).

A cooperative could be one of:

- a group of workers sharing labour and the profits from their labour – a worker cooperative
- a group of producers who have joined together to sell their produce – a producer cooperative
- a group of consumers who have joined together to bring about lower prices – a consumer cooperative
- a group of people who have joined together to provide financial benefits – a mutual organisation.

Worker cooperatives

Worker cooperatives are where a group of workers decide to share the work, decision-making and profits of an enterprise between them. Sometimes workers faced with the threat of closure will use their redundancy money to buy the firm that they work for but

> ### NUMERACY activity 1
>
> The original point of consumer cooperatives was to lower prices. Compare your local cooperative with other stores to see if this is still true. You will need to choose a basket of goods to price, say bread, milk, eggs, fish, cheese, butter and jam. Write down the price of each item at the Co-op. Add up the total to gain an index price of 100. Price the goods at other stores (making sure that you are comparing like with like) and compare the totals. Show the results on pie charts.
>
> (N2.2, N2.3)

this is not the only way in which worker cooperatives are formed.

In Scandinavia, for example, it is a very common form of ownership and is known as the 'third way' between communism and capitalism. The major features of worker cooperatives are shared decision-making, shared risk and shared profit.

In a small organisation shared decision-making may be possible; a meeting of all the workers in a small business may mean that decisions are made totally democratically. However, this is not very efficient and either delegates or managers may need to be appointed. A delegate would be sent to a meeting to speak for a group of workers. A manager would be employed to take operational decisions.

With shared risk and shared profit, each worker puts in an equal amount of money, has an equal say in the decisions and takes an equal share of the profit.

Worker cooperatives have less chance of industrial relations problems, produce better motivation in workers as they are working for themselves, and tend to be more aware of their responsibilities to the local community where the workers live. On the other hand, growth of the organisation is difficult; it is hard to raise capital and, with mutuals, there were restrictions on the amount of capital they were allowed to raise – this is one of the main reasons why Scottish Widows has decided to demutualise. A further problem is that all members are entitled to a say in decision-making and sometimes this will lead to disagreement and internal tensions – not every member will be qualified to speak on every issue but all will have a right to; at the same time there may be a reluctance to employ personnel from 'outside' who do have the expertise.

Producer cooperatives

Producers who join together to share resources and/or marketing are a common feature of many societies. In parts of Africa, for example, several villages will join together at harvest time in order to gain mutual benefits. In South America, smaller producers of coffee (and most farms are small) have joined together to cooperate in the branding and marketing of their own produce.

They have been helped in this by charities whose aim is to ensure that small producers are not being exploited. Café Direct is one such firm – a cooperative of small coffee producers. Their combined crop shares facilities, marketing, packaging and distribution where this would not be economical for any one of them. Such organisations are not unknown in the richer parts of the world – growers of oranges, lemons and limes in California have joined together to market under the cooperative 'Sunkist' label.

> **COMMUNICATIONS** *activity*
>
> Mr Wilks, Mr Jones and Mrs Edwards own dairy farms that are next to each other. Each has a small herd of dairy cattle and each supplies a bottling and distribution plant with raw milk. Draw up an agreement between the farmers that each will sign because it shows the advantages that forming a cooperative can bring. You will need to think of ways in which sharing would bring advantages and write them in the form of an agreement.
>
> (C1.3)

Such groups may find a number of benefits from cooperation. Large or expensive machinery can be shared, preparation, processing and packaging plants can gain economies by drawing from several suppliers and there are benefits of shared marketing.

Consumer cooperatives

The Rochdale Pioneers, as outlined before, were the forerunners of the modern cooperative movement. The Cooperative Retail Society (CRS) has a turnover in excess of £8,000 million and 5,000 retail outlets nationwide. The CRS has adopted the principles that were laid down by the Rochdale Pioneers:

- Each member has only one vote, regardless of how many shares in the society s/he owns.
- Anyone may buy a share and become a member of the society, regardless of race, colour, creed or religion.
- Goods and services are sold at reasonable prices. After usual business expenses have been paid, the profit or surplus is returned to the members in proportion to the amount of money that they have spent with the society. This profit is divided equally and is therefore called a dividend (at one time it was given out at the point of sale as a dividend stamp, issued according to how much you had spent).

The Co-operative Union

In 1869, 25 years after the founding of the original Rochdale cooperative, the Co-operative Union was formed. This is a body that helps and advises on the formation of new cooperative enterprises. It now forms an umbrella body under which are the CRS, the Co-operative Wholesale Society and other cooperative enterprises, such as Co-operative Funeral Service, Co-operative Insurance Society, Co-operative Press, Co-operative Bank and Co-operative Travel. The Industrial Common Ownership Society will give help and advice to worker cooperatives.

Mutual societies

The two main groups of mutual societies are insurance companies and building societies. Insurance companies work on the principle that everyone pays a fee – a premium – into a central fund and anyone who suffers a misfortune is compensated from this funds. As not everyone will suffer a loss, the society should be able to cover the losses that are made. In some cases, funds were set up to cover things that were going to happen – death, funeral expenses, retirement. Building societies were originally set up so that people could cooperate in the building of houses and, when every member in a group had a house, the society would be closed. The point of mutual societies is that they have the interests of their membership at heart whereas other forms of organisation will be more concerned with profits and the interests of shareholders.

The deregulation of the financial services market has led to a number of mutual societies seeking to demutualise so that they can compete in the new markets. For example, building societies were allowed to operate current accounts and issue credit and debit cards and banks were allowed to issue mortgages (loans for house purchase). Some societies, such as Scottish Widows, have demutualised – with cash or shareholding benefits going to members – others have resisted and remained as mutuals.

PROGRESS CHECK

1. ▶ Describe the different types of cooperative.

2. ▶ Explain what you think is the purpose of each type of cooperative.

3. ▶▶ In what ways might the business objectives of a cooperative differ from those of any other business that you have studied?

4. ▶▶▶ Cooperatives are sometimes called the 'third way' – give a detailed explanation of what this means.

5. ▶▶▶ Research the trends among mutual societies. What is the current trend? Do you see this continuing or not?

Key terms

COOPERATIVES – groups of workers, producers, consumers, investors who join together for mutual benefit.

MUTUAL SOCIETIES – generally building societies, pension funds and insurance companies.

DEMUTUALISATION – the process of turning from being a mutual into being a company.

DIVIDEND – a share of the divided profits.

STUDENT CHECKLIST

1. Cooperatives occur in producer, consumer and labour markets.

2. Worker cooperatives have some drawbacks associated with communication and management.

3. Mutuals can be seen as financial cooperatives.

4. The Co-operative Union provides support for cooperative enterprises.

Section C Business context and influences

CHAPTER 25

Industrial sectors

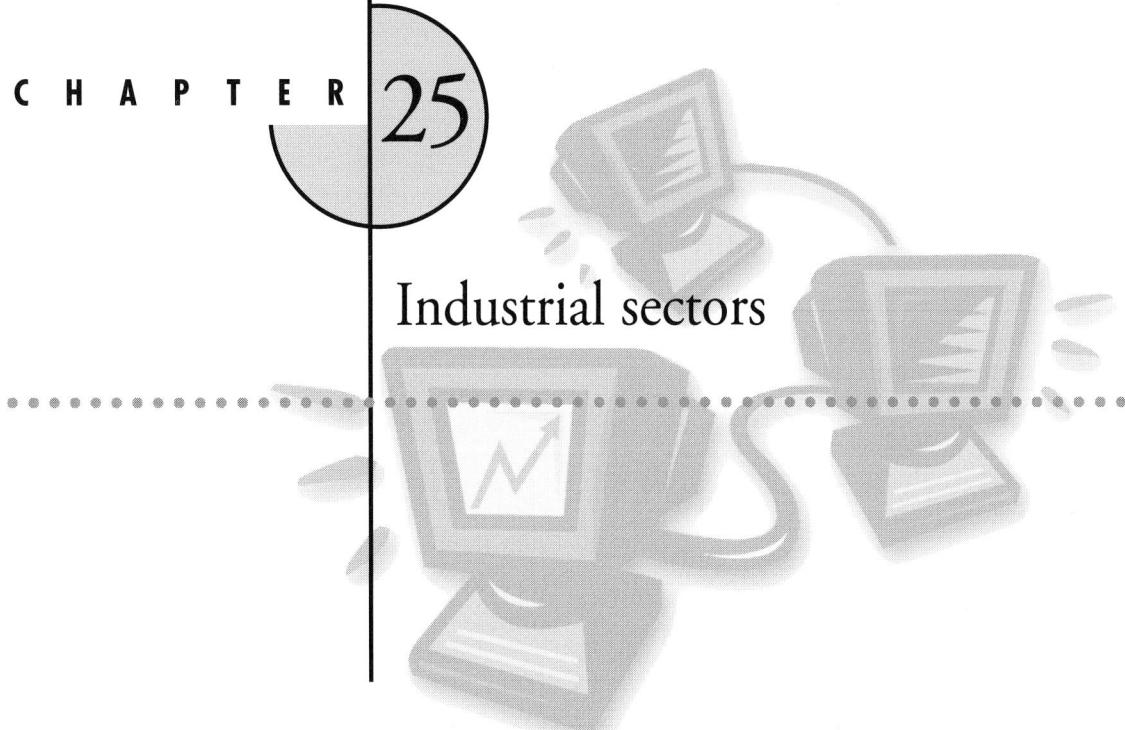

From Seaforth to breakfast table

As a product is made, it passes through several stages along a chain of production. At each stage, the producing firm will be trying to add value until the product is sold to its final consumer. One well-known example is the production of Kelloggs breakfast cereals. It begins with the planting, ripening and harvesting of maize. This is imported into the UK where it arrives at Seaforth. After storage it is then milled to remove the parts that would harm freshness and taste. The milled 'grits' are taken by road to Manchester where it is flavoured, cooked and dried. At each stage it is checked for quality. The next stage is to roll the maize into flakes, which are then toasted at high temperatures. At last, the cereal can be put into inner liners and then packed into cartons. The cartons are collected into cases for storage in the warehouse before being transported by road to the country's supermarkets and then on to consumers' breakfast tables.

What you need to do

- **To gain a pass** you need to describe the industrial sectors and identify the broad growth or decline of the sectors in the UK.
- **To gain a merit** you need to explain how trends in the growth or decline of a business sector in the UK are affecting one business you are investigating.
- **To gain a distinction** – no specific statements for this level.

Chain of production

Every product has a chain of production with each stage linked to the next. There might be a different number of stages but these may be grouped under three main headings or industrial sectors – the primary, secondary and tertiary sectors.

Primary sector

Virtually every product will start back in the primary sector. This is where the raw material is extracted. Industries involved in the extraction of raw materials are quite varied. The most obvious examples would be the mining of coal and the extraction from quarries of such things as iron ore, granite and limestone.

Other industries that are particularly important for the UK are the Oil and Natural Gas extraction. Forestry in all its forms will also be part of the primary sector. This will include the felling and logging of trees but could also include rubber plantations where rubber trees are tapped and rubber resin is collected in pots from each tree. Agriculture will cover the most obvious Western world farming activities of animal rearing and arable production; but worldwide, a huge number of crops will be grown from tea to cotton, and from coffee to rice. A final industry to recall in this sector is fishing.

Secondary sector

Once the raw material has been 'harvested' it will enter the secondary sector where it is processed or manufactured into a finished product. In this sector there may be a very large number of production stages before the final product is ready for sale. The more complex the product the more stages it is likely to go through. This sector also covers a large number of different industries and activities.

Some products will need to be processed such as that described for cornflakes at the start of this chapter. This might also apply to both oil and beer where the product has to be refined from the original raw materials. Some products will have to be 'simply' assembled from pre-produced items and in the modern day car plant this is the general rule. Many of those car parts have to be manufactured at some point and this secondary stage of production is often referred to as the manufacturing stage. A final industry to include in the secondary stage is construction, both the building of houses, factories and shops.

Tertiary sector

Finally, the product will enter the tertiary sector where the product will be distributed to organisations prepared to sell it on to the final consumer. Tertiary production includes all types of services, such as the commercial services of banking and advertising, and the

> **GET IT RIGHT!** ✓
>
> Some records of employment that are published include figures for the utilities of gas, electricity and gas alongside mining. This is misleading because such utilities are not normally thought of as part of the primary sector. It is more acceptable to think of firms in these industries as part of the secondary sector, although they do have characteristics of all three sectors.

direct, personal services of doctors and hairdressers.

These stages of production are said to be part of a chain because they are linked together as illustrated in Table 25.1. You should remember, of course, that various services will also be needed at each stage to help production take place. For example, the services of a bank will be needed by virtually every firm involved in the chain, as will transport.

CHAIN OF PRODUCTION FOR WOOD FURNITURE

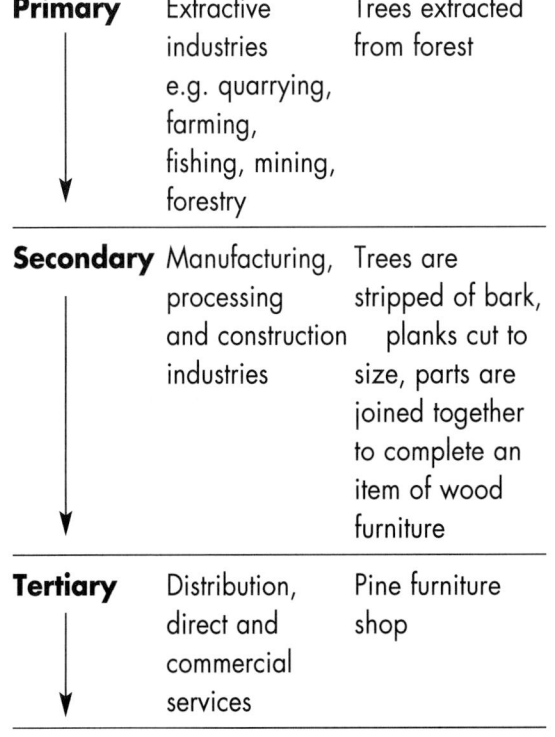

Primary	Extractive industries e.g. quarrying, farming, fishing, mining, forestry	Trees extracted from forest
Secondary	Manufacturing, processing and construction industries	Trees are stripped of bark, planks cut to size, parts are joined together to complete an item of wood furniture
Tertiary	Distribution, direct and commercial services	Pine furniture shop
Consumer		Consumer

TABLE 25.1

PROGRESS CHECK

1. ▶ Use the descriptions of the three sectors, the data on page 168 and your own research on trends in employment and output in the three sectors to produce a table that explains and compares the three sectors. In particular, try to build up a picture of employment in the three sectors in your area or region of the country.

2. ▶▶ Plan your table before using IT resources to produce a hard copy of your comparison.

3. ▶▶▶ Illustrate the table using suitable images drawn from real world sources or from computer picture banks.

(N2.1, C2.3, N2.3, IT1, IT2.2, IT2.3)

Key terms

PRIMARY PRODUCTION – a first stage of production where raw materials are extracted.

SECONDARY PRODUCTION – at this stage, raw materials are manufactured and processed into the final good.

TERTIARY PRODUCTION – this is the provision of services of all kinds both to business and to the general public.

VALUE ADDED – this is the difference between the value paid for the inputs used in production and the value of a firm's output.

STUDENT CHECKLIST

1. There are many stages involved in producing most goods with value added as the product moves from raw material to finished product sold to the consumer.

2. These stages may be placed into one of three sectors – primary, secondary or tertiary.

3. For most products these sectors are linked together in a chain of production.

4. Recent trends suggest a continuing decline in employment in both primary and manufacturing sectors while tertiary employment continues to increase.

CHAPTER 26

Business activity

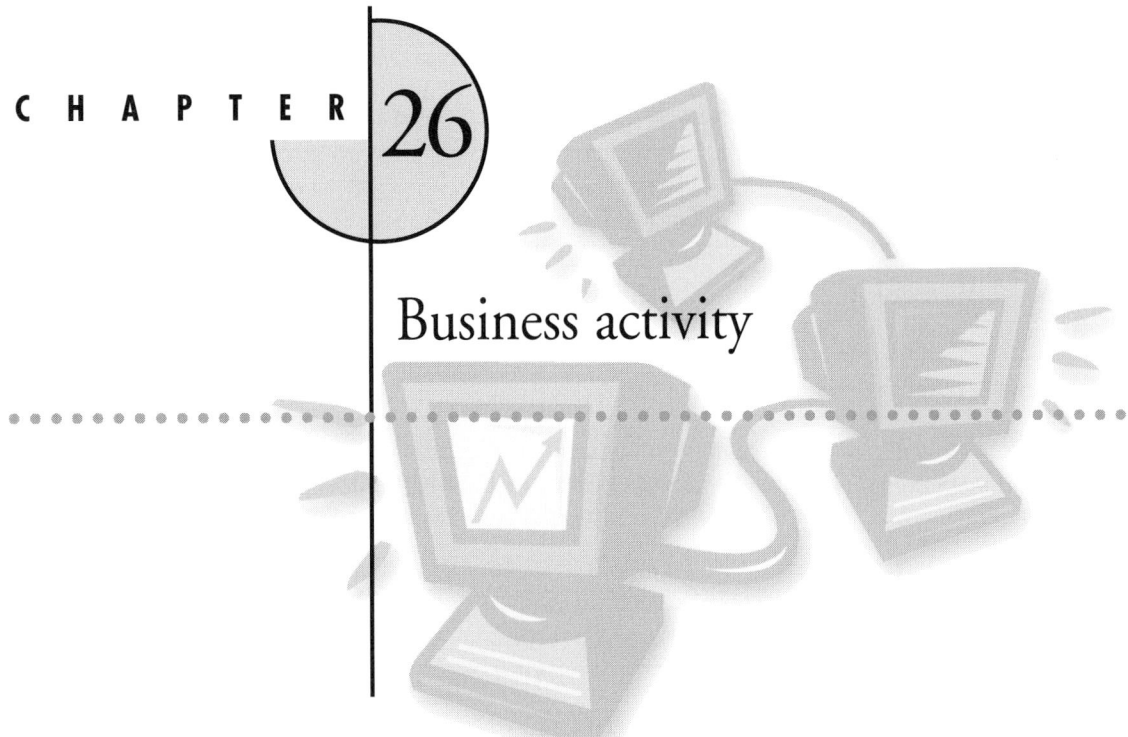

Death of the salesman?

Every day consumers purchase millions of goods and services from supplying firms in the UK. In most cases these transactions have required a face-to-face interaction, or perhaps a voice-to-voice interaction when the deal has been done over the telephone. This may end sooner than we expect if sales through the Internet continue to expand at present rates. Current predictions for transactions via the Internet in the UK during 1999 are just under £1 billion. By 2005 this is predicted to rise to a staggering £18 billion. Direct sales avoiding our traditional outlets will mean the death of the salesperson. Every firm in the country will have to start planning for a new way to organise their business activity and new tactics are being launched, for example, the AA giving 10% discounts for customers buying insurance on-line and the Prudentials Egg finance provider will now only accept new customers through the Internet.

What you need to do

- **To gain a pass** you need to describe the main activities of business, how they are carried out and describe the UK trends of growth or decline in the activities of two businesses.
- **To gain a merit** – there are no specific statements for this level.
- **To gain a distinction** – there are no specific statements for this level.

Changes in employment

In the previous chapter, you were intro-

INDUSTRY	1990	1991	1992	1993	1994	1995	1996	1997	1998
Agriculture, forestry, fishing	294	287	290	307	280	253	261	275	282
Mining etc, electricity, gas, water	396	370	333	289	255	231	222	221	211
Manufacturing	4605	4196	3983	3808	3823	3918	4002	4055	4033
Construction	1114	1025	925	840	840	814	859	940	1066
Wholesale & retail trade	3574	3512	3503	3483	3570	3619	3728	3840	3928
Hotels and restaurants	1242	1215	1200	1162	1173	1235	1245	1270	1276
Transport, storage, post, telecom	1371	1352	1334	1297	1293	1285	1302	1322	1376
Financial services	1045	1024	992	961	966	984	959	982	1014
Real estate, renting, computer	2395	2355	2363	2442	2455	2604	2945	3137	3262
Public administration & defence	1385	1404	1406	1400	1382	1345	1346	1299	1272
Education and health services	4062	4103	4146	4139	4172	4221	4237	4268	4280
Other services	900	885	913	939	932	943	1024	1047	1081
Total	22383	21728	21387	21066	21141	21452	22128	22657	23080

NB All figures are in '000s, are for the whole of Great Britain and are recorded in June of each year.

TABLE 26.1

duced to the three main industrial or production sectors – primary, secondary and tertiary. These sectors are rather too broad to use effectively when we want to examine and explore the range of business activities. In particular, by breaking the sectors down into more parts we can see in more detail the employment changes taking place. This is shown in Table 26.1 based on data from the Monthly Digest of Statistics.

In some ways, this table is not that useful as a tool for making comparisons as it is difficult to spot the trends both for each industry and between industries. One way of improving the usefulness of this information would be to plot the figures for each industry over the nine years as a series of line graphs.

IT activity

Your task is to use this table of employment by industry to present a chart of 12 line graphs for each category of industry over the nine-year period. Do not produce a graph for the total employment figures. Each line needs to be labelled and differentiated from the others. Choose a suitable scale for the employment figures to show the changes to best effect.

(IT2.3)

Even this graph is still limited in allowing you to make a comparison of the real changes over time. It is often more useful to show the percentage changes over time as this allows more useful comparisons to be made between industries. For example, the Labour Market Survey produced these figures for the industrial employment. The table below shows the percentage change in job creation by industry between September 1997 and September 1998.

Construction	+9.8%
Transport & communications	+5.1%
Banking, finance & insurance	+3.6%
Distribution, hotels & restaurants	+3.1%
Other services	+2.2%
Public administration, education & health	+0.1%
Manufacturing	−0.8%
Energy & water	−2.2%
Agriculture & fishing	−8.5%
Total services	+2.3%
All jobs	**+1.9%**

TABLE 26.2

This is certainly a useful piece of data to compare the employment changes between industries, but it would be even more useful if we knew the actual size of those changes. For example, the largest increase is 9.8% in construction but the actual numbers may be very small if few people are employed in construction.

IT activity

1. **Go back to Table 26.1 and turn the figures for each industry in 1990 into a percentage of the total employment for that year. Repeat the exercise for 1998. Put the results in a table and describe the changes that you can observe over the nine years.**

2. **Use a spreadsheet program to do these calculations for you but in this task do the calculations for all nine years. Print a hard copy of your table.**

3. **Using your spreadsheet data, create a line graph of the percentage changes for each industry over the nine-year period. How does this compare with the line graph you completed for the Information Technology activity?**

There is no information included in this data on the trends in full-time and part-time working. It is expected that the increases in part-time working will mainly come from retailing, distribution and catering where part-time working is already very strong. There is also expected to be an increase in part-time work in the more professional activities of consultancy, computing and financial services. In other words, such people may be expected to combine a number of part-time posts or activities to create the equivalent of a full-time position. Some estimates suggest that by 2010 there will be nearly 8.75 million part-time jobs which compares with 6.84 million in 1998 and just 4.8 million in 1980.

Other data that you might find useful in analysing changes in business activities relates to the small business market. For example:

- 99% of UK businesses employ less than 100 people
- 98% of businesses employ less than 250 people
- those 98% account for 60% of the employed UK workforce
- a staggering 2.5 million businesses employ no-one, with 13% of the workforce classed as self-employed

Figures for start-ups in 1997 give some indication of the popularity of the various type of business activity chosen. In 1997, retailing saw 17% of start-ups, leisure 16%, production 14%, construction 10%, business and professional 17% and other 26%.

Typical business activity

There are many equally valid ways of grouping or classifying business activity. The list of start-ups above gives one indication as analysed by one bank. To help you think about business activity, descriptions of seven typical activities are given below.

1 Retailing

In simple terms this involves the selling of a good or service to a consumer, usually at a shop or some other outlet. The range of retailing outlets is quite extensive and the range of goods and services being offered is almost beyond belief. There are still the one-off traders with a single outlet offering personal service or a small range of items, such as hairdressers and small newsagents. A common sight on today's high street is the variety chain or multiple offering several different types of goods and operating from a large number of branches located throughout the region or nation.

Marks and Spencer, Woolworths and Littlewoods could all be placed in this category although all three have had their problems over the years and have had to relaunch themselves or their products. While Woolworths is ever present in most high streets, Littlewoods has sold off several of its shops and developed clearer links with its home catalogue business by extending its Index catalogue sales at its high-street shops. Marks and Spencer has found itself with many new competitors and has had to develop at out-of-town shopping centres as well as in the major high streets.

Most supermarkets have moved into becoming superstores selling much wider product ranges from ever bigger outlets with ever bigger car parks alongside. The development of discount retailers and hypermarkets has been more uneven with firms, such as electrical retailers Comet, maintaining steady sales patterns, while furniture firms, such as MFI, seemed to have reached a peak and fallen back. The DIY business is a very buoyant one but the structure of the industry is undergoing much change as mergers and sell-offs have created new opportunities for some well-known names such as B&Q or Homebase.

Most high streets have a wide range of specialist retailers with many being part of a multiple organisation. Restaurants, opticians, bakers, travel agents, estate agents, banks and building societies probably make up the biggest proportion of retailers on your high street but even here change seems to be speeding up. For example, many banks are closing smaller branches as television and Internet banking services seem to be on an ever upward curve.

2 Health

This area of business activity includes the more obvious elements of personal service, such as general practitioners, hospitals, dentists, physiotherapists and opticians. One obvious trend at one end of this personal care industry is the more direct marketing to the public of some parts of health care. BUPA advertises its private medical schemes including its own hospitals, while both opticians and dentists are a far more noticeable part of high-street outlets. With clinics offering tattoo removal or various forms of plastic surgery and even general practitioners setting mission statements, the whole health care industry is undergoing rapid change in its activities.

3 Leisure and sport

This is a growth activity with definite increases in specialist leisure providers such as gyms and dance studios, in leisure clubs linked to hotels, in the creation of golf clubs and finally in team sports. The growth of premier league football clubs and their spin-off commercial enterprises is also reflected in other team sports, most notably the move to professional rugby union.

4 Manufacturing

This title of business activity covers a multitude of firms producing a multitude of products but even so some broad types may be picked out. Clothing manufacture is one industry involving particular production techniques and skills while the food industry covers two areas – processed and frozen food production. One large section will include the manufacture and assembly of consumer durables ranging from cars to fridges, and from televisions to microwave ovens. Other industries include the refining and distilling of diverse products such as oil, beer and alcoholic spirits. A final industry that needs to be identified is the capital goods industry – making machinery and equipment that may be used to make other goods and services.

5 Transport and communications

The trends in these industries are a little difficult to plot with real certainty. In general, there is an increase in demand for the products and services of both industries but, while rail transport seems to be benefiting from an increase in demand, bus transport seems to have stagnated. The demand for communications products such as mobile phones has still not peaked and the demand for Internet-related communications is really beginning to take off.

PROGRESS CHECK

1. ▶ Carry out research into your local area to identify and describe trends in employment in the main types of business activities.

2. ▶▶ Consider the different forms of business activity in your local area. Establish some categories of business

activities and identify one example of a firm for each of the activities you have identified.

3. ▶▶ Give a description of the size of each business activity you have identified, suggest reasons for their locations and how these reasons might have changed over time.

4. ▶▶ Describe the processes used by each of your businesses to provide the product or service.

5. ▶▶▶ Describe the main competitors for each of your chosen businesses and suggest any external factors and trends that might be affecting the businesses.

STUDENT CHECKLIST

1. Businesses carry out one or more business activities.

2. Many firms will have a core business activity dealing with products, services or both.

3. Business activities include retail services, manufacturing goods, transport, communications, agriculture, forestry, fishing, mining, health care services, sports and leisure services, financial services, and other services.

4. Some activities are growing, some declining and some are quite stable.

CHAPTER 27

Stakeholders

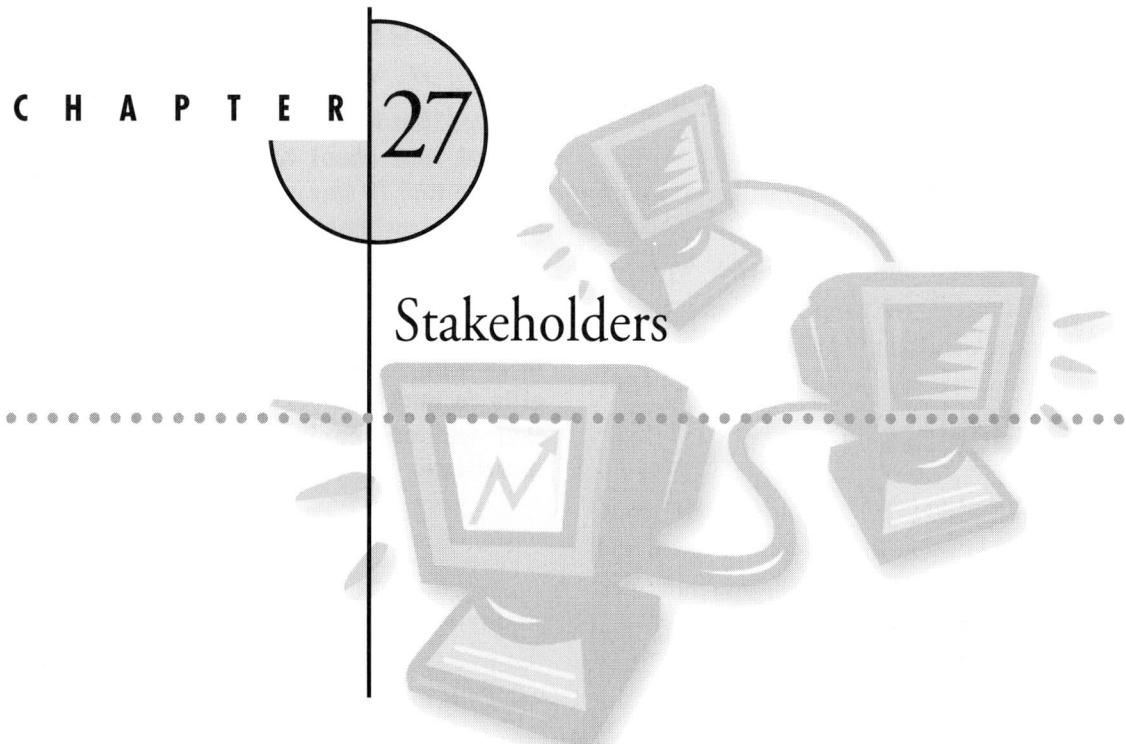

Kodak recognises stakeholders

Any modern and forward-looking company needs to recognise that it depends on the commitment and goodwill of more than just one group of people. Kodak is a multi-million-dollar multinational corporation, the leader in its field. Kodak deals not just in cameras and film but in all kinds of photographic images and ways of making them. Its mission statement says that it wants to 'build a world class, results-oriented culture by providing solutions to capture, store, process, output and communicate images to people and machines anywhere, anytime …'. The company recognises that it has a huge number of stakeholders, not only its customers – all the people who rely on Kodak from your holiday snaps to sophisticated image-making and manipulation – but also its suppliers, its shareholders and even its employees. In fact, it sets such high store by its employees that it recognises the contribution that they make in its company literature, acknowledging that progress will be made 'through a diverse range of energetic employees with the world-class talent and skills necessary to sustain Kodak as the world leader in imaging.'

What you need to do

- **To gain a pass** you will need to know and understand what a stakeholder is; describe the range of stakeholders that exists; describe the range of influences of stakeholders in two selected businesses, one from Group 1 and one from Group 2; and describe how businesses respond to the changing requirements of stakeholders.

- **To gain a merit** you will also need to compare the influence of stakeholders on one selected business with the other business selected.
- **To gain a distinction** you will also need to explain the developments taking place in one selected business; explain why the developments are happening; and explain what the developments might achieve.

Stakeholders

The stakeholders in a business are those people who have an interest in how well the business performs. They include customers, owners, managers, employees and suppliers.

Stakeholders can be split into a number of groups, some within the firm, some outside it:

- customers
- owners
- employees
- suppliers
- other businesses
- the local community.

Stakeholders' objectives

Each group of stakeholders may have different objectives, sometimes these will be in conflict with one another. Each group and their possible objectives is described below.

Customers

A customer's stake in a business will be linked to the goods or services that the business produces. They will want reliability, quality, con-

COMMUNICATIONS activity

Imagine that Kodak, or a firm that you have studied, was about to launch a major new product and it was your job to inform the directors, customers and employees of the new range. It will mean overtime for employees, more profits for the company and a better choice for customers. Prepare three different documents outlining the benefits to each stakeholder and a short talk that will outline the benefits at a press conference.

tinuity of supply and speed of service. Perhaps the overriding aim of the customer is to get value for money.

Owners

The owner of a business may be a single person (a sole trader), a small group of two or more persons (a partnership or cooperative) or shareholders (a company). Each group may have differing objectives.

In the case of sole traders and partnerships, the owners are likely to be aiming for targets such as survival, personal satisfaction and a reasonable income for their efforts – enough money to live on, for example.

In companies, the shareholders, as the owners of the firm, are likely to want the company to aim for the maximum return for the money that they have spent on shares.

Owners may also want to see their business expand, or take a particular share of the market, or achieve other measures of success. In Kodak's case this includes being and remaining the world leader in 'imaging'.

Employees

Employees are likely to want a decent income that allows them a reasonable standard of living. However, they will also want such things as decent working conditions, a holiday allowance and a pension entitlement. In addition, they may feel that they are entitled to other 'perks' ranging from interest-free season ticket loans and car parking spaces to special discounts on the business's products or services. Kodak shows through its mission statement that it is interested in the welfare of its employees and sees them as one of its major assets.

Suppliers

Suppliers want regular repeat orders (and will offer special terms for those businesses that trade with them on a regular basis, as this helps them to manage stock). They also want businesses who are going to be reliable in paying in full and on time. Again, there are generally special discounts for those who pay early.

The supplier will also, of course, want to sell as much as possible at the highest price that they can get.

Visit the Kodak website (www.Kodak.com) and find as much information as you can about product lines and new developments.

Other businesses

Suppliers are just one specific type of other business that may have a stake in a business's success. Others may include lending institutions, such as banks and building societies, and specialists that the business will have to buy from, such as insurance companies.

If a business is providing local employment, then income is being generated to spend in other local businesses. A successful employer like Kodak will generate spending in local shops and with leisure outlets and service providers.

There may well also be additional direct expenditure by the firm on other specialist services which are taken 'out-of-house'. These may be direct services, such as printing and catering, or services provided by specialist agencies, such as maintenance, recruitment and training.

The local community

The local community may rely on a business for a number of reasons. While the main reason may well be employment there are other reasons why the community has a stake in success.

- Reputation – an area may have a good reputation because of a local business or set of businesses, Sheffield for steel, Stoke for pottery, for example.
- Local needs – local businesses may provide particular goods or services that are essential to a specific community (a Muslim butchers providing Halal meat, for instance).
- Links with other organisations – a good local reputation can be of positive benefit to a business. Links may be established with local schools, colleges or universities in order to provide specific training or encouragement into a particular industry. This also benefits the business if they can gain the best possible staff for the business from the local area.

- Environmental factors – businesses may help to enhance their reputation by being 'good neighbours' in the local community, for example being involved in environmental projects and other campaigns that generate positive publicity. Often the publicity that can be generated from such 'selfless' actions as tree planting or 'greening' an area is cheaper and more effective than bought publicity or advertising.

> **GET IT RIGHT!** ✓
>
> Remember there is a difference between satisficing and maximising targets. A satisficing target is where a stakeholder reaches a point where they are satisfied – happy – for example, a sole trader is making enough to be able to afford to work less hours. A maximising target is where a stakeholder is able to get the most or maximum – a manufacturer is producing the maximum possible output from machinery, for example.

Stakeholders' differing objectives

Each type of stakeholder will exert a particular influence on a business according to the objectives that they want to reach. As these objectives are reached, or changed, the business will need to respond to the changes. The major objectives are summarised below:

1. **Customers**
   Value for money, reliability, service.

2. **Owners**
   Satisficing or maximising targets. The initial target for any business will be survival, then break even and then profit. Businesses may also wish to expand.

3. **Employees**
   Employees' objectives will centre around pay and conditions of work. They will expect the accepted rate for the job. They will expect (and have a right to) comfortable and safe working conditions.

4. **Suppliers**
   Suppliers will seek continuity of demand for their goods or services. They will want a business to pay and pay on time. Some suppliers may depend solely on the success of another business – a firm supplying component parts to a manufacturer, for example.

5. **Other businesses**
   Other businesses are likely to have both satisficing and maximising targets. In most cases, other businesses will be looking for the firm to stay successful. In some cases, of course, where competitor firms are involved, it is possible for businesses to gain a positive effect through the decline of a firm.

6. **The local community**
   The local community is likely to have a vested interest in the business being successful and therefore a local employer. They will also want the business to be involved in the community in positive ways, from providing a small service (such as a local business hosting a church or club noticeboard) to major influences on the local environment or area.

Responding to changing stakeholders' influences

Businesses need to be aware of what the various stakeholder groups' objectives are and try to balance the needs of one group against those of another.

Problems may occur if the business is not meeting stakeholders' aims. For example:

- Shareholders who do not receive adequate return on investments may sell shares to move their investments elsewhere.
- A local community who have little or no faith in a company will not seek employment there.
- Suppliers who find that a company does not pay on time, or is inefficient in its dealings, may not wish to supply the business.
- Customers who feel that they are not getting the service (or the value for money) that they seek, will take their trade elsewhere.
- Employees who lack motivation due to poor working conditions will not be working hard for the business.

PROGRESS CHECK

1. ▶ List the stakeholders in Kodak and another firm that you have studied.

2. ▶ For each one list the main objective or objectives that they are likely to want.

3. ▶▶ Choose three pairs of stakeholders from your list for each company and explain how their objectives might conflict.

4. ▶▶▶ Explain which of these conflicts is likely to cause the biggest problem for the business.

5. ▶▶▶ Explain how you would advise the business to respond to changes in stakeholders' objectives.

Key terms

STAKEHOLDER – anyone with an interest, financial or otherwise, in the successful progress of a business.

MAXIMISING – reaching a target that is the maximum, or most that can be reached.

SATISFICING – reaching a target that is enough to satisfy the aims.

MOTIVATION – wanting to work harder or better because of incentives or working conditions provided by the employer.

STUDENT CHECKLIST

1. Stakeholders are any group with a stake in a business success.

2. Stakeholders include other businesses, such as customers and suppliers, and anyone with a financial stake in the business, such as shareholders or lenders.

3. The biggest group of stakeholders is likely to be the firm's employees.

4. Businesses need to recognise the changing objectives of stakeholders and respond to them.

5. Stakeholders may not always have the same objectives – sometimes objectives conflict.

CHAPTER 28

Location

Nissan chooses out the North East

Nissan Motor Manufacturing (UK) Ltd started to build its production plant at the old Sunderland Airfield in 1984. The reasons for choosing this site were quite complex but there are several key reasons that stand out. The geography of the site itself was very important since it offered a large expanse of flat land allowing new buildings to be built easily and quickly. This was essential for a company that planned to expand rapidly. The location of the site also offered excellent infrastructure with immediate access to the A19 and close proximity to both the A1 and nearby deep water ports.

As a large and expanding labour force was going to be essential to Nissan, the fact that the area was well known for its engineering background and the excellence of its training colleges was a factor in deciding to locate there.

More difficult to measure was the attitude of the people living in this part of the North East. Nissan's research suggested that there was a very positive attitude among the local people towards the development of such a site and the support of trade unions was also a positive feature. As the site was part of an enterprise zone there were a number of positive benefits for locating at Sunderland, and not least was the availability of grants worth £100 million. As Nissan points out, however, this was not an overwhelming factor since the company itself planned to invest over £900 million in the first few years.

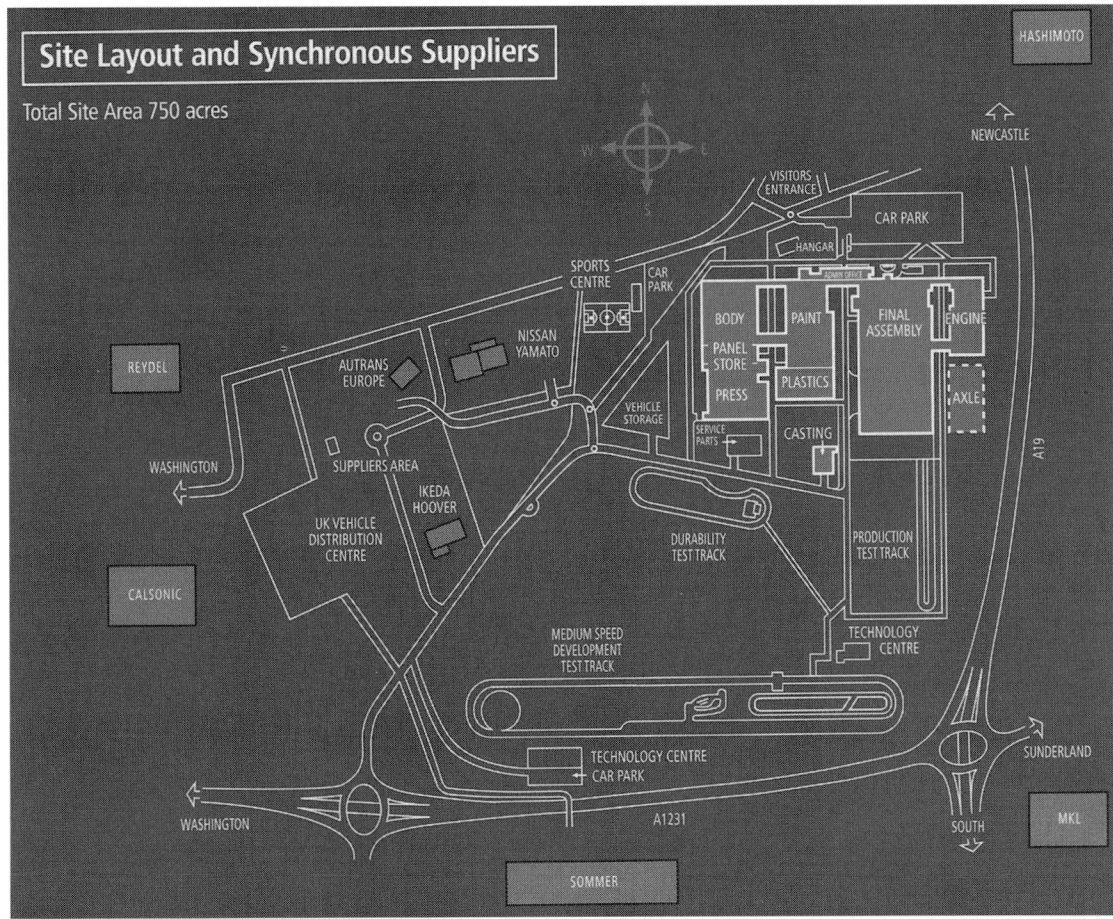

FIGURE 28.1 *Map of Nissan site*

What you need to do

- **To gain a pass** you need to describe the key features of the location of each business and explain why each business has chosen its location; and explain which influences are the most significant for the business now.
- **To gain a merit** – there are no specific statements for this level.
- **To gain a distinction** you also need to show an understanding of how and why external influences in the UK are influencing the location of the businesses.

Factors to consider

When a firm is planning to start up a new operation or when it is planning a major expansion, one of the most important decisions it has to take is where to locate its business. Whether it is manufacturing a product or providing a service, and whether it is small, medium or large, a firm must consider a number of factors. Ideally, the location will keep costs to a minimum while helping to generate maximum revenue since the overall aim is to be successful. Some factors affecting location decisions will be under the firm's control while others will be quite outside its power. Sometimes, decisions about location will be influenced by outside bodies, such as the government, European Union, development agencies and local councils.

What factors should a firm consider before deciding the best location?

There are a wide variety of factors that ought to be considered. For some firms, only a few factors will be really important. Other firms may have to consider and balance a complex mixture of location factors. Possible location factors may be grouped under the following eight headings and the decisions facing firms are expressed as questions that the firms might need to answer.

1 Supply of a suitable labour force
- Is there an adequate supply of workers?
- Do those potential workers have the right skills?
- Are there training facilities nearby if needed?
- Will the wage rates the firm feels able to pay attract enough workers? Firms may find they can pay lower wage rates in areas of high unemployment.
- Do the local people have a positive attitude towards the development of the firm?

2 Cost of the site and buildings
A firm will need to consider such things as:
- How long will the site/building be needed and should it therefore be rented or purchased?
- Will the site need to be drained and levelled?
- Is it a greenfield site, disused or on a well-developed industrial park?
- What are the level of rates payable to the local council?
- Are there extra risks with the site/building, and will these raise the insurance premiums?
- Is there room for expansion?

3 Financial help from the government and other external agencies
Throughout the twentieth century, there have been some regions in the UK with higher rates of unemployment than others. Within these problem regions there have often been small areas with very high rates of unemployment. It was not until after 1945 that governments began to use measures to help reduce unemployment in the problem regions. Most of these measures aimed to persuade firms to locate in the regions of high unemployment. Such regions were called assisted areas because financial assistance was available to many firms either expanding in or relocating to those areas. Over the last 50 years, the types, amount and sources of assistance have changed and so have the regions identified as having unemployment problems. The major forms of assistance include the following.

Advice and information
- County Councils' Business Development Units provide funding advice and practical assistance in assembling business plans for firms proposing to create or safeguard jobs.
- District Councils have economic development officers to give advice on local development issues and opportunities.

- Learning and Skills Councils (LCSs) have subsidiary organisations giving information and counselling support to all types of business.
- The Rural Development Commission (RDC) supports firms with between 5 and 50 employees in manufacturing, service, tourism and some retailing. Support includes training courses on both rural skills and business skills.

Financial assistance
- British Coal Enterprises Ltd provides loans or investment capital for job-creating projects in former coal field districts. The support is limited to 25% of the total funding package or £5000 per job created over three years.
- The Department of Trade and Industry can provide various forms of financial help for firms in the assisted areas. Regional Selective Assistance for manufacturing and some service businesses of any size is available for investment projects. The level of grant is the minimum for the project to proceed and is linked to the number of jobs created or safeguarded. Regional Enterprise Grants may also be available in some parts of the assisted areas for small firms undertaking investment projects or innovation projects. There is special support for firms with up to 250 employees developing new products.
- LSCs can provide a mixture of grants and interest-free loans to new firms.
- The RDC can offer top-up loans at fixed interest rates for projects in rural communities.
- There are a number of other organisations both in the private and public sectors who offer loans and grants. These include:
  - the commercial banks such as Barclays
  - Northern Enterprise Ltd
  - Northern Venture Managers Ltd
  - the Prince's Youth Trust
  - the Royal British Legion
  - some of the District Councils.

4 Premises
Business Development Units at County Councils keep a register of all advance factories and industrial sites in their county. There are a wide variety of units available for purchase or on lease. These are provided by organisations in both the public and private sector, including the County Council, the District Councils, English Partnerships and the RDC.

5 Business training
This form of help is often forgotten about and yet is very important. Again there are a number of organisations providing a wide range of training. Providers include the TECs, University Business Schools and specialist training organisations like Entrust.

6 Help from the European Union
Parts of the country are able to receive financial assistance from the EU.

7 Other forms of help
There is one other way in which the Government tries to influence the location of industry. This is through the creation of Enterprise Zones. These are quite small areas, which often have pockets of particularly high unemployment. The area may have suffered from the decline of a major

industry and it may have a number of derelict business properties or industrial estates. The idea is to make them like 'mini-Hong Kongs'; in other words to encourage a lot of new enterprise so that as the area becomes more prosperous the benefits spread out to surrounding neighbourhoods. Over 24 such zones have been created since 1981. The major help that is available is:

- Rates are free for up to ten years.
- There are tax advantages to locating in a zone.
- There are easier planning controls on new premises so it should be quicker to build and start operating.
- There may be other financial help available such as that indicated in the assisted areas but this depends where the zone is located.

8 Transport links for supplies and distribution

- Are there adequate transport systems for the site – road, rail, air, river/canal, ports?
- How far are the transport links from the site?
- Are there adequate communication systems, especially telephone facilities?
- Are there ancillary firms to help production take place? For example, are there firms to deal with waste disposal, repair machinery, transport the finished product and supply computer services?

The need to be where suppliers and raw materials are based

If the product loses bulk or weight as it goes through the production process, then a firm will achieve the lowest transport costs by locating as near the supply of raw materials as possible. If these materials or parts are imported then a firm will wish to locate near deep water ports. It may be that the assembly of the product requires a large number of small parts and components. In this case, the firm will want to locate near to other firms supplying these items; and you can see from the map of Nissan's site (see Figure 28.1) that it has several suppliers very close to its main factory.

Other more geographical factors to consider include:

- Water supplies – will there be adequate supplies of clean water? This is very important for firms using large quantities of water like paper manufacture, pharmaceuticals and electricity generation.
- Prevailing wind – which direction does the wind usually blow? For some firms that create smell, smoke or dust during the production process, it might be important for the usual wind direction to take these pollutants away from areas of population.
- Waste disposal – are there adequate facilities for dealing with the waste created during the production process? Some firms create a good deal of waste during production. Various laws strictly control how this should be disposed of safely.
- Safety – are there any specific safety issues to consider when considering location?

Some firms make products that are dangerous or use production processes that are dangerous to the public. These firms will need a site well away from people's homes. Typical examples ought to include firework factories, nuclear plants, chemical processors and petrol refineries.

The need to compete with other businesses in the same activity

Many firms are attracted to site their operations close to their main competitors. In some instances this might be because the labour supply in that area has the necessary skills. In other cases it might be because that is where the market is located. Sometimes, firms may wish to share knowledge or even research projects leading to the need to be in close proximity. Generally, as an industry develops, firms often find that all the necessary extra facilities and experience grow with it. This might be ancillary firms such as machine repairers or transport firms; or it might be the expertise of local banks and advertising agencies to deal with the needs of that type of industry.

The need to be where customers are

If a product gains bulk or weight during the production process, transport costs may be kept down by locating near large centres of population, ie the people who are going to buy the products in largest quantities.

Even where this is not the case, firms who depend on large sales to mass markets will wish to locate near the largest centres of population. The spread of the car and better roads has made this a little less important and hence the development of the out-of-town shopping centre.

History and traditions

In the past, sources of power supplies were a very important consideration when locating a business. The early woollen mills located next to rivers so that water power could drive the early looms. Steam power generated by coal soon took over, thus leading to so many industries locating in the coalfield areas of the country. The creation of electricity and North Sea gas together with a national grid system for distribution has helped most firms become more footloose when considering power supplies ('footloose' is a term used to describe businesses that can locate almost wherever they wish).

For some industries, the original reasons for location have disappeared. For example, the centre of the pottery industry is in the Midlands but the reserves of china clay were exhausted long ago. The area now has other benefits that outweigh the extra costs of transporting in china clay. New firms will be attracted by the skilled labour force, by the firms experienced in dealing with the needs of the industry, and by the tradition of the area.

Sometimes a firm locates at a particular site by chance. For example, many of our oldest firms became established in an area because the original owner happened to live there.

PROGRESS CHECK

1. Whichever businesses you choose to investigate and report on for your portfolio, you need to:

   1 Identify which of the above factors might have influenced the location of the particular businesses.

   2 Discover whether any of the reasons for the chosen location are changing and how this might affect the businesses.

2. Carry out research into the kind of help and assistance available to firms in your locality.

3. Explain how this help and assistance might influence firms' location decisions using examples of real firms.

 STUDENT CHECKLIST

1. There are a large number of factors that might influence the location of both a whole industry and a single firm.

2. Most firms will try to look for the best location that keeps costs to the minimum while helping maximise revenue.

3. Most firms will be influenced by a mixture of six or seven factors.

4. One of the most important factors for some firms is the availability of government and other external aid.

5. Some firms remain rooted in their traditional locations.

Section D Case studies

CASE STUDY 3

Sole trader

Set yourself up!

After leaving school or college, you have decided that you would like to set yourself up in business. You will have the advantage of knowing the pros and cons of various types of ownership from your studies. You will need to decide on various issues, such as the type of business, the location, the amount of money that you might need to borrow for start-up capital and so on. You will have an advantage if you choose as a business interest an area where you have either interest or expertise. The business that you choose does not have to be a retailer, but could be any business which could, sensibly, be started as a sole trader (the manufacture of aeroplanes or setting up a chain of stores are not, therefore, likely options). You could be providing a service – and this includes services such as managing a band, illustrating books or providing legal or financial advice, as well as the more common household services such as plumbing, gardening, wiring and painting or general services such as taxi driving.

Your knowledge of industrial sectors and their relative growth and decline will enable

FIGURE CS III.1

you to make an informed choice as to the type of goods or services that you will sell.

This work should be included in your portfolio and carefully indexed so that you know which parts of the course it is covering. Instead of a business of your own devising, you could base the questions and tasks on a sole trader that you know or have contacts with. If you do this, it is important that you respect their time – you will have to speak to them at a time that is convenient to them – and their privacy.

Remember that the financial details of a sole trader do not have to be made public (this is one of the advantages of being a sole trader, after all) so you should not ask questions that require information on financial detail. You could ask general questions such as whether the owner is making enough profit to be able to say that they have reached a satisficing target or what the basic sources of their initial finance were (but not the actual figures).

1 From your knowledge of industrial sectors, choose an area that is becoming more important. Say what the changes have been in this area over the past few years and what changes you would predict for the future.

2 Identify all the sole traders that you can find in your local town, shopping precinct or geographical area (this might be a village, a high street in a big town, or a borough of a city, for example). Explain on what evidence you have decided that they are sole traders. Explain which ones you think are in expanding markets and which in declining markets. In setting up as a sole trader you would have certain short-, medium- and long-term objectives. These objectives might be quite general or really specific. They might be satisficing objectives or could be maximising objectives.

3 Outline the reasons why each of the businesses that you have found might be a sole trader. You could check your theory against facts by seeing what sort of business objectives each business has through interview or questionnaire techniques. Remember to respect time and privacy.

Outline the advantages and disadvantages of operating as a sole trader. What, in your opinion is the biggest advantage, what is the biggest disadvantage?

Outline what objectives you will have as a sole trader. Say which are satisficing, which are maximising and which are more important to you.

4 As a sole trader you will have a number of important business decisions to make. List all the decisions that you will have to make and then put them in order of priority. The picture will give you some clues.

FIGURE CS III.2

Having decided what you are going to trade in you now need to decide on the location of your business. You will need to collect information on possible sites that will give you rent or purchase costs and rateable values. If operating a service you will need to find out what the tax position is if you operate a business from your home rather than from designated business premises. You will also need to look at possible competition.

5 Look at the local area and decide on a suitable location. State the reasons why you have chosen this location. If it is a service that you will be providing then outline which local area you will be operating in and why. Outline the costs you will have to pay to buy, rent or run the premises.

You will need to purchase stock or tools and equipment. Find an appropriate catalogue – specific to the line of business that you are considering – that can give you costs for the basic items that you will need. Although you may gain some benefits from buying stock in bulk, you will also have to consider storage areas and costs if it is not to be sold or used in a short time.

6 Estimate your fixed and variable costs for the first six months of operation. How much money do you need to borrow? Where will you get it from? Who else will be involved as a stakeholder in your business?

7 Draw up a detailed business plan for your own business – one that you could confidently present to a bank manager to ask for a loan. (You could invite a bank manager in to give you advice and a judgement on the plan.) Alternatively, draw up a plan for the expansion of a sole trader that you are working with.

Remember – all this work should be carefully labelled and inserted at the appropriate place in your portfolio. If you complete the following tasks you are on course for a **pass**.

TASK	COMPLETE (DATE)
1 Describe the main features of a sole trader to include a clear description of liability and legal status.	
2 Show that you understand why small traders are generally the size that they are.	
3 Relate the business to the industrial sector that it is in.	
4 Show a full understanding of the process of providing a product or service and relate this to the business.	

If you complete the following tasks, you are on course for a **merit**.

TASK	COMPLETE (DATE)
1 Look at the trends in the industrial sector that the business is in.	
2 Look at the likely stakeholders in the business and show an understanding of their different objectives.	
3 Use a wide variety of source material, accurately logging the way it has been used to build the portfolio.	

If you complete the following tasks, you are on course for a **distinction**.

TASK	COMPLETE (DATE)
1 Draw together all the external influences on the business, including ownership, location and stakeholders, and comment on their relative importance.	
2 Choose relevant points of comparison between this business and another one and show a critical understanding of the context in which the businesses operate.	

CASE STUDY 4

Growth of a firm: the influence on one firm's expansion plans

Cookswell Garage Ltd

Cookswell Garage Ltd is a small family business established 50 years ago. It is currently a Citroen franchised dealer, having evolved from an Esso petrol station, with workshops and used vehicle sales, to a Polski Fiat dealer. The business is located at Pegswood Village, just one mile from the market town of Morpeth, Northumberland.

In December 1996, the company decided to expand, and so in February 1997 – after numerous meetings with company shareholders, ideas, investment appraisals, profit forecasts and planning – work started on a new, additional garage location. The garage, completed in July 1997, is located in the town of Ashington, three miles from Pegswood.

This case study looks at why the firm decided to invest, what its options were, the factors influencing each option, and why they chose to opt for a used car garage.

Why grow?

There were four main reasons:

1. The firm's primary reason for expansion was in order to utilise its unused capital (retained profit) in the most profitable way. It was felt that investment in the firm itself would be more profitable than leaving the capital to earn interest in a bank account.

2. The company's original site at Pegswood had physical constraints as it was impossible to sell any more cars due to a lack of storage area. This meant that the company

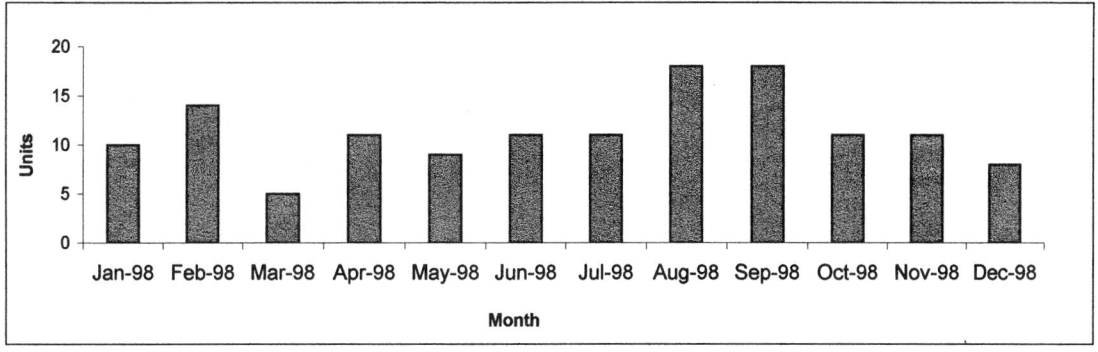

FIGURE CS IV.1 *Predicted car sales from a new car garage*

found itself forced to trade (sell) many vehicles to other motor dealers at much lower prices than if it had sold the cars to the public. Thus, profit margins were reduced and the potential of the business was held back. The company found that it was suffering a multiplier effect. Potential sales to the public were not being made, the firm's customer base was restrained, which meant that there were fewer people to return to buy another car, and less customers were bringing their vehicles in for servicing.

3 The company owned land in Ashington that it had previously rented out. When the tenants came to the end of their agreement they decided to leave, and so Cookswell was left with money tied up in unemployed resource.

4 Finally, independent reviews of the market that Cookswell was operating indicated that the garage could gain a larger share of the local market for car sales. Consumers who lived within the firm's territory were moving outside it to make a vehicle purchase. If Cookswell had more capacity to retail more units (cars), it would stop these leaks from its market into other ones.

What were the options for growth?

Option 1
The company seriously considered finding another tenant to occupy its unused land in Ashington. This would have relatively little risk, and monthly income would benefit the company quickly.

Option 2
This involved using the land in Ashington to build a new franchised dealership. This would allow the company to benefit from another profit centre, not just Citroen. A different franchise would attract a different type of customer to the business and would ensure that the new dealership would not compete with the existing one. It would certainly help Cookswell to increase market share locally. Starting a new franchise would involve large extra costs, in particular, new workshops would be required along with a new parts service; but this would also provide an opportunity to further increase income and hopefully profits.

Option 3
This involved using the land in Ashington to build a used car garage. The existing building

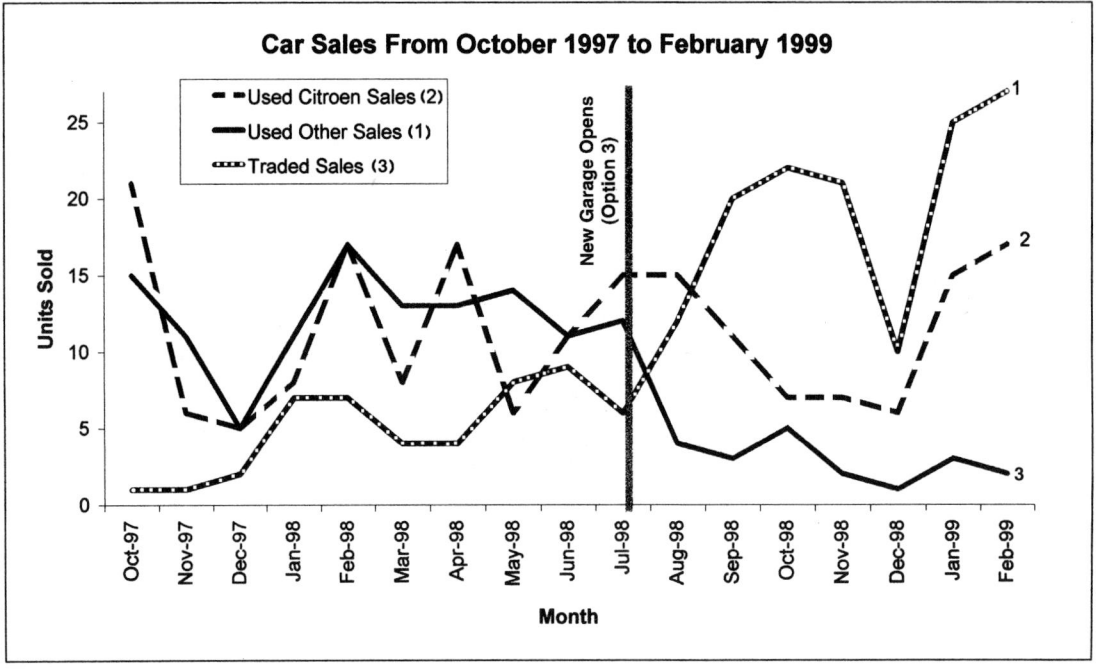

FIGURE CS IV.2 *Actual and estimated sales from Pegswood site*

on the site could be converted at low cost although other costs would be incurred – notably tarmac on the large forecourt, security and lighting systems. The new site would act as an extension to the existing Pegswood garage, and release some of the pressure from the workforce there. This would mean that the new site was not in competition with the Citroen dealership for new car sales. Efficiency benefits were expected since marketing and accounting functions for both sites could be carried jointly. Less capital would be needed to start this business as there would be fewer capital costs in terms of both building work and machinery, and there would be less labour costs as little labour retraining would be needed.

The Decision

After a lot of research, consideration, and tactical and strategic decision-making, the directors decided that the best choice would be option 3. While option 1 might give a steady stream of income, Cookswell thought that the site had too much potential to limit it to this option. The company lacked confidence in opening a new car franchise (option 2) at a time when the car industry was undergoing a great deal of change. The car manufacturers were themselves reluctant to build an outlet in the area and the directors were not convinced that option 2 could give them sufficient long-term profitability, especially as this would require the largest initial capital investment. The directors believed that Option 3 offered reasonable expectations for profitability from a minimum investment, and it would still leave

	OPTION 2 £		OPTION 3 £
Capital requirements			
Capital cost (buildings etc)	245,000		40,000
Investment in stock etc	293,000		200,000
Total capital investment required	538,000		240,000
Capital sources			
Mortgage	245,000		–
Retained profit	100,000		100,000
Stocking loan	193,000		140,000
Total	538,000		240,000
Estimated costs			
Wages	5,400		1,500
Interest	3,005		700
Rates	300		250
Advertising	1,000		100
Other	2,315		1,510
Total per month	12,020		4,060
Total per year	144,240		48,720
Estimated revenue (per year)			
Sales of cars (revenue – purchase costs expected average of £300 per car) (cars)		(cars)	
New car sales 110	33,000	0	–
Used car sales 120	36,000	200	60,000
Revenue from car sales	69,000		60,000
Net revenue workshop services	51,825		–
Total revenue	120,825		60,000
Estimated profit and loss			
Annual trading profit/loss from new activities	(23,415)		11,280

TABLE CS IV.1 *A comparison of estimated revenue, costs, profit and capital requirements for options 2 and 3*

The old site which was previously rented

The new showroom

Land which was used as a forecourt

The new forecourt

FIGURE CS IV.3 *Before and after*

options open for the future. Many outside the company welcomed the development as it meant removing a building that to many was an eyesore, opposite a large residential area.

1 Draw up a table that:
   a identifies the likely stakeholders with an interest in the growth of this company and its planned development
   b describes the interest of each stakeholder group in this planned growth and development.

2 Describe the location factors Cookswell might have to consider when choosing a suitable site for a new garage development.

3 Use the data and your own knowledge to describe the likely business activities and services being offered by Cookswell Garages Ltd.

4 Cookswell had three options. Each had a number of advantages and disadvantages for the company.
   a Identify and describe all the factors influencing each option.
   b Explain which factors are likely to have been the most important in helping the directors to make the final decision to go ahead with option 3.

5 Explain the possible ways in which the fact that Cookswell was a private limited company might have both helped and hindered it in its planned expansion.

Unit 3 Business finance

SECTION A

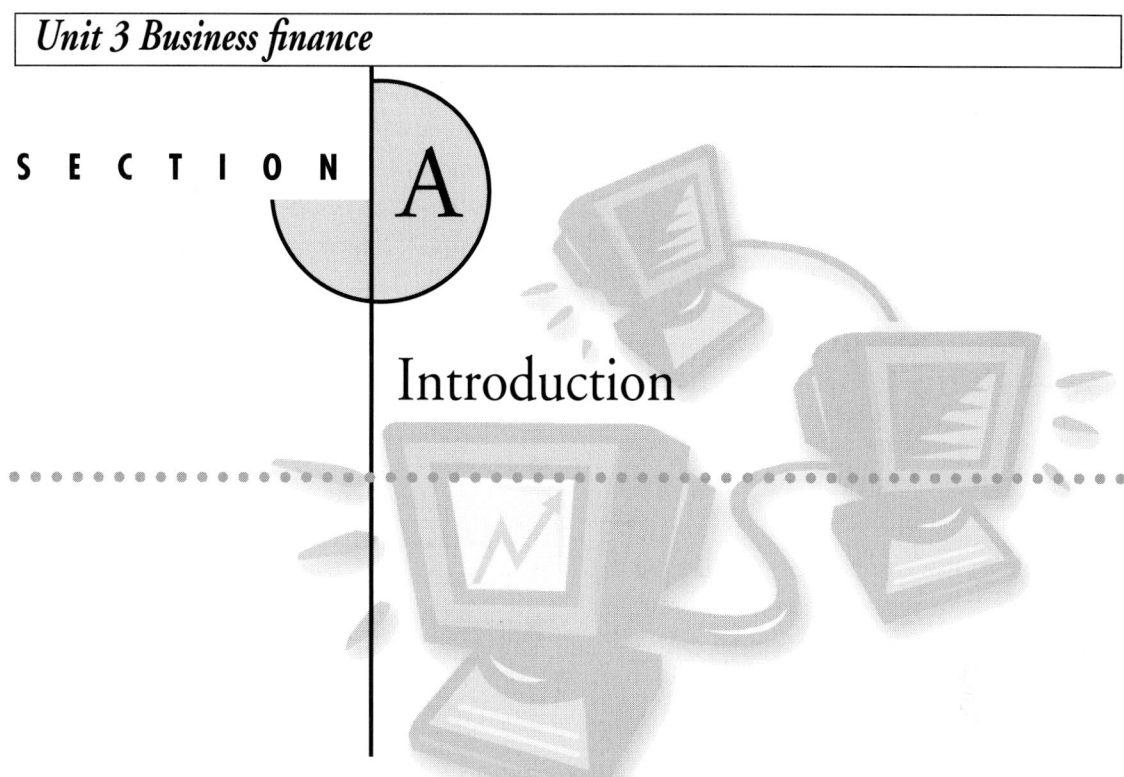

Introduction

This final mandatory unit is the only one that is going to be externally assessed. Whatever grade you achieve on that assessment will be your grade for the unit. This means that you have to approach the work and the content of this unit slightly differently to the first two units. You do not have to collect evidence towards a portfolio but you still need to do a number of tasks and exercises that build up your knowledge and understanding of the content and then allow you to use and apply that knowledge to solve problems linked to business finance.

To help you do this, the chapters in this unit are very similar to those for the first two units. Terms and concepts are explained and described and applied to realistic or real world situations experienced by firms. By completing the tasks in each progress check, you will be building up your knowledge and understanding of the content and, in effect, you will be gathering evidence that could go towards a portfolio. But as this is not needed the tasks in the progress checks are helping you to prepare yourself for the methods of external assessment that will be used by your institution's awarding body. You must also remember, however, that some of the tasks will also be gathering evidence towards your key skills portfolio, so it is vitally important that you complete all the tasks in the chapters or, alternatively, others supplied by your teachers and lecturers.

As with the other units, your teachers will supply you with full details of the requirements of the unit; and the explanation that follows attempts to summarise and integrate all the small details to give you an overview of what you need to for this unit.

So, what do you need to learn? The chapters for unit 3 clearly show the broad headings for the content of this unit. Costs and revenue, Break-even, Cash flow forecasts, Profit and loss statements, Business documents for buying in resources and Business documents for selling goods and services are the six main content areas for unit 3. In more detail, you need to:

- be able to identify and explain typical fixed, variable, start-up and running costs of a variety of businesses
- be able to use cost figures to calculate the total costs for producing a certain number of goods and the unit (average) costs of a single good
- be able to explain how information about costs can help a firm make decisions about producing new products
- be able to explain how revenue may be calculated and show how such figures help firms make decisions about producing new products
- be able to calculate a firm's break-even point
- be able to create and use break-even graphs to calculate break-even and show the effects of changes in the fixed costs, variable costs and the price of the good or service
- be able to understand how to prepare a cash flow forecast by identifying the main elements of a forecast and then entering data to complete it
- be able to explain the uses of a cash flow forecast
- be able to estimate a firm's gross and net profit figures using values for revenue, cost of sales and expenses or overheads
- be able to explain the purpose and use of financial documents both for purchasing resources to use in production and to use in selling the finished products
- be able to complete accurately examples of all the documents listed mentioned in the chapters
- be able to explain the importance of accuracy in the completion of these documents
- be able to describe a computerised finance system, including any advantages and disadvantages, that will complete such documents and undertake other financial tasks
- be able to use spreadsheets and other programs to complete calculations on costs, revenue, break-even, cash flow, and profit and loss tasks
- be able to describe the advantages and disadvantages of using computers for these tasks.

Wherever possible, try to obtain real data from firms to help build your understanding. Such information may be quite sensitive, however, and you will need to use your common sense when identifying likely costs and revenue figures that will then help you perform the various financial tasks. If you have problems collecting real world data, all the chapters include enough data to enable you to meet the demand of this unit. Some data will be available in the annual accounts of public limited companies but you will need your teachers' guidance in selecting such data.

When you read and use each chapter, pay particular attention to the description of what you need to do to achieve a pass, merit and distinction. Remember, for this unit the external form of assessment will be designed to test these specific skills and items of knowledge. Questions and tasks will be targeted at each description, so if your aim is, for example, a distinction, you need to be prepared to complete tasks that ask you why a firm's costs and revenue might change and how changes in costs and price will affect break-even.

Also use the checklists at the end of each chapter to ensure that you have covered everything and that your knowledge matches the desired content.

The communications key skills signposted for this unit include research notes and a short talk illustrated by pictures on the costs and revenue of a firm's new product. In addition, the calculations for break-even, cash flow and profit and loss are also signposted for both the number key skills and the IT key skills. So do not forget to complete them, include evidence in your portfolio and record the coverage of the key skills on your record or map of key skills completion.

Section B Financial accounts

CHAPTER 29

Costs and revenue

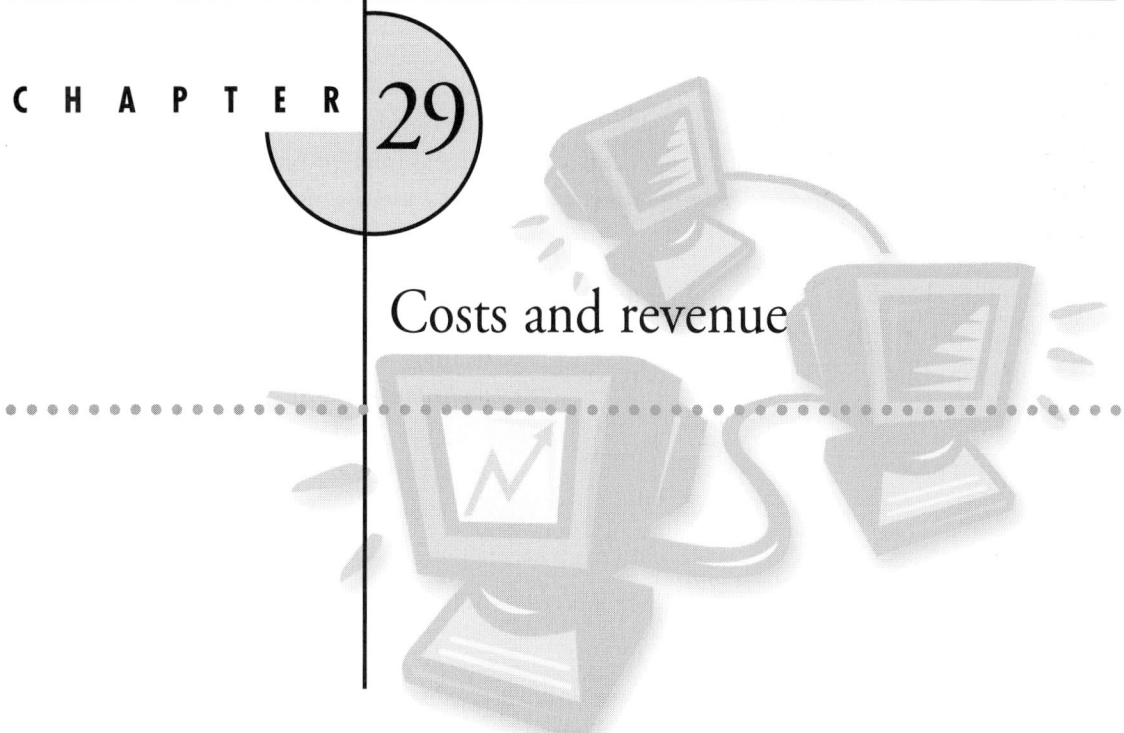

Kent goes mobile

Kent Clarke has run his own hairdressing business in Ashington, Northumberland, for the last 25 years. During this time he has often employed a fully trained assistant at his small salon, just down from the town's main high street. In the last few years, Kent has been the main stylist and has depended on a succession of trainees to do the less skilled tasks. He has found it increasingly difficult to take holidays and, when he has, it has meant closing the business. This has affected his trade and he has still had to pay all his overheads for that time.

In his leisure time, Kent likes to perform in local pubs and clubs with his friends in a rock band and he has found it quite difficult to balance this with the need to keep his hairdressing business running. Meanwhile, competition in the hairdressing trade in Ashington has become quite intense. So, for some time, Kent has been considering closing the salon and opting for the extra flexibility of operating as a mobile hairdresser. One of the other main advantages will be that he will reduce his overheads.

In the months leading up to the closure of the salon in September 1999, Kent asked his customers if they would continue to support him if he went mobile. Over 90% of his customers said they would, and some even suggested that other members of their families would probably use his services while he was at their homes. After a short holiday, Kent started his new mobile hairdressing business in early October of 1999 helped by Clare who he has helped to train up over the last two years.

What you need to do

- **To gain a pass** you will need to understand the difference between start-up and running costs; understand the difference between revenue from the sale of goods and the sale of services; identify typical items of cost and revenue; and understand fixed and variable costs.
- **To gain a merit** you will also need to identify typical costs and revenue for specific types of business; and calculate accurately from given data total and average costs.
- **To gain a distinction** you will also need to explain the reasons why costs and revenues might change.

What are costs?

Any business, whether it is making and selling a good or whether it is providing a service, will require a large number of resources. These resources are likely to include workers, land and buildings, machinery and equipment, raw materials and parts or components. It is unlikely that these resources will be obtained 'free of charge' and most firms will have to pay either to purchase or to hire them. Such payments for these resources are known as 'costs of production' or more simply as 'costs'.

What are the typical costs of a business?

The types of costs that a business faces will depend on its size and on the nature of the good or service it is offering for sale. Some broad categories of costs, however, may be identified if we think of the typical groups of resources that a business will use.

GET IT RIGHT! ✓

A lot of people when they go into a sweet shop might ask, 'What is the cost of that bar of chocolate?' What they should be asking is, 'What is the price of that bar of chocolate?' It is important to think of costs and price from the point of view of a business. Costs are the payments a business makes to buy or hire resources to make and sell goods or provide services. When the good or service is sold the business will set a price that will bring in income or revenue to the firm before any costs are taken away.

- labour – salaries, wages, training, bonuses, fringe benefits
- land – rent or purchase price
- buildings – rent or purchase price, business rates, water rates, insurance
- power – heating, lighting
- equipment – hire or purchase price, maintenance/repairs, machinery/tools, furniture/furnishings, vehicles
- communications – telephone, post, stationery
- raw materials
- ingredients
- parts
- components
- depreciation
- interest on loans

GET IT RIGHT! ✓

Depreciation is a special type of cost that will be included on a profit and loss account. Capital equipment, e.g. plant, machinery, tools and vehicles, will gradually lose value. They lose value as they become older, worn out and out of date or obsolete. This is like a cost or expense to the firm and so a figure showing the amount of depreciation in a year is included as an expense on a firm's annual profit and loss account.

What are the main types of revenue earned by a firm?

Revenue is income that is earned by a firm selling either the goods it makes or the services it offers. Some firms in primary industry will earn revenue by extracting and selling raw materials. For example, quarries might extract and sell stone, mines might extract and sell coal, while farms will grow and sell crops. Manufacturing firms will make or assemble goods and earn revenue mainly by selling them to other firms. Retail firms will earn revenue mainly by selling goods or services to its customers from the general public. Other firms in the tertiary sector will earn revenue by selling services either to the public or to other firms.

From these examples, you can see that a firm's revenue is income received direct from its main production or trading activities. Sometimes, such revenue is called 'turnover' or even 'sales turnover', particularly when stocks are bought in and then sold on to customers.

A firm might change the revenue it earns in a number of ways. It might change the price of the good or service. A lower price will bring in less revenue for each good or service sold but the firm would hope that it would gain so many more customers that, overall, revenue would rise. Raising the price of a good would bring in extra revenue for each item sold, but if sales fell, some revenue would be lost. The firm therefore would have to consider any price change very carefully. Other ways to earn more revenue might involve changes to the product, the use of promotion and advertising to boost sales or alternative ways to distribute the product to the consumer. All methods would have to be considered carefully to see if the extra revenue would more than pay for any extra costs. A firm might receive other income that is not directly linked to such activities. For example, a retailer might rent out a flat above its shop or a manufacturer might move to new premises and make a profit from selling its old factory. These sorts of income will not normally be included as part of revenue or turnover.

GET IT RIGHT! ✓

Do not confuse revenue with profit. Revenue is income to a firm before any costs are taken away. A profit is calculated by taking costs away from revenue.

COMMUNICATIONS
activity

Either think of a product or service that a firm has recently started to make or provide in your home town or near to your school; or think of a product you would like to make and sell or a service you would like to offer to your local community.

1. **Research both the possible costs and revenue of your chosen product or service.**
2. **Estimate the likely figures for these costs and revenue for a certain period of time.**
3. **Prepare a talk for the students in your teaching group that will explain these costs and revenue. Your talk must be illustrated with pictures of the product/service and with charts of the costs and revenue.**
4. **Deliver your talk, answer any questions and discuss your performance with the rest of the group.**

(C2.1b)

What are the differences between start-up and running costs?

Start-up costs are any costs that a firm needs to pay out before it starts to make and sell its goods or provide its services. Obvious examples of such costs will include the purchase of premises, equipment, vehicles and furniture. Some of these items might be leased and will probably involve the payment of a sum of money as a form of deposit in advance. Other start-up costs might include market research, or payments for the installation of services such as electricity, water and telephones. A manufacturer will need to buy in a stock of raw materials, parts and components before it can start production; while a retailer will need to stock its shelves with goods before it opens its doors to customers.

Running costs are the costs a business needs to pay out for its day-to-day operations as it makes the goods or provides its services. Some of these costs will be quite different to those paid to start up the business. For example, wages will have to be paid once workers start to manufacture goods or serve customers. Electricity and perhaps gas will be needed once machinery starts to operate. Many running costs will, however, be start-up costs as well. If the building or machinery is leased then rent will have to be paid out at regular intervals. Additional stock will have to be bought as production takes place or as customers make their purchases.

IT *activity*

Go back to the Communication activity earlier in this chapter where you discovered the costs of making a good or providing a service.

1. **Create a three-column grid with the headings 'Start-up costs', 'Running costs' and 'Both start-up and running'.**
2. **Place each of the costs identified for your chosen business in the appropriate column. If you have access to a colour printer use a different colour for each column.**
3. **Where possible, select some appropriate clip art to illustrate some of the costs.**
4. **Make a hard copy of the completed grid and make sure you save your work – you will need the file again.**

(IT2.2, IT2.3)

What are fixed and variable costs?

It is sometimes quite useful for a firm to divide its costs into those that are either fixed or variable. For a manufacturing firm making candlestick holders, its fixed costs are costs that will not change even when the level of its output changes. These fixed costs will stay the same whether the firm's output is 500 or 1000 candlesticks per week. If the firm produces no candlesticks one week, it will still have to pay its fixed costs. A restaurant faces a similar situation. It will have some costs that are fixed and will not vary with the number of meals or customers served on any day. These fixed costs will be the same whether 50 meals are served, 100 meals are served or no meals are served in a day.

Variable costs are the costs that change when the level of output changes. The firm making candlestick holders will find that it will have some costs that change directly with the number of candlesticks it makes. A restaurant will be in the same situation in that its variable costs will change as it serves either more or less meals to its customers. Strictly speaking, when no candlesticks are being made or there are no customers to serve, each firm will have zero variable costs.

There are some types of costs that will be fixed for one firm and variable for another. For example, those firms that pay wages that are directly linked to the amount of goods made will view them as variable costs. Other firms and organisations may pay wages or salaries that cannot be linked to the amount of goods produced or services provided and these will be classed as fixed costs. In some cases, a particular cost might have an element of both fixed and variable. For example, the power costs of a hairdresser will include the fixed cost of heating and lighting the premises and will have to be paid even if no customers turn up to have their hair cut. Then, when customers do arrive, the hairdresser will have variable power costs as water is heated and dryers are used.

GET IT RIGHT! ✓

Remember that even fixed costs might change at some point. For example, the owner of the building you are using as a factory or a shop might put up the rent at the start of the next year; or the insurance company might have to raise its premiums because bad weather has lead to an increase in claims for flooding and so the increase costs are passed on to all firms. The point is that these costs are not changing because of any changes in the level of output of goods or services.

IT *activity*

Look back at the list of costs you have already created and the table you created for the last IT activity.

1. Create a three-column table with the headings 'Fixed costs', 'Variable costs' and 'Fixed or variable'.

2. Place each of the costs you have already created under the correct headings. You can do this part of the exercise by starting with the file you have already saved and amending the table.

3. Remember to save your new table with a new filename and print a hard copy.

4. Discuss with your colleagues in the class the differences between this table and the one you produced earlier for the IT activity.

(IT2.2, IT2.3)

Total costs and unit costs

To find out the total costs of producing a certain number of goods or the total costs of providing a particular service, a firm would need to add together the fixed costs and the variable costs of that level of output. If it did this for different levels of output, the firm could compare its range of total costs with the range of total revenue earned if it sold those output levels. As a result the firm could start to estimate the amount of profit (or loss) it could make. It would also help the firm to consider the possible effects of any changes to either its fixed or variable costs.

A final calculation would be to find out the average or unit cost of making a single item or unit of production. The simple formula for

$$\text{unit costs} = \frac{\text{total costs}}{\text{output produced}}$$

This calculation could be repeated for each level of output and then plotted on a graph to show the most efficient level of output. This would be where the unit costs are at a minimum.

All of these may be shown in a table and graphs plotted to show the relationships for the production of candlesticks in one week (see Table 29.1).

Any increases in either category of costs will increase a firm's total cost of producing a certain level of output. Some of these costs might be outside the control of the business itself. For example, a rise in raw material costs will result from a supplier putting up its prices. Some costs might be set outside the business but could be influenced inside the firm. For example, electricity prices might be increased by the supplier but a firm might try to economise on its use of such power. Some costs like wages are mainly under the control of the business itself so any increase in wage rates will usually be the internal responsibility of the firm. Any increase in costs, however caused, is likely to put up the unit cost of production unless output can be increased to help pay for this.

IT activity

1. **Use Table 29.1 to create your own spreadsheet of the data and then draw the graphs shown below the table using your spreadsheet data. Save and print the table and graphs.**

2. **Now change the fixed costs to £28,000 and reduce the variable costs for each level of output by £1,000. If you used formulas in the spreadsheet correctly, new totals should have been recalculated. Redraw the graphs and save and print.**

OUTPUT (CANDLESTICKS)	FIXED COSTS £	VARIABLE COSTS £	TOTAL COSTS £	UNIT COSTS £
0	25,000	0	25,000	–
1,000	25,000	2,000	27,000	27
2,000	25,000	3,000	28,000	14
3,000	25,000	5,000	30,000	10
4,000	25,000	9,000	34,000	8.50
5,000	25,000	20,000	45,000	9

TABLE 29.1 *Costs for candlestick production in one week*

3. Compare the original graphs with the new ones. How do they differ?

4. Why might the fixed costs have changed?

5. Why might the variable costs have changed?

(IT2.2, IT2.3)

PROGRESS CHECK

This exercise is designed to check your knowledge and understanding of the main costs and revenues involved in business. Go back to the beginning of this chapter and reread the opening information about Kent Clarke and his hairdressing business.

1. ▶▶ Make a list of the likely costs of running a hairdressing salon.

2. ▶ Break these costs down into three columns – fixed, variable, and fixed or variable.

3. ▶▶ Make a list of the likely costs that Kent will face setting up as a mobile hairdresser and then make a list of his likely running costs.

4. ▶▶ How might Kent have tried to check the viability of his new business?

5. ▶▶▶ Why might Kent's transport costs rise and how might his new business be affected by this?

6. ▶▶▶ How might Kent try to increase the revenue he earns from his new mobile hairdressing business?

Key terms

COSTS – payments by firms for the purchase or hire of resources used to make and sell goods and services.

RUNNING COSTS – costs that a business needs to pay out for its day-to-day operations to make goods or provide services.

START-UP COSTS – costs that a business needs to pay out before its starts to make and sell goods and services.

FIXED COSTS – costs that do not change with the number of goods or services being made and sold.

VARIABLE COSTS – costs that change with the number of goods or services being made and sold.

UNIT COSTS – the average costs of making a single item or unit of output.

REVENUE – income that is received by a business selling its goods or services.

STUDENT CHECKLIST

1. Costs are payments for the purchase or hire of resources.

2. The costs of businesses may be divided up into start-up and running costs or into fixed and variable costs.

3. Unit costs measure the average cost of making a single item or unit.

4. Changes in costs will affect the profitability of business.

5. Revenue – a firm's income – may be earned either by making and selling goods or from selling services.

6. Revenue might change as the result of changes in price and through changes in consumers' views on the goods or services being sold.

7. Changes in revenue will also affect a firm's profitability.

CHAPTER 30

Break-even

Firm is more than the flavour of the month

Kell and McGrane Ltd has been making and selling boiled sweets in the Borders area of Scotland for the past 40 years. It produces 30 different flavours of boiled sweets including pineapple chunks, raspberries, blackcurrants, and its best line rhubarb and custards. The process for making each flavour is very similar and the company uses two small production lines. Each production line specialises in one flavour of sweet usually for one or two days. The production lines are then cleaned and quickly prepared for the next flavour. In this way Kell and McGrane are able to manufacture all 30 flavours each month. Stock is sold and sent out each day to wholesalers throughout southern Scotland.

Kell and McGrane Ltd has set itself a number of objectives. One of its basic targets is to at least break even each month. The company has calculated that its fixed costs each month are £50,000. The basic ingredients for each flavour of boiled sweet are virtually the same so variable costs are calculated to be £1.40 per kilogram of sweets. Kell and McGrane sells all flavours to wholesalers at the same price of £3 per kilogram. It uses all these figures to create a break-even chart, which is then used to interpret the effects of any changes to its costs and the possible implications of a change to the price it charges for its sweets. The company monitors production and sales very carefully to ensure that it will reach its monthly minimum target to break even.

What you need to do

- **To gain a pass** you will need to create break-even charts; and interpret break-even charts.
- **To gain a merit** you will also need to calculate accurately from given data break-even points.
- **To gain a distinction** you will also need to show the effects of changes in fixed costs, variable costs and prices on the break-even point.

What is the break-even point?

This is the level of sales where the total costs of making and selling items of output equals the total revenue from selling them. Sales above this point will mean a firm is making a profit but sales below the break-even point will result in a loss. This makes the break-even point an important target or objective for a firm. Such a target is particularly important for small firms because it can be the difference between survival and closure. Medium to large firms may also target break-even when a new production line is started or a new product is introduced to the market. It may also be an important target for firms selling a service as well as for those making and selling goods.

How are break-even charts created?

These charts, and the graphs drawn from them, are created from five lots of data:

- numbers of items sold
- fixed costs
- variable costs
- total costs
- total revenue.

All the figures have to be for a certain period of time; and this could be for a day, a week, a month or even for a year. The actual break-even period will depend on the type and size of firm and the good or service being sold. A firm should be able to create a break-even chart using either its own real figures from its business records or figures estimated from its plans.

The break-even graph may then be drawn from this data. Costs and revenue are identified on the vertical axis and sales on the horizontal one. Normally, three lines are plotted; those for fixed costs, total costs and total revenue. The break-even point is located where the total cost and total revenue lines cross or intersect. Dropping down from this point to the bottom axis, the publishing firm can see what level of sales are needed to break even each day.

NUMBER OF NEWSPAPERS SOLD ('000S)	0	100	200	300	400	500
Fixed costs (£'000s)	250	250	250	250	250	250
Variable costs (£'000s)	0	20	40	60	80	100
Total costs (£'000s)	250	270	290	310	330	350
Total revenue (£'000s)	0	90	180	270	360	450

TABLE 30.1 *Break-even table for a newspaper publisher*

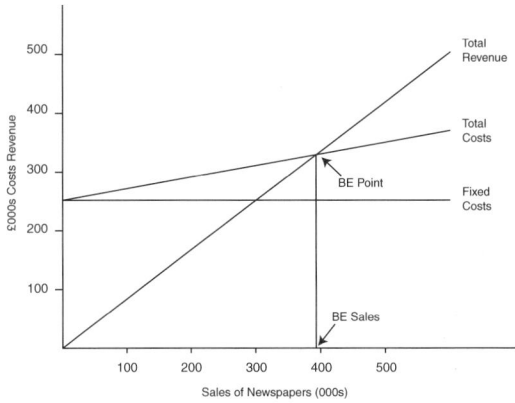

FIGURE 30.1 *Break-even graph for a newspaper publisher*

What does this graph show the newspaper publisher?

It shows the newspaper publisher that it needs to sell just over 357,000 newspapers each day to break-even.

Sales below this would mean the firm was making a loss. For example, sales of 200,000 would earn the publisher £180,000 of revenue but its total costs would be £290,000 and result in a loss that day of £110,000.

On the other hand, if it achieved sales of 500,000, revenue would be £450,000, while costs would only be £350,000, thus earning a daily profit of £100,000. These figures can be seen both by using the table and by analysing the graph.

The main drawback of calculating the break-even point using a graph is that the figures may not be exact. It is difficult to see from the graph whether 357,000 sales are needed to break-even or whether it is nearer 358,000. The graph method does have one big advantage and that is in showing the effects of changes both in costs and price on break-even.

On graph paper create your own break-even graph using Table 30.1 for the daily sale of newspapers. Make sure you choose an appropriate scale, label everything correctly and give the graph an appropriate heading.

(N2.2c, N2.2d)

1. **Use a spreadsheet program to create the break-even table making sure you use formulas where appropriate. Save your work using a suitable filename.**

2. **Using the data in this spreadsheet file, create a break-even graph. Save and print your work.**

(IT2.2, IT2.3)

GET IT RIGHT! ✓

In the external assessment you might have to calculate the cost and revenue figures and then use them to draw out a break-even graph. Always make sure you choose a suitable scale for each axis and always label each one. Draw each line as accurately as you can and label each line and the break-even point and level of sales. Add a suitable heading for the graph.

How will changes in costs and price affect break-even?

A change in fixed costs will cause a parallel shift in this line. An increase in fixed costs will shift the line up the vertical axis and a decrease will allow the line to move down. The total costs would then start wherever the new fixed costs line starts. Higher fixed costs will raise the break-even point while lower fixed costs will reduce it.

A change in variable costs will affect the slope of the total costs line, but the total costs line will always start from the fixed costs line. A rise in variable costs will raise the slope of the

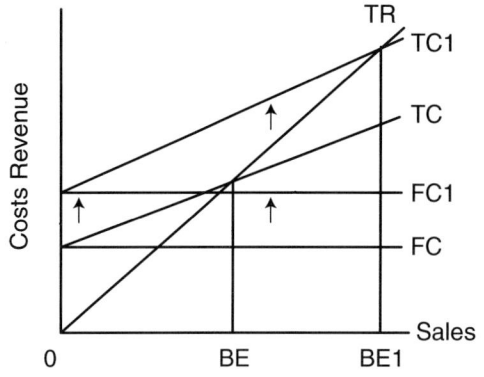

FIGURE 30.2 *A rise in fixed costs*

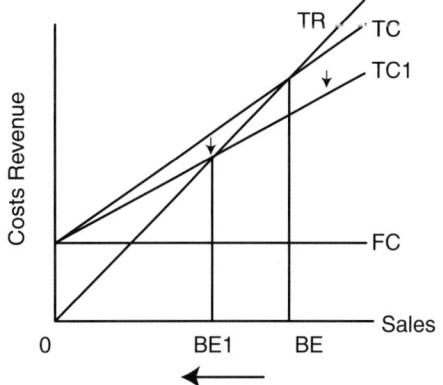

FIGURE 30.3 *A fall in variable costs*

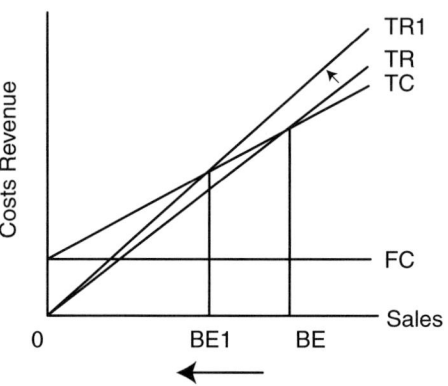

FIGURE 30.4 *An increase in price*

total costs line while a fall in variable costs would flatten the total costs line. Rises in costs will mean that the publisher has to sell more newspapers to break-even each day.

An increase in the price of each newspaper will increase the slope or gradient of the total revenue line and will mean the publisher does not need to sell as many newspapers each day to break even. Any fall in price would flatten the total revenue line and mean the publisher would need to sell more newspapers each day to break even. Many firms will find themselves facing a number of such changes and will need to analyse them on a break-even graph.

NUMERACY activity 1

The newspaper publisher finds that its fixed costs rise to £260,000 while its variable costs rise to 22p per newspaper. To help pay for these costs, the publisher decides to raise the price of the newspaper to 92p.

1. **Use these new figures to create a new break-even table.**

2. **Using the new table, create a new break-even graph.**

3. Compare the two graphs and explain in detail the changes between the two.

4. Identify the level of loss or profit at sales of (a) 250,000 newspapers (b) 450,000 newspapers.

(N2.2c, N2.2d, N2.1, N2.3)

IT
activity

1. Use the spreadsheet file you created earlier to input the changes to the publisher's costs and price. Save your work using a new filename.

2. Use this changed table to create a new break-even graph. Save and print your work.

3. Use the spreadsheet files to create the two break-even graphs on the same page.

(IT2.2, IT2.3)

How may the break-even point be calculated?

To overcome the problems of inaccurate calculation using graphs, a simple formula may be used. This is often called the contribution method since part of it involves calculating the contribution the production and sale of each unit makes to a firm's fixed costs. There are two parts to the formula:

1 Price per unit − variable cost per unit = contribution to fixed costs

2 $\dfrac{\text{Fixed costs}}{\text{Contribution}}$ = break-even level of sales

As with the graph, these figures must be for a certain period of time. This method may be illustrated using the first set of figures for the newspaper publisher: price per newspaper 90p, variable costs per newspaper 20p, fixed costs per day £250,000.

1 (Price per unit) − (variable cost per unit) = (contribution)

£0.90 − £0.20 = £0.70

2 $\dfrac{\text{(Fixed costs)}}{\text{(Contribution)}}$ = (break-even sales)

$\dfrac{£250,000}{£0.70}$ = 357,143 newspapers have to be sold each day to break-even

It is worth pausing at this point to consider the significance of calculation errors. In the case of break-even, it might mean a firm is aiming for the wrong sales targets and unexpected losses might result instead of profits. If it does not identify this quickly enough, a firm may find itself in serious financial difficulties.

> **GET IT RIGHT!** ✓
>
> In the external assessment you will not need to remember the actual formula for the contribution method but you must make sure you show all your working and use a calculator to give an accurate answer. Always round any answer up to the nearest whole unit for the break-even figure.

NUMERACY activity

Calculate the break-even point for the newspaper publisher when its fixed costs are £260,000, its variable costs are 22p per newspaper, and the price of each newspaper has risen to 92p.

PROGRESS CHECK

This exercise is designed to check your knowledge and understanding of break-even. Go back to the beginning of this chapter and reread the opening information about Kell and McGrane Ltd.

1. ▸ Create a break-even table for Kell and McGrane Ltd using the information in the data calculating costs and sales revenue for sales figures of 0, 5,000, 10,000, 15,000, 20,000, 25,000, 30,000, 35,000 and 40,000.

2. ▸ Create a labelled break-even chart from this table.

3. ▸ Use the break-even chart to estimate the level of profit or loss if the actual level of sales in a month is (a) 27,000 and (b) 37,000.

4. ▸▸ Calculate an accurate figure for the break-even point using the contribution method.

5. ▸▸▸ Show the effects on break-even if fixed costs rise to £54,000 per month, variable costs fall to £1.25 per kilogram of sweets and Kell and McGrane raises its price to £3.10 per kilogram of sweets.

6. ▸▸▸ Why might fixed costs have risen and variable costs fallen?

7. ▸▸▸ To what extent do you think Kell and McGrane were sensible in raising the price of sweets by 10p per kilogram?

Key terms

BREAK-EVEN POINT – the level of sales at which total revenue earned from those sales equals the total cost of making those goods or services.

CONTRIBUTION – the sales revenue of an item (its price) minus the variable cost of making and selling that item.

STUDENT CHECKLIST

1. Break-even may be calculated using the contribution method or formula.

2. Data on sales, revenue, fixed costs, variable costs and total revenue may be used to create a break-even table and graph to show the break-even point.

3. The break-even point is for a particular period of time.

4. The break-even point will be increased by lower prices and by higher fixed and variable costs.

5. The break-even point will be reduced by higher prices and by lower fixed and variable costs.

CHAPTER 31

Cash flow forecasts

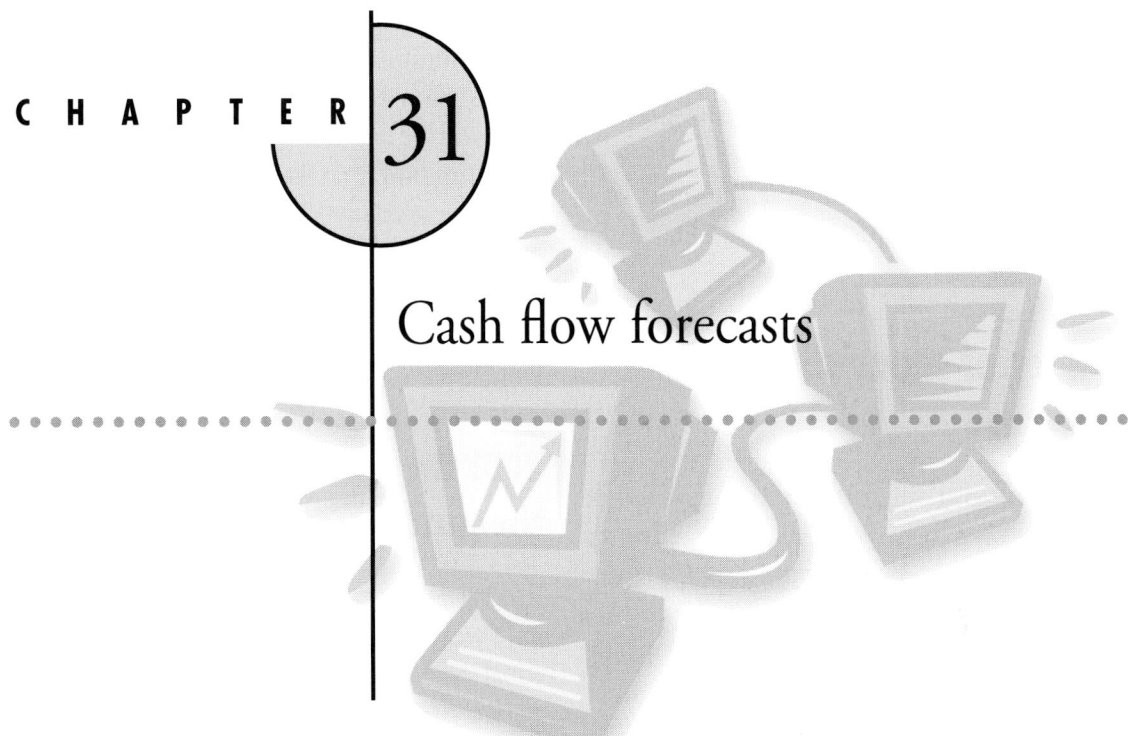

Revenues out of sync with costs

In Chapter 30 you were introduced to Kell and McGrane Ltd – a manufacturer of boiled sweets based in the borders area of Scotland. Its main inflow of cash comes from the sale of its boiled sweets to a number of wholesalers in southern Scotland. Most of these wholesalers expect at least two months credit while some can take more than three months to settle their bills.

Most of Kell and McGrane's outflows of cash include amounts that have to be paid out regularly, either weekly or monthly. The largest item is the wage bill followed by overheads, such as power, rent and rates. Ingredients are the main variable cost with sugar topping the list. Kell and Mcgrane receives a small discount if it pays its ingredients' suppliers within 14 days.

While Kell and McGrane has a regular demand and is certainly profitable, it does have some problems with its cash flow. It is able to finance the regular monthly net outflow through a sizeable overdraft which it has negotiated with its bank. Nevertheless, Kell and McGrane would like to reduce this overdraft and improve cash flow.

What you need to do

- **To gain a pass** you will need to identify which flows of money come into and out of a business; complete the main parts of a cash flow forecast; and explain the advantages and disadvantages of using a computer spreadsheet for financial calculations.

- **To gain a merit** – there are no specific statements for this level.
- **To gain a distinction** you will also need to explain why it is important to prepare a cash flow forecast; and understand the significance of making errors in calculating financial data.

Flows of money into a business

Inflows of cash will start when a business is being set up or when it is being expanded in some way. Owners will put some of their money into a business and they may be able to obtain grants from various organisations to help pay for the land, buildings and equipment. If there is a shortage of capital, loans might be arranged from banks and other financial institutions to help provide the necessary cash to pay for the start-up costs and some of the later running costs of the business. Once the business is running, a firm's main income will be received from the sale of its goods or services, although the actual arrival of cash into the business might be delayed or might vary from day to day or week to week. The firm might have other sources of income, such as rent from parts of its premises that it no longer needs to use itself.

Flows of cash out of a business

When a business is being set up, the main outflow of cash will be for all the start-up costs. If the business is already operating and it expands or introduces a new product, then again the main outflow of cash will be for these additional start-up costs. Once the business is ready to operate, the main outflow of cash will be for the firm's running costs. It will also find that cash flows out to repay loans, to give owners a share of any profits and to pay any tax due through its business activities. All these outflows will be of quite different amounts and will take place at irregular times.

Will the inflow of cash equal the outflow of cash?

It is extremely unlikely that on any particular day, week or month the inflow of cash will equal or balance the outflow of cash. One week a firm may have a cash surplus but find the next week that it has a cash deficit. This is likely to be the case both for new and old firms, and for small, medium and large firms. The problem is any shortage of cash may prevent a firm paying its immediate debts. As a result, the firm might find it difficult to obtain new stocks of materials or may even find it difficult to pay wages to its workers. Overdrafts from banks will help the short-term situation but the interest rates on these are quite high. A bank will usually put an upper limit on the size of the overdraft. If the net cash outflow becomes too large the bank may refuse to honour cheques made out by the firm with the overdraft. In extreme cases, a firm might have to stop trading because of a cash shortage even though it is relatively profitable. More businesses close because they have cash flow problems than through low profitability.

How will a cash flow forecast help?

A shortage of cash is not necessarily a problem as long as it has been forecast and planned for. Such planning will start with the creation of a cash flow forecast that estimates the likely flows of cash into and out of the business usually over several months. The forecast will help the firm to predict when it might suffer from cash shortages and this knowledge will help it to control its business and financial operations. If the firm compares this forecast with the actual flow of cash it will identify when it:

- needs to speed up the flow of cash into the business
- needs to slow down the flow of cash out of the business
- can afford to pay off some debts
- can afford to order new stocks/equipment
- needs to negotiate an increase in overdraft facilities at its bank.

How is a cash flow forecast created?

Each firm and each set of accountants is likely to devise its own individual style of cash flow forecast to suit its own needs. Whatever the actual style, there are five key parts to any cash flow forecast and these are shown in Table 31.1.

From this cash flow forecast table we can see the firm – Smylie and Stephenson Partners, providing secretarial services – starts month 1 with £400 in the bank. Over that first month, it estimates that it will earn and receive £900 of revenue from selling its services. This means that it has £1,300 cash available over this month to pay for its costs. The partnership estimates that it will pay out £1,450 during the month meaning that it will be overdrawn at the bank by £150 – shown by a brackets around the figure. This figure is then carried forward to the start of month 2. By the end of month 3, the partnership estimates that it will have a surplus of cash back in the bank of £50 and will no longer be paying interest on its overdraft.

MONTH	1	2	3
A Bank balance brought forward	£400	(£150)	(£350)
B Cash from sales	£900	£1,100	£1,550
C Total cash available (A+B)	£1,300	£950	£1,200
D Total cash out	£1,450	£1,300	£1,150
E Bank balance carried forward (C−D)	(£150)	(£350)	£50

TABLE 31.1 *A simple cash flow forecast table for Smylie and Stephenson Partners*

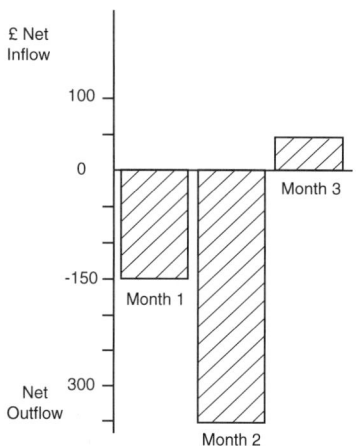

FIGURE 31.1 *Net cash flow for Smylie and Stephenson partners*

This may also be shown in a graph of the cash flow forecast showing the net inflow or outflow each month. This will be the bank balance carried forward at the end of the month and can show the overall trend over a period of time.

A detailed cash flow forecast

The previous table and graph show the main sections for Smylie and Stephenson but the partners will wish to see a more detailed breakdown, in particular showing the main categories of cash flowing out. This is shown in Table 31.2.

This more detailed table will allow the partners to identify expected changes in individual figures and will allow them to analyse the possible effects of both predicted events and those it cannot forecast.

 NUMERACY *activity*

Look at the three-monthly cash flow forecast, including the graph of net flows, for Smylie and Stephenson Partners and describe the changes taking place over the three-month period. Use figures to support your descriptions.

(N2.1)

MONTH	1	2	3
Bank balance brought forward	£400	(£150)	(£350)
Revenue from secretarial services	£800	£950	£1,350
Income from photocopying service	£100	£150	£200
Total cash in	£900	£1,100	£1,550
Total cash available	£1,300	£950	£1,200
Cash out			
Rent and Rates	£100	£100	£100
Transport	£50	£55	£60
Power	£40	£45	£40
Stationery	£40	£45	£50
Insurance	£150	£0	£0
Wages	£970	£955	£800
Other	£100	£100	£100
Total cash out	£1,450	£1,300	£1,150
Bank balance carried forward	(£150)	(£350)	£50

TABLE 31.2 *A detailed cash flow forecast table for Smylie and Stephenson Partners*

trends and analyse performance – just as you did in the Numeracy activity above. Public limited companies could compare their accounts with those of other plcs using the published annual reports.

IT
activity

1. **Using a spreadsheet program, create the full version of the profit and loss account for Lockey's for the year ended 31 January 1999. Make sure you use formulae to calculate the totals. Save this using a suitable file name and print a hard copy.**

2. **Create a second file showing the figures for the year ended 31 January 2000 in separate columns to the right of the 1999 figures. Either change the figures for 1999 to italics or use bold for the 2000 figures. Again make sure you use formulae for calculating the totals. Save using a new filename and print a hard copy.**

3. **Explain the problems that would result from calculation errors. Illustrate this by producing a copy of the 1999 account alone with two errors in – one in expenses and one in sales revenue.**

(IT2.2, IT2.3)

What factors might affect profitability?

There are a range of factors that might affect a firm's profits. Changes in costs will have an obvious effect, either because supplying firms have changed their prices or because the firm itself allows the costs to change. For example, a shortage of coffee worldwide would almost certainly push up the price of coffee being sold in shops and restaurants; while a firm would have to decide itself whether to award pay rises to its employees and therefore push up the wage cost element of making a good. Expansion plans will involve a whole new set of costs that will have to be paid for and it may take some time before enough income is generated to pay for them fully.

Changes in demand will have an obvious influence on profits:

- This might be the result of the firm's own actions, such as greater promotion of its products or changes in prices.
- It might be the result of the actions of other competing firms who decide to change their prices, products and promotions.
- It might even be the actions of the government or of the European Union that have an effect on a firm's profits.
- New taxes or laws for example might affect both a firm's costs and sales.

What happens to net profit?

There are three broad uses of net profit. Initially, the Inland Revenue will tax a proportion of profit. Profit after tax may then be used to reward the owners for risking their money in the business. In addition, some of the profit may be retained in the company either as a cash reserve or more usually for investment in new buildings and equipment.

PROGRESS CHECK

This exercise is designed to check your knowledge and understanding of profit and loss accounts. Go back to the start of this chapter and re-read the opening information on Virgin Atlantic.

1. ▶ Why will a company like Virgin Atlantic produce a profit and loss account?

2. ▶ Suggest typical items for Virgin Atlantic's cost of sales and expenses.

3. ▶▶ Produce a statement that compares the company's profitability in 1999 with its expected profitability in 2000.

4. ▶▶▶ Virgin Atlantic's profitability in 2000 is being affected by four factors. Explain in detail how each of these factors is likely to affect profitability for the company.

STUDENT CHECKLIST

1. A profit and loss account is a record of a firm's past financial performance, although estimates of future accounts may also be created.

2. Sales revenue less all the costs of production will give a firm its level of net profit (or loss).

3. The five main elements of a profit and loss account at this level are sales revenue, cost of sales, gross profit, expenses and net profit.

4. Records of both sales revenue and payments for costs of production need to be kept and used to create an annual profit and loss account.

5. Changes in costs, changes in price and changes in demand for the good or service will all affect the actual level of profit that a firm makes.

6. Calculation errors and incorrect procedures in computer spreadsheet programs will lead to serious mistakes in maintaining accurate records of profit and loss.

Key terms

SALES REVENUE – income to the business from selling the good or service before any costs are deducted.

COST OF SALES – the cost of purchasing stocks of raw materials, parts, components, ingredients and other inputs that go into the actual making of the product.

EXPENSES – all other costs or overheads, including wages, that are involved in making and selling the good or service.

GROSS PROFIT – the difference between a firm's sales revenue and its cost of sales.

NET PROFIT – the difference between a firm's gross profit and its expenses.

CHAPTER 33

Financial documents used for buying goods and services

Kell and McGrane Ltd, the manufacturer of boiled sweets, was introduced to you in chapters 30 and 31. As you will recall, one of its main purchases of raw materials is sugar, particularly caster sugar. Other types of sugar are also required, as are flavourings and colourings. These items are usually bought from three main suppliers operating in southern Scotland. It is vital that Kell and McGrane keeps an accurate record of its purchases and of the payments for these ingredients. Records of purchases of other items and especially services also need to be kept but such things as telephone bills, insurance premiums and business rates demands arrive virtually automatically from the providers of these services.

To help keep these financial records and to help monitor stock levels of ingredients, Kell and McGrane uses a number of financial documents in its purchasing activities, particularly when buying in stocks of ingredients. In the descriptions of purchasing documents that follow, an example of Kell and McGrane buying caster sugar from one if its three main suppliers, Canebeat Ltd, is used to illustrate the *purchasing* process and its documentation.

What you need to do

- **To gain a pass** you will need to understand the use of financial documents including who uses them, when and why; and recognise financial documents, transfer given financial data accurately to complete these documents and check them for accuracy.

- **To gain a merit** you will also need to understand the sequence in which financial documents are most commonly used; and explain the advantages and disadvantages of using a computerised accounting system to generate financial documents.

- **To gain a distinction** you will also need to understand the significance of making errors in completing financial documents.

GET IT RIGHT! ✓

Each individual firm will have its own personalised version of these purchasing documents. The versions used here are typical examples of actual documents and the information that is required; but some firms may require additional sections on a document and other firms may require less. Be prepared to identify different versions and be prepared to complete them in slightly different ways. If possible, visit firms and ask them to explain the documentation that they use.

What documents are needed to buy goods and services?

Purchase order

The most common use of documents for a firm like Kell and McGrane Ltd will be to buy in the raw materials needed to make sweets. The first important document it generates and uses is the purchase order. This is a form that requests another firm to supply Kell and McGrane with a particular number and type of goods. It will be sent in the post or perhaps via a fax machine to the potential supplier. In some cases, it might be the written confirmation of an order made by telephone, especially if Kell and McGrane make regular purchases from the supplier. If the good is a piece of equipment that the company only buys occasionally then Kell and McGrane might request some written quotations before sending out a purchase order to the 'best' supplier.

You will notice that a purchase order has several sections that need to be completed. If any one section is incomplete then delays may well occur in the goods actually reaching Kell and McGrane. The name, address and telephone number of Kell and McGrane will be in a prominent position so that the company receiving the order knows who has sent it.

Kell and McGrane also include the name and address of the firm to whom it is sending the purchase order to help avoid mistakes and to help with its record keeping. It is also then able to use envelopes with a clear address window, which display this name and address on the paper and saves the address being written on the envelope.

An order number is used and the date of the order is located next to this, both helping with record keeping. The main body of the order form has details of the goods to be purchased.

- The reference number is used to record any specific identification that the supplying company uses for the goods. This may be particularly important if there is a large catalogue of goods to choose from.
- The quantity and description then help to confirm the exact goods required together with the unit price that has either been agreed for each unit or that Kell and McGrane normally expects to pay.
- The amount is then calculated by multiplying the quantity by the unit price.

- Finally, a space is left for any special instructions perhaps about the timing of deliveries and the purchase order has to be signed by a person authorised to make the order.

A completed purchase order is shown in Figure 33.1. Check that you understand each part before you move on to the next document.

As this purchase order shows, Kell and McGrane are ordering 1,000kg of caster sugar from Canebeat Ltd. Kell and McGrane use three copies of the purchase order. One copy is sent to Canebeat, one copy is kept by the purchasing department and one copy is sent to the accounts department in Kell and McGrane.

Delivery note

Assuming that Canebeat Ltd is willing and able to supply the sugar to Kell and McGrane, the next documents that will be needed will be generated by Canebeat Ltd itself. Firstly, once the order is put together Canebeat will create and send out with the order a delivery note that specifies the exact goods being supplied. A typical delivery note used by Canebeat Ltd is shown in Figure 33.2.

As you can see, Canebeat's name and other details are shown at the top of the page followed by the name of the company to which it is sending the goods. Other details show the order number of the firm requesting the goods and the exact details of the goods being delivered.

PURCHASE ORDER

Kell and McGrane Ltd
Borders Industrial Estate
Kelso KA4 9LT
Tel: (01234) 56789. Fax: (01234) 98765.

To: Canebeat Ltd
Burns Business Park
Hawick HE7 4TC

Order No: KM: 42–37
Date: 29 March 2000
Delivery: Above address

QUANTITY	REF, NO	DESCRIPTION	UNIT PRICE	AMOUNT
1000kg	—	Caster Sugar	£1.15	£11.50
			TOTAL	£ 11.50

Special Instructions: Please ensure delivery within 7 days of order date

Order Authorised by: J. Murray

FIGURE 33.1 *Completed Kell and McGrane purchase order*

```
                        DELIVERY NOTE

                         CANEBEAT Ltd
                      BURNS BUSINESS PARK
                        HAWICK  HE7 4TC
                 Tel: (01456) 78910. Fax: (01456) 10798
```

To: Kell and McGrane Ltd   Your order no: KM: 42-37
     Borders Industrial Estate   Date: 4 April 2000
     Kelso KA4 9LT   Delivery no: CBD-9403

DELIVERY INSTRUCTIONS:

REF NO	DESCRIPTION	QUANTITY
—	CASTER SUGAR	900kg

NB

100kg of caster sugar to be sent within 48 hours of above date

Packed by: R Prosser   (sig)   Date: 3/4/2000
Delivered by: Fastrucks Ltd   (FIRM)   Sig: P Jones   Date: 4/4/2000
Received by: P Burke   (sig)(Date: 4/4/2000

FIGURE 33.2 *Completed Canbeat delivery note*

Most delivery notes will not include details of the price or the value of the order, but they may indicate if something has been ordered and cannot be included with the delivery, for example perhaps because it is out of stock. The actual signatures required will depend on the system being operated. If one copy each is to be retained by the company receiving the goods, by the company supplying the goods and by the company doing the actual delivery then three signatures might be required. This is the system operated by Canebeat Ltd and each signature has space for a date.

The completed delivery note shows 900kg of caster sugar being delivered to Kell and McGrane by Fastrucks Ltd on behalf of Canebeat. Notice how the delivery note states that the other 100kg of caster sugar ordered by Kell and McGrane will follow on within 48 hours.

Sales invoice

Once the delivery leaves the Canebeat warehouse its accounts department will be notified and a sales invoice prepared and sent to Kell and McGrane. This is, in simple terms, the bill for the goods sent.

Canebeat's name and key details will head the page followed by the name and details of the firm that has purchased the goods. The exact description of the goods ordered and sent should match the purchase order and the delivery note, unless something could not be delivered. The price and value of the goods will partly depend on whether a fixed price had been agreed at the time of the order, and some firms may choose to charge for delivery. If VAT has to be charged on the goods being sent this will be shown in the section showing the sub-totals and amount due. The firm preparing the invoice may also state the maximum amount of time it is prepared to wait for payment. In this case, Canebeat offers a 3% discount on the value of the sugar if payment is received within 14 days. As sugar is classified as a food there is no requirement to charge VAT on it.

Canebeat's sales invoice for the caster sugar sent to Kell and McGrane is shown in Figure 33.3. This will be sent to the accounts department at Kell and McGrane soon after the goods are dispatched. Some firms may include the sales invoice with the delivery

---

SALES INVOICE

CANEBEAT Ltd
Burns Business Park
Hawick HE7 4TC
Tel: (01456) 78910. Fax: (01456) 10789.

VAT Reg No: 987-654321

Sold to: Kell and McGrane Ltd
Borders Industrial Estate
Kelso KA4 9LT
Invoice Number: CBI-4094

Your Order No: KM: 42-37
Order Date: 29/3/2000
Dispatch Date: 4/4/2000
Invoice Date: 5/4/2000

Ref No	Description	Quantity	Price per unit	TOTAL
—	CASTER SUGAR	1000kg	£1.15	£11.50

Terms:
Payment must be made within 30 days of invoiced date, 3% discount applies if payment received within 14 days

Gross Value	£11.50
Less 3% discount	£34.50
Sub total	£11,15.50
Plus VAT at 17.5%	—
Invoice Total	£11,15.50

FIGURE 33.3 *Completed Canebeat invoice*

note when the goods are delivered to reduce postage and speed up the payment process.

You will notice that the invoice is for the full 1000kg of caster sugar ordered by Kell and McGrane and shows the invoice total as net of 3% discount. If it is not paid within the 14 days Canebeat would expect the full £1,150 to be paid.

Goods received note

Once Kell and McGrane Ltd receives the goods it will complete a goods received note for its own internal use. This will inform the department requesting the goods that they have arrived. The note shows the typical information included about the goods received, in this example as used by Kell and McGrane.

One copy of the note will go to the department ordering the goods and one copy will go to the accounts department. The key information on this note should match the information on the original purchase order. Both the purchasing department and the accounts department at Kell and McGrane will use the note to check that all the details are correct. For the accounts department, it will be particularly important to check the details before it pays Canebeat Ltd the amount shown on the sales invoice for the caster sugar.

GOODS RECEIVED NOTE

Kell and McGrane Ltd

GRN NO: KM/RN-4921
Date: 4/4/2000
Delivery Note No CBD-9403

Supplier: Canebeat Ltd
Delivered by: Fastrucks Ltd

Order No	Quantity	Description	Ref No
KM: 42-37	900kg	Caster Sugar	—

Received by P Barke
Action/Comments:
Sugar deposited in main warehouse, section A.

FIGURE 33.4 *Completed Kell and McGrane goods received note*

Credit note

When the accounts department at Kell and McGrane checks this sales invoice against the original purchase order and the goods received note, it will notice that the invoice is for the full order of 1000kg of caster sugar, while the goods received note will record the receipt of only 900kg. If the missing 100kg do not arrive within the stated time delay, Kell and McGrane may decide to obtain additional sugar from another company. If it does this, the accounts department will contact Canebeat to inform it of this and Canebeat will issue a credit note for the undelivered 100kg. This credit note will decrease the amount outstanding on the original sales invoice and saves Canebeat producing a replacement sales invoice for the 900kg of caster sugar. A completed credit note is shown in Figure 33.5.

Cheque and remittance advice slip

Once the accounts department at Kell and McGrane is happy that all the details of the transaction are correct it will be prepared to pay for the goods received. This will involve

CREDIT NOTE
Canebeat Ltd
Burns Business Park
Hawick HE7 4TC
Tel: (01456) 78910. Fax: (01456) 10798.
VAT Reg No: 987-654321

To: Kell & McGrane Ltd
Borders Industrial Estate
Kelso KA4 9LT
Credit Note No: CB/CN-421

Date: 8/4/2000

Invoice No: CBI-4094

Ref No	Quality	Description	UNIT PRICE	TOTAL
—	100kg	Caster Sugar	£1.15	£115
			Gross Value	£115
			Less 3% discount	£3.45
			Subtotal	£111.55
			Plus VAT at 17.5%	—
			Credit value	£111.55

FIGURE 33.5 *Completed Canebeat credit note*

writing a cheque and completing a remittance advice slip. Both of these are shown in Figures 33.6 and 33.7.

The cheque is a standard one issued by a bank in books of 30 or 60. Larger organisations may have their names clearly printed on part of the cheque as well as the name and address of the bank. In this case, you will notice in the bottom corner underneath the space for the signature that it states the cheque is written on behalf of Kell and McGrane Ltd. The remittance advice slip is created by Kell and McGrane to send with the payment explaining clearly what is being paid for. It will keep a copy for its own accounts records so that it knows which goods and services have been paid and it may be used as an additional check alongside the firm's cheque book record.

You will notice that the cheque includes the amount in both words and numbers, that it is made payable to Canebeat Ltd who will have to pay it into its account because the cheque is crossed with two parallel lines. The cheque has to be signed and dated to make it completely valid. The remittance advice slip matches the amount of the cheque and details what goods are being paid for. Some firms

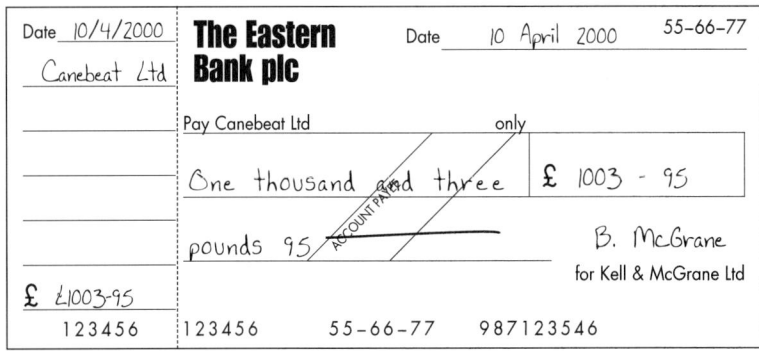

FIGURE 33.6 *Completed Kell and McGrane cheque*

```
                        REMITTANCE ADVICE SLIP

                          Kell and MacGrane Ltd
                          Borders Industrial Estate
                              Kelso KA4 9LT
                   Tel: (01234) 56789. Fax: (01234) 98765.

To:  Canebeat Ltd                              Our Order No:KM: 42-37
     Burns Business Park                       Your Invoice No    CBI-4094
     Hawick HE7 4TC

For: 900kg Caster Sugar
Payment enclosed: £1003-95
Cheque No: 123456
Date: 10 April 2000

All queries should be addressed to the Accounts Department.
```

FIGURE 33.7 *Completed Kell and McGrane remittance advice slip*

PURCHASE ORDER

Allsweets Ltd
Guardsman Industrial Park
Coldstream CO4 9TS
Tel: (01678) 93210 Fax: (01678) 93220.

To: Kell & McGrane Ltd
  Borders Industrial Estate
  Kelso KA4 9LT

Oder No: AL/4929
Date: 10/5/2000
Delivery: Above address

QUANTITY	REF NO	DESCRIPTION	UNT PRICE	AMOUNT
20kg	PC-24	Pineapple Chunks	£3 per kg	£60.00
25kg	RB-36	Raspberry & Blackcurrants	£3 per kg	£75.00
45kg	RC-48	Rhubarb & custard	£3 per kg	£135.00
			subtotal	270.00
			+17.5% VAT	47.25
			TOTAL	£317.25

Special Instructions: Deliveries accepted between 10.00 and 16.00 Monday–Thursday

Order Authorised by: L. McGregor

FIGURE 34.1 *Completed Allsweets purchase order*

used in the sales process as well as an individual number and date for the sales invoice itself.

It is important that Kell and McGrane states the maximum period of credit – in this case 60 days – and because sweets are not classified as a food item VAT must be charged on their gross value. The current rate of VAT is 17.5% and, when this is added on, the total amount payable on this invoice by Allsweets is £317.25. Kell and McGrane will send this invoice to the wholesaler shortly after delivery has been made with its accounts department keeping a copy as part of its records. This will enable it to investigate in case of queries, to chase up any late payment and will enable it to complete financial accounts such as a profit and loss account. The accounts department at Allsweets will also check the invoice against both a copy of the original order and a copy of the delivery note. If all is in order it will store the document until it is ready to pay the invoice.

Business statement of account

Kell and McGrane uses these with its main customers both to help it keep track of sales and the payments it receives and to help to remind the purchasing organisations that they owe it money. A statement of account is produced for each wholesaler

```
                         DELIVERY NOTE

                       Kell and McGrane Ltd
                       Borders Industrial estate
                          Kelso KA4 9LT
                 Tel: (01234) 56789. Fax: (01234) 98765.
```

To: Allsweets Ltd   Your order no: AL/4929
     Guardsman Industrial Park   Date: 10/5/2000
     Coldstream CO4 9TS   Delivery no: KMD/591

DELIVERY INSTRUCTIONS: 1000–1600 Monday–Thursday

REF NO	DESCRIPTION	QUANTITY
PC-24	Pineapple Chunks	20kg
RB-36	Raspberry and Blackcurrants	25kg
RC-48	Rhubarb and Custard	45kg

Packed by: L Gainford   (sig)   Date: 13/5/2000
Delivered by: P Hall   (sig)   Date: 14/5/2000
Received by: M Duthie   (sig)   Date: 14/5/2000

FIGURE 34.2 *Completed Kell and McGrane delivery note*

on a six-week basis. This shows both the value of the goods being sold on each date against a specific invoice number and a record of payments during this six-week period for specific sales. The differences between these debits and credits allows Kell and McGrane to show a series of running balances and the outstanding balance at the end of the six-week period. An example of a business statement of account is shown in Figure 34.4.

Kell and McGrane may use these statements to monitor trends in sales and speed of payments over the whole year. They might also help it to identify possible cash flow problems at particular times of year. They will certainly help to identify 'slow payers' and those who might need some encouragement to settle accounts more rapidly. A spreadsheet program is useful to Kell and McGrane in creating these statements.

Cheque and remittance advice slip

At various intervals Kell and McGrane will receive payment for the sweets it has sold to Allsweets Ltd. Such payments will normally be by a bank cheque, which will be accompanied by a remittance advice slip. This slip will show Kell and McGrane which invoice and order is being paid and will include the number of the cheque in case of queries. Examples of both documents are shown here

SALES INVOICE

Kell and McGrane Ltd
Borders Industrial Estate
Kelso KA4 9LT
Tel: (01234) 56789. Fax: (01234) 98765.
VAT Reg No: 994-362415

Sold to: Allsweets Ltd
Guardsman Industrial Estate
Coldstream CO 9TS
Invoice Number: K-00-10144

Your Order No: AL/4929
Order Date: 10/5/2000
Dispatch Date: 15/5/2000
Invoice Date: 16/5/2000

Ref No	Description	Quantity	Price per unit	TOTAL
PC-24	Pineapple Chunks	20kg	£3pkg	£60.00
RB-36	Raspberry & Blackcurrant	25kg	£3pkg	£75.00
RC-48	Rhubarb & Custard	45kg	£3pkg	£135.00

Terms:
Payment must be made within 60 days of invoice date

Gross value	270.00
Plus VAT at 17.5%	47.25
Invoice Total	317.25

FIGURE 34.3 *Completed Kell and McGrane invoice*

and you should be able to identify the amount involved on the business statement of account in Figure 34.3.

Receipt

Kell and McGrane might issue a receipt for this payment although it is more likely to use the statement of account to show Allsweets Ltd that it has received the payment. Some small sweet retailers prefer to buy their sweets direct from Kell and McGrane by calling at the factory. In these cases, the company will issue a receipt, especially if it is for a cash payment as is the case in the completed receipt shown in Figure 34.7.

STATEMENT OF ACCOUNT

Account name: Allsweets Ltd
Account No: 456-9215
Date: 18/6/2000

Kell and McGrane Ltd
Borders Industrial Estate
Kelso KA4 9LT
Tel (01234) 56789.
Fax: (01234) 98765.
VAT Registration Number: 994-362415

INVOICE NO	DATE	DEBIT	DATE	CREDIT	BALANCE
K-00-10123	3/5/2000	232-55	1/5/200		1020-45
K-00-10099					1253-00
K-00-10144	16/5/200	317-25	8/5/2000	370-40	882-60
K-00-10103					119-85
K-00-10159	30/5/200	234-14	23/5/200	541-67	658-18
					892-32
			15/6/2000	424-19	468-13

Total balance outstanding
£ 468-33

TERMS
Payment must be made within 60 days of invoice date.

FIGURE 33.4 *Completed Kell and McGrane statement of account*

Date 22/5/2000
Kell McGrane
Invoice
K-00-10103

£ 54-67
654321

The Northern Bank plc
Date 22/5/2000   22-33-44
Pay Kell & McGrane Ltd only
Five hundred and forty one   £ 541-67
pounds 67 pence
for Allsweets Ltd
654321   22-33-44   654231879

FIGURE 34.5 *Completed Allsweets cheque*

REMITTANCE ADVICE SLIP

Allsweets Ltd
Guardsman Industrial Park
Coldstream CO4 9TS
Tel: (01678) 93210. Fax: (01678) 93220.

To: Kell & McGrane Ltd
Borders Industrial Estate
Kelso KA4 9LT

Our Order No: AL/4901
Your Invoice No T-00-10103

Payment enclosed: £541.67
Cheque No: 654321
Date: 22/5/2000

All queries should be addressed to the Accounts Department.

FIGURE 34.6 *Completed Allsweets remittance advice slip*

FINANCIAL DOCUMENTS USED TO SELL GOODS AND SERVICES

```
Date  9/5/2000                RECEIPT
No  20/124          No 20/124    Date  9/5/2000
From  Butler's      Received from  Butler's Sweet Shop
  Sweet Shop
Amount £  250-00   Amount £  250-00
Cash  250-00       Cash 250-00  Credit Card No _____
Cheque No          Cheque Number _____
Credit Card No     Signed B. Beattie  for Kell & McGrane Ltd
```

FIGURE 34.7 *Completed Kell and McGrane receipt*

PROGRESS CHECK

This exercise is designed to check your knowledge and understanding of the main documents used in the selling of a good or service. Go back to the beginning of this chapter and reread the opening information on Kell and McGrane Ltd. You might also reread the information on the company at the start of chapters 30, 31 and 33.

The blank documents needed to complete these tasks are included in the teachers' book that accompanies this student book. These documents may be photocopied for you to complete.

1. ▶ Complete a purchase order on behalf of Allsweets Ltd to Kell and McGrane for 35kg of rhubarb and custard sweets, 40kg of mint humbugs and 15kg of pineapple chunks. The reference number for the mint humbugs is MH60 and the other reference numbers are the same as shown on the previous order form. The last order number was AL/5234 and date the order as the day you start this exercise. Prices are now £3.10 per kg and VAT is 17.5% unless it has been changed by the government in the mean time.

2. ▶ Complete a delivery note and invoice to match the above order. The next delivery number is KMD/643 and the next invoice number is K-00-10356. Date the two documents according to the date you started these tasks.

3. ▶ Complete a cheque and remittance advice slip on behalf of Allsweets Ltd for the amount of the invoice 30 days after the invoice date.

STUDENT CHECKLIST

1. The use of purchase orders, cheques and remittance advice slips used by a purchasing organisation.

2. The use of delivery notes, sales invoices, business statements of account and receipts by organisations selling goods and services.

3. The normal flow and order of documents in the selling process.

4. The importance of accurate calculation and completion and the problems that will result from mistakes.

5. The possible use of computer software for operating purchasing and selling processes.

Section C Case studies

CASE STUDY 5

Hardings Ltd

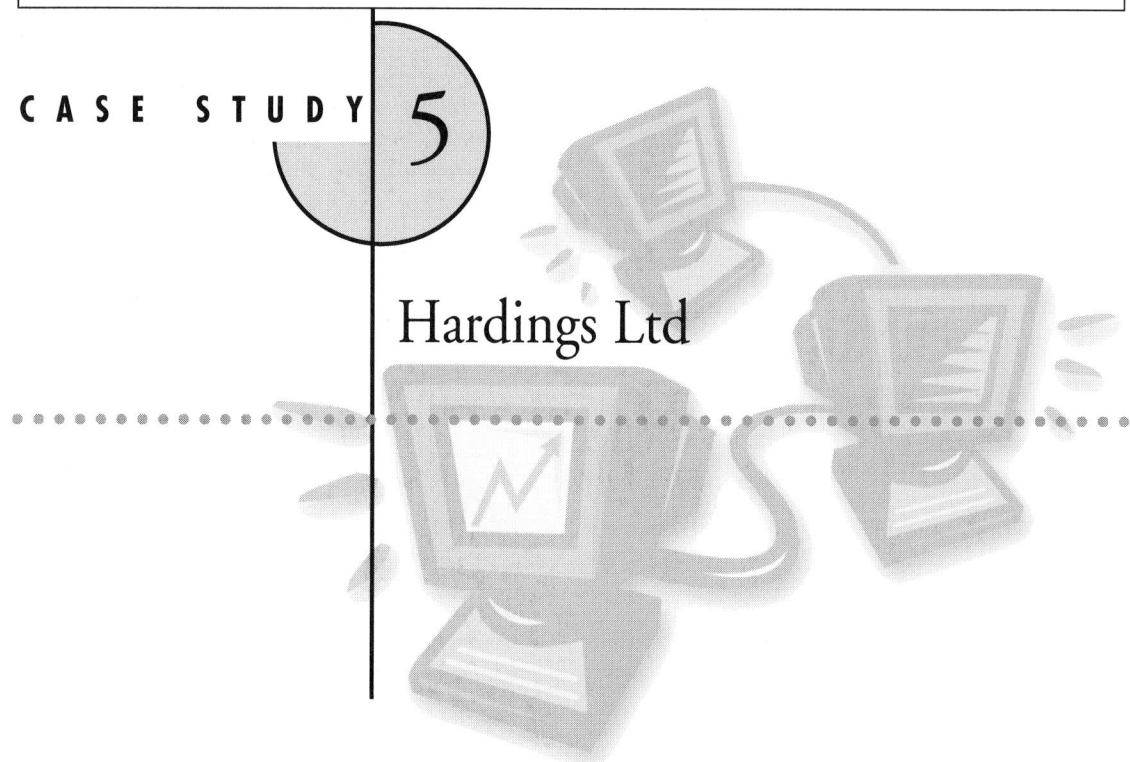

Hardings Ltd is a small brewery making real ale for sale in public houses in Cumbria and Northumberland. In early 1999, it undertook a small expansion in its existing brewery plant and this has helped it increase both sales and profitability. For example, in December 1998, prior to expansion, its monthly revenue was £34,000 with cost of sales that month at £7,500 and expenses at £23,400. The end-of-month figures for December 1999 were revenue of £45,000, with cost of sales at £10,500 and expenses at £28,300.

1 Use these figures to calculate gross and net profit for the two months. Compare the figures and your calculations to comment on the extent of the changes.

Hardings believes that these figures show that a further expansion may also prove to be profitable. This time Hardings will need an additional building to house the extra brewing facilities. It starts to collect some information on likely costs.

There is a suitable building on an adjacent site that is available for rent. Hardings will have to put up an initial bond of £4,000 for the building with the monthly rent set at £1,200 while rates to the local council will work out at £600 per month. Additional utilities, such as power and water supplies, will need to be installed and current estimates for these are £5,000.

The biggest cost is for the additional brewing equipment and Hardings has a quote of £50,000 for this. Installation of the equipment will cost a further £10,000. Hardings remembers that increased brewing facilities will also require additional equipment, such as beer barrels, and it estimates £4,000 for this, while extra transport will be needed amounting to hire costs of £400 per month.

Eight workers will be needed to run the new brewing plant costing some £8,000 per month, while extra power and water usage will increase these costs by £1,800 each month. In addition to using some of its retained profit, Hardings plans to borrow some of the necessary capital from a bank and this will mean monthly interest payments of £200. It believes other costs will amount to £3,000 per month.

2 Use this information on Hardings' expansion plans to calculate the likely setting up costs of the expansion and its estimated monthly running costs. Also suggest what items of costs might Hardings include in the 'other costs' category.

One of the pubs that buys some of its beer from Hardings is 'The Wild Rover' located at Kirkleyside on the Northumberland/Cumbria border. 'The Wild Rover' is owned by partners Stewart and Jane Jones. On average they find that each pint of beer is sold at

FIGURE CS V.1 *The Wild Rover pub*

£1.95 while the variable costs per pint average out at £1.10. Over a six-monthly period the total fixed costs of the pub amount to £85,000.

3 Calculate the break-even point for beer sales in 'The Wild Rover' over a six-month period.

STARTERS	MENU	PUDDING
FARMHOUSE VEGETABLE SOUP 60P		APPLE PIE AND CREAM............£1.20
PATE 90P		RHUBARB CRUMBLE............£1.20
		ICE CREAM............£1.40
MAIN DISHES		GATEAU............£1.50
SHEPHERD'S PIE £1.85		CHEESE AND BISCUITS............£1.40
LASAGNE £1.30		
STEAK AND KIDNEY PIE £2.45		DRINKS
PLAICE AND CHIPS £3.20		COFFEE............90P
EGG AND CHIPS £1.80		TEA............80P
CHICKEN IN THE BASKET............£2.90		FRUIT JUICE............90P
STABLE FUNCTION ROOM AVAILABLE FOR HIRE		

FIGURE CS V.4 *Pub menu*

4 Explain how the break-even point would be affected if:
- the average price of the beer sold in the pub rose to £2.05
- the variable costs of each pint rose on average to £1.15
- if the six-monthly fixed costs rose to £90,000
- all three changes took place at the same time.

5 When Stewart Jones wants to order a supply of beer from Hardings he rings the company up but does not confirm this with a written purchase order. As a result, he has found the occasional mistake in the order. Create a suitable order form for 'The Wild Rover' pub and illustrate the form by ordering 50 gallons of Hardings best bitter, which, at current cost before VAT, is £7.50 per gallon. Remember that VAT will be charged by Hardings.

6 Create and complete both a sales invoice and a delivery note that Hardings might use as part of its documentation for these 50 gallons of best bitter.

7 Explain why it will be particulary important for Hardings to maintain detailed and accurate records of its purchasing and sales documentation.

8 How might a computerised system help the company?

'The Wild Rover' does not just depend on the sales of drinks to create revenue for Stewart and Jane Jones. They have a major source of income in the form of the sale of lunches and evening meals; and a minor source of income from the occasional hiring out of a function room built in an old stable across the car park. The partnership has had some cash flow problems and has been advised to create and use a cash flow forecast.

9 Plan out a suitable cash flow forecast table that could be used for 'The Wild Rover' pub. Remember the three sources of income and start and end each month with a balance. Decide the main categories of costs and expenses and include these in the section for detailing the types of cash out. Design the table for four months starting from April 2000.

10 You could test out your cash flow forecast table by suggesting some likely figures or you might do some research to find out typical figures for such a business.

CASE STUDY 6

Nugardens Ltd

Nugardens Ltd makes a range of garden furniture and other novelties for sale through garden centres across the country. Having completed a detailed break-even analysis of its garden gnomes operation, Nugardens decides to carry out a similar process with its range of wooden garden furniture. The average price for an item of wooden garden furniture is £45 with variable costs averaging £15 per item. Fixed costs for this operation are £42,000 for a three-month period.

1 Using the contribution method, calculate the break-even level of sales for the three-month period.

2 Draw a graph of this break-even point.

3 Show the effects on the break-even graph both of a rise in fixed costs to £44,000 and a rise in variable costs to £16 per item.

4 Nugardens knows that it can offset these cost increases by raising the average price charged for the garden furniture. Estimate from the graph how much Nugardens would have to raise its average price to continue to break-even at the same level of sales over the three-month period. Check your answer by using the contribution method with the new values.

5 Explain the possible problems to Nugardens if it does raise its price of garden furniture.

6 Suggest the likely types of costs which make up Nugardens':
   - variable costs
   - fixed costs.

7 Which costs might be included under both headings?

Over the financial year ended on 31 March 2000, Nugardens earned sales revenue of £350,000 from the sale of wooden garden furniture and £210,000 from the sale of gnomes. Cost of sales amounted to £130,000 for the furniture and £49,000 for the gnomes. Expenses over the year were £144,000 for the gnome production and £168,000 for garden furniture.

8 Calculate Nugardens':
   - gross profit
   - net profit for the year ended 31 March 2000.

9 How might Nugardens be affected by a fall in the sales of garden gnomes?

10 Describe possible actions that Nugardens could take in response to any fall in the sale of its garden gnomes.

Nugardens finds that it has to pay most of its bills for materials and other services within 28 days of receiving the invoice. The company finds that some of the garden centres can take up to three months before settling their accounts.

11 What sort of problems is Nugardens likely to suffer as a result of this situation?

12 Describe how Nugardens might try to overcome these problems.

As part of its business documentation, Nugardens completes and issues a business statement of account for its main customers every two months. It has the following data ready to complete a statement of account for one of the garden centres it deals with, Farmgates Garden Centre Ltd (see table following).

Note that the balance owed by Farmgates Garden Centre to Nugardens was £362 on the 1 April 2000.

The address for Nugardens is Newbewick, Rothbury-on-the-Moor, NE45 5TG and it has a joint phone/fax number of 01245 67854. The address for Farmgates garden centre is Wicklington Town, WE44 5GY.

INVOICES SENT AND AWAITING PAYMENT		
DATE	INVOICE NUMBER	AMOUNT
3/4/2000	NUI-00-12456	£1500
10/4/2000	NUI-00-12465	£800
25/4/2000	NUI-00-12485	£450
8/5/2000	NUI-00-12501	£230
23/5/2000	NUI-00-12516	£345
28/5/2000	NUI-00-12523	£105
INVOICES PAID WITHIN THIS PERIOD		
DATE	INVOICE NUMBER	AMOUNT
2/4/2000	NUI-00-11983	£255
16/4/2000	NUI-00-12019	£342
30/4/2000	NUI-00-12065	£263
15/5/2000	NU-00-12101	£368

13 Design a suitable business statement of account for Nugardens. Complete the account for its customer Farmgates Garden Centre Ltd using the information given here.

14 Explain both the importance of accurate completion and how a spreadsheet program might be used to help produce such accounts and other financial documents, such as profit and loss statements and cash flow forecasts.

Key skills consolidation – Case studies

CASE STUDY 7

Communication

The National stadium: should it be for more than soccer?

Introduction

This unit is about applying your communications skills to deal with straightforward subjects and extended written material. You will show you can:

- contribute to a discussion
- give a short talk
- read and summarise information
- write different types of documents.

There are three parts to the unit. The detailed information on each of these three parts is produced in an integrated table format at the end of this introduction. Activities allowing you to collect evidence for your Communication Key Skills might include:

- carrying out an investigation, project or assignment
- dealing with enquiries from customers or clients
- exchanging information and ideas with work colleagues or other students.

Evidence may be built up across a number of activities throughout the course, and remember, one activity might provide several examples of evidence.

Your skills need to be practised as you prepare for assessment. Some of your written material and images may be produced using IT and you could also use this to support your talk.

Communication case study

The famous twin towers of Wembley Stadium in London have been host to many major sporting and entertainment events. While being primarily a football venue, the stadium has also hosted major athletics events and pop concerts (including the massive Live Aid concert in 1985). It was built in 1923 and hosted the 1948 Olympic Games. It had an official capacity of 78,000, reduced by the necessity to become an all-seater stadium after the Hillsborough disaster and the subsequent Taylor Report. Its maximum crowd, for the first FA Cup Final staged at Wembley, was 126,047. The stadium is part of a complex of venues including Wembley Arena, an indoor arena, a concert venue and a conference centre that holds 10,000 people. It was decided in the mid-1990s that a new national stadium should be built and a competition was held as to where it should be sited. The decision finally went to London's bid for a new, revamped Wembley Stadium in 1997.

There was then a further competition for designs and the contract was won by Norman Foster's (Lord Foster) firm of architects. This design originally appeared to gain acceptance but its future has been thrown into doubt by the fact that there is no running track, ruling out its use for athletics.

Some useful websites are listed below:

www.wembleynationalstadium.com
www.new.whatsonstage.com/wos/seating/wembleystadium.html
www.ft.com (library of information and articles)

The players

- Lord Foster, architect, has designed a national stadium that has no permanent running track. The architects have said that a running track could be installed along with additional seating but that this would mean major work and the closure of the new stadium for at least six months.
- Kate Hoey MP, who is the Minister for Sport who replaced Tony Banks, and who decided to have the report by American specialists drawn up.
- Ken Bates, Chairman of Chelsea Football Club has been appointed as an independent observer to oversee the design process. He is chairman of Wembley National Stadium Ltd.
- Chris Smith MP and Cabinet Minister has told members of parliament that the design does not have sufficient provision for athletics and is not a suitable venue for an Olympic bid.

The Organisations

- The Football Association. Their contract to play matches at Wembley Stadium runs out in 2002. They can then choose to play fixtures such as England internationals and the FA Cup Final at any venue that they choose. The Football Association will also play a major role in England's bid to host the 2006 Football World Cup.
- Sport England (formerly the English Sports Council) administers National Lottery money for sport.
- Wembley National Stadium Ltd is a

wholly owned subsidiary of the Football Association, which has been set up to handle Lottery money, oversee the design and raise the rest of the money needed.
- Brent Council. This is the local council for Wembley and has a say in what goes on because they have to pass the stadium for safety, access and planning regulations, such as access for disabled fans. They wanted a 75,000 capacity stadium for a combined World Athletics Championship and Olympic bid. They are concerned about who should pay for upgrading of local train and underground stations and about the impact on the local area. They have asked for £30m from Wembley National Stadium Ltd to cover planning expenses.
- Athletics UK (formerly the British Athletics Federation), who will be central to the bid for England to host the 2005 Athletics World Championships and the Olympic Games of 2012.
- Ellerbe Beckett, an American firm of consultants who are experts in the field of stadium building and management, and who have produced a report criticising the narrow (football only) focus of the stadium.
- The International Olympic Committee who insist on a capacity of at least 80,000 for the opening and closing ceremonies.

The problems

- The design that has been accepted has already cost a great deal of money. There is a reluctance to try to change this.
- The government has cast doubt on whether it will accept a stadium that is not capable of hosting major athletics events.
- No permanent running track – putting one in reduces the seating capacity below that required by the Olympic Association. While the football stadium could seat 90,000 people, the addition of an athletics track would reduce the capacity to 67,500.
- If the design is altered to incorporate a running track, the opening date of mid-2003 would probably be missed and the bid for the 2006 Football World Cup damaged.
- Brent Council may withhold planning permission, especially if they do not receive funding for what they see as necessary infrastructure changes.

The figures

- £120m from the National Lottery – a grant that is dependent on the new stadium being able to hold major athletics events.
- £355m from Wembley National Stadium Ltd; to be raised in the year 2000 in the City. If the money is not raised, the grant can be recalled.
- £13m paid to top architect Lord Foster to draw up the designs for the new stadium.
- £280m in building costs – material, labour etc.
- £75m to build a new hotel and office block.
- £107m to buy the site that Wembley Stadium stands on.

1 Find out as much as you can about the development of Wembley Stadium from various sources and form an opinion on

the question of whether the new stadium should be for soccer only or for soccer, athletics and other events. Express your opinion to a partner and then join in a group discussion, sharing both information and opinions. The way in which you conduct and contribute to the discussion will determine what level you may be awarded. To achieve level 3 you will need to present a complicated and logical line of reasoning and to be able to listen attentively and actively as well as speak.

2 Present a short report that outlines your opinion and the reasons why you hold it, using any images and other information that you can find. You should be able to give a short illustrated talk and to write a letter to a national newspaper expressing your view. You should proofread your work and check it carefully.

3 Select the material that is relevant to the discussion from the material here and from the information that you have collected. Identify the main points made in the information and use these to make a summary.

4 Imagine that the people of Brent were to be involved in a referendum to decide whether the stadium should include athletics. Prepare two leaflets, one for each side of the campaign, to try to persuade them to vote one way or another.

5 Using the summaries and leaflets as a base, write a lengthy report that details both sides of the argument. You should then include a closing paragraph that summarises the main information for both sides and in which you state and support your own opinion.

CASE STUDY 8

Application of number
Garden centres

Introduction

This unit is about applying your number skills in a substantial activity that involves a series of straightforward tasks. You will show you can:

- interpret information from different sources
- carry out calculations
- interpret results and present findings.

There are three parts to this unit.

The detailed information on each of these parts is produced in an integrated table format at the end of this introduction.

Activities allowing you to collect evidence for Application of Number Key skills might include:

- carrying out and reporting findings from an investigation or project
- designing something, measuring up or costing a job
- following up enquiries from customers or clients.

One activity must allow you to follow through the tasks for N2.1, 2.2 and 2.3. Other evidence may be built up throughout the course using the signposted opportunities for key skills in the vocational units. These signposts are of two types – opportunities for assessed evidence and opportunities for you to develop skills.

Information for your activities in application of number may be obtained first-hand by your own measurement or observations but may also come from already produced written sources. You may use IT to present your findings but you must show you understand what you have presented. In all of this, you need to think about the quality of your application of number skills and check that your evidence covers all the requirements of Part B – what you must do.

Case Study: Gill Robson's Garden Nursery and Greenwoods Garden Centre

The following data relates to garden centres and nurseries and in particular to two businesses operating in this market: Gill Robson's Garden Nursery and Greenwoods Garden

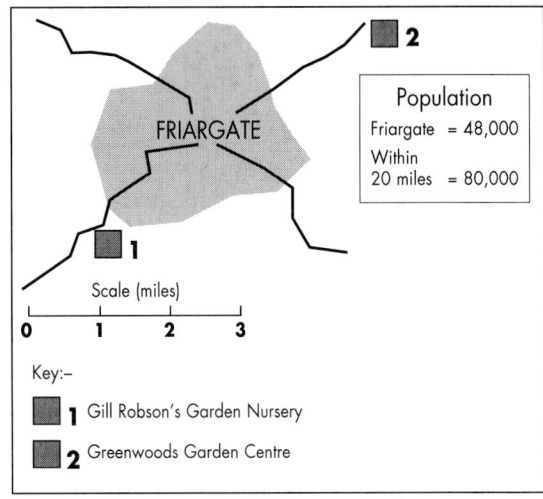

FIGURE CS VIII.1 *Map of Friargate and surrounding area showing the relative locations of Gill Robson's Garden Nursery and Greenwoods Garden Centre*

Centre. Read through all the data and then undertake the activity.

Comments from Gill Robson on her garden nursery

Gill Robson

'I started my business five years ago. I have a love for gardening and many years of experience working for various garden centres and nurseries. When my last employer closed down, I used my redundancy money, a medium-term bank loan and my own savings to start up the business. Each year, I try to retain some of my profits to pay for a small expansion, such as a new range of plants. I felt that additional loans would be too risky in my early years of operation.

I now employ five full-time and three part-time staff. Due to our small size, everyone has to be prepared to do a range of jobs and all must be able to give sound advice to customers.'

'I have tried to specialise in a limited range of top-quality plants and seedlings, many grown in our own nursery. I feel we can offer individual help and advice to our customers and sell good-quality compost, fertiliser and other plant care to back this up. Our prices are a little higher than Greenwoods but many of our customers are very loyal and are attracted back by the quality. The 'pick-your-own fruits' is a useful additional source of revenue in the early summer months. Nevertheless, trying to compete and maintain our level of business is a continuous struggle.'

PRODUCT GROUP	GREENWOODS GARDEN CENTRE (%)	GILL ROBSON (%)
Plants, seedlings	40	85
Compost, fertilisers, seeds, plant care	10	10
Gardening equipment	14	–
Bricks, paving, gravel	9	–
Seats, fountains, fencing	5	–
Sheds, greenhouses conservatories	8	–
Dried flowers, novelties, cards, pottery	8	–
Seasonal products, e.g. Christmas decorations	6	–
Pick-your-own fruit	–	5

TABLE CS VIII.1 *Contribution to revenue for the two garden centres for the year ended 31/12/1998*

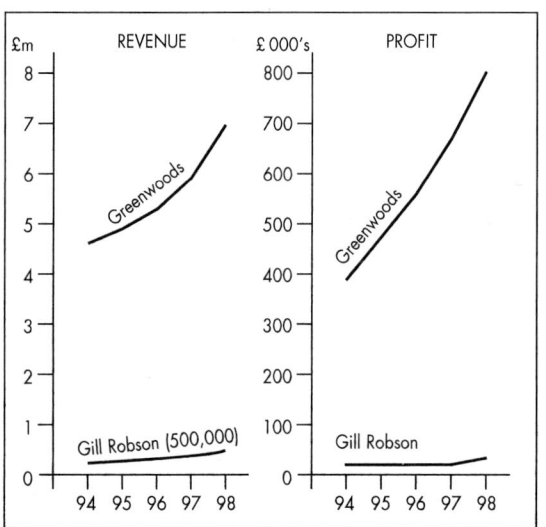

FIGURE CS VIII.2 *Comparison of revenue and profit earned by the two garden centres over the last five years*

Gill Robson of Friargate

Your friendly, local garden nursery

Top-quality plants and seedlings available now to make your gardens a BLOOMING success this summer.

Ask for advice from our helpful, expert staff.

Top-quality plant care products for all your needs.

Throughout May and June soft fruits are available – so come and 'Pick-your-own'

FIGURE CS VIII.3 *A recent advertisement placed by Gill Robson in the local newspaper*

Part of a talk given by Jim Askell, Greenwoods' manager, and Selina Modi, his assistant, to a group of GCSE Business Studies students on a visit to the garden centre at Friargate

Jim Askell

'This particular business started as a family concern back in 1974. It became part of the Greenwoods Garden Centre chain in 1986, which helped reduce some of the financial risks. Additional investment by the public limited company and specialised business experience helped to develop and expand the garden centre at Friargate.

We aim to stock a wide range of products to suit all pockets and try to introduce a new development each year. Three new developments – animal care, the café and the fruit and vegetable shop – are operated by other firms. These firms financed the development and pay Greenwoods a fee for the use of the building.'

Selina Modi

'We now have 25 full-time staff with another 45 part-timers to give us the flexibility to meet peak demand, such as spring and summer weekends. The full-time staff specialise in particular sales areas so that we can offer some experience and help to our customers.

While we are able to offer some discount prices to customers for buying in bulk, we believe most people want quality. We usually price in the mid to upper range. We use a range of special offers on our own brand products and this helps us in our general promotions. We need a wide range of products so that we attract a variety of customers.'

For all your gardening needs come to

Greenwoods Garden Centre near Friargate

It's a great day out for all the family, open 7 days a week

- Ample free parking
- Use our home delivery service
- Family picnic area and play facilities for the kids
- Eat in our new country café
- Treat your family pets too!
- **Just opened – our Fresh Fruit and Vegetable Shop**

Up to 15% off

- Lawnmowers
- Hedgetrimmers
- Most garden tools

- Conservatories
- Garden sheds
- Green houses
- Ornaments
- See our restyled show areas for the latest models at very special prices

For a limited period only

Greenwoods Garden Centre Compost – Buy 2 of our 75 litre bags and get 1 free

Free with this voucher

1 Pair of Greenwoods Garden Centre gardening gloves

Valid until the end of July

Free with this voucher

Greenwoods Garden Centre 2 kilogram pack of general garden fertiliser

Valid until the end of June

FIGURE CS VIII.4 *Extracts from a promotional leaflet for Greenwoods Garden Centre distributed with a local free newspaper*

Market research into the buying habits of consumers purchasing gardening-related products in the Friargate area

AGE RANGE	%	AVERAGE TIME SPENT PER VISIT
20–25	15	1.0 hours
26–35	30	2.0 hours
36–45	40	1.5 hours
46–55	48	1.5 hours
56–65	61	2.0 hours
66+	58	2.0 hours

TABLE CS VIII.2 *Percentage of local population visiting a garden centre or nursery at least five times a year*

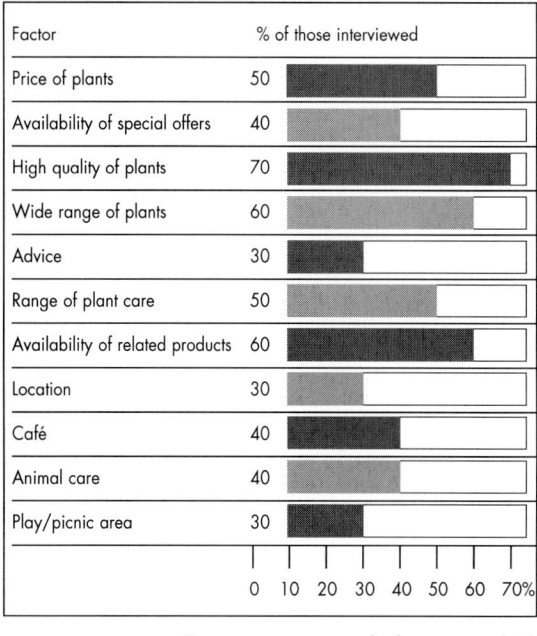

Factor	% of those interviewed
Price of plants	50
Availability of special offers	40
High quality of plants	70
Wide range of plants	60
Advice	30
Range of plant care	50
Availability of related products	60
Location	30
Café	40
Animal care	40
Play/picnic area	30

FIGURE CS VIII.5 *Consumers were asked to say which factors were important in their choice of garden centre/nursery*

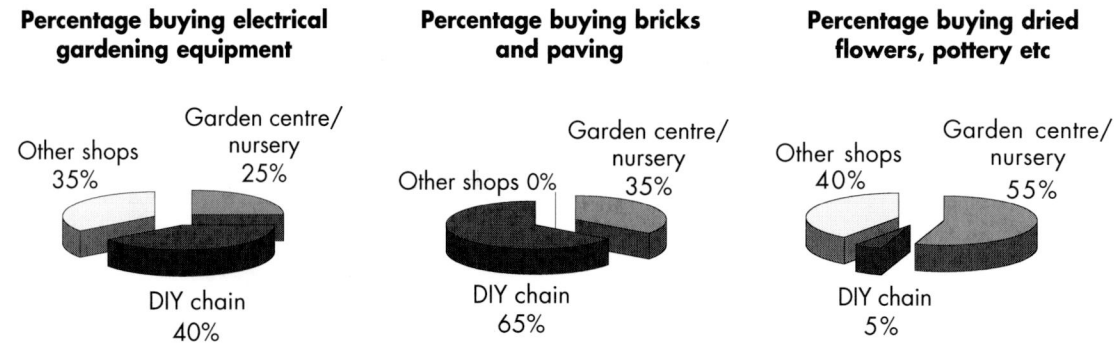

Percentage buying electrical gardening equipment
- Other shops 35%
- Garden centre/nursery 25%
- DIY chain 40%

Percentage buying bricks and paving
- Other shops 0%
- Garden centre/nursery 35%
- DIY chain 65%

Percentage buying dried flowers, pottery etc
- Other shops 40%
- Garden centre/nursery 55%
- DIY chain 5%

FIGURE CS VIII.6 *Consumers were asked to say which type of outlet they used to purchase certain items*

Population figures for Friargate

125,000 people live in Friargate or within 20 miles of the town. The age distribution is as follows:

Age	
0–19	28%
20–25	7%
26–35	14%
36–45	13%
46–55	12%
56–65	11%
66+	15%

Number of residents surveyed for the market research = 500 people

The Activity

Prepare a report that:

1 Compares the two businesses of Gill Robson's Garden Nursery and Greenwoods Garden Centre. This should include:
- the distances of each business from the centre of Friargate
- the proportion of full-time to part-time staff in each business
- the relative size of each business in terms of employees, revenue and profits
- the amounts of revenue earned in 1998 from each product group.

2 Analyse the purchasing habits at garden centres of the population living in Friargate and within 20 miles of Friargate. This should include:
- the numbers in each age range visiting a garden centre at least five times a year
- the total hours spent per average visit by each age group
- a chart placing the factors that are classed as important by consumers in their choice of garden centre or nursery in descending order according to the number of interviewees
- three pie charts for the type of retail outlet used to purchase different products, illustrating the information, using an alternative format and adding information about the number of people the % figures represent.

Remember to refer back to the general advice on what you need to know, do and include in your evidence for this key skill of Application of number.

CASE STUDY 9

Information technology
Masterspeak and JET

Introduction

This unit is about you applying your information technology skills to suit different purposes. You will show you can:

- search for and select information
- explore and develop information and derive new information
- present combined information including text, images and numbers.

There are three parts to the unit.

The detailed information on each of these three parts is produced in an integrated table format at the end of this introduction.

Activities that will allow you to develop and apply your IT skills during your work or studies will include:

- researching and reporting findings from a project or assignment
- researching and designing a product
- dealing with enquiries from customers or clients
- exchanging information and ideas with work colleagues or other students.

You will need to practise your skills in preparation for assessment. Remember using IT can contribute evidence towards the other key skills – Communications and Application of number.

Case Study: Masterspeak

Masterspeak are a company based in Yorkshire who specialise in providing graduate students for the Japanese 'JET' programme. This programme – it stands for

Japanese Exchange and Teaching – is designed to improve Japanese skill in conversational English. Japan has been accused of being a 'mute superpower' because of its failure to speak the international business language of English and is attempting to correct this problem. In 1998, over 5,000 recruits were sent, at a salary of approximately £20,000 a year, on one-year contracts to Japan. Approximately one fifth of these were recruited by Masterspeak and, after a recent Japanese government announcement that the programme is to be extended, the company is seeking ways to expand its involvement.

The directors have decided that they will invite a group of Japanese businesspeople, who have started to learn English through the JET programme, to visit England for a week, to get a better feel for the country and its language.

Before the visitors arrive, the firm has decided that all its employees should know as much as possible about the country and customs of Japan.

1 Find out as much information as you can about Japan. Use published resources, CD-ROM information and the Internet to compile a list of information and images. Sort the information into an order that puts what you think is the most useful information at the top of the list. Some of the information that is at the bottom can be eliminated.

2 Make up a leaflet for Masterspeak. Use the company logo shown in a prominent position and ensure that your leaflet is consistent in its use of style. You should include figures relating to Japan (e.g. size, population, figures relating to the economy), images and explanations. Your leaflet should be no more than four sides of A4, so you will need to be careful to choose only relevant information and images. Check your finished document, save it and print off a copy. Let a colleague in your class or group look at your copy and suggest improvements. You should do the same for another colleague.

Once the Japanese party (ten men and their wives) arrive, you will need a programme of visits and entertainment for the seven days that they are in England. They are interested in visiting the area where you live and either London or York and in seeing entertainment that is in English to help them with their language studies. You will need to book them into appropriate four-star hotel accommodation for each night of their stay.

3 Put together an itinerary for the visitors, which includes:
- hotel names, addresses and prices
- choices of entertainment
- the mileage between stops.

4 The information from your itinerary should be entered onto a spreadsheet so that you can work out a budget. Use the spreadsheet to predict the variations in price so that you can present budget demands that are:
- the highest you could possibly need (the best hotels, best seats and first-class transport)
- the lowest you could possibly need (four-star hotels, cheaper seats, cheaper transport arrangements)
- two budgets in between these extremes.

5 Link the budget information with some of

the information that you prepared for the leaflet on Japan and present this as a request to your financial department for the appropriate budget. Your finance department will need to see the percentages that you intend to spend on each part of the itinerary – accommodation, transport, entertainment, hospitality etc. Find the best way to present this information and incorporate it in your documentation. Recommend to your financial department which itinerary you think is best to justify your budget request. Use the relevant parts of the information that you have collected to make up a leaflet for the visitors. The front page must include the Japanese writing for 'welcome' and the company logo.

6 You are now going to prepare and present the entire detailed proposal as a single document for the directors of the business. Prepare all relevant documentation in an appropriate way using the company logo and Japanese symbols where necessary. The documents should show a consistency of approach, colour and style that may be achieved through the use of automated routines, such as the use of macros for headings and subheadings and standard layouts for figures, frames for images etc. Include the following:

- a letter to JET groups in five cities spread across Japan with personal invite to a named JET student
- a leaflet for employees in the UK
- a letter requesting hotel accommodation
- a standard letter requesting tickets for events
- a full itinerary, with maps, times and distances
- relevant more detailed location maps for each destination
- a speech of welcome to be made by a director on the visitors' arrival
- an alternative itinerary, providing different entertainment so that there is a choice, if necessary
- all relevant costings, including contingencies for cancellations or changes to the programme
- anything else that is relevant.

7 Once you have prepared a first draft of the proposal, give it to a colleague to check and suggest improvements. Then, acting on this feedback, prepare and present final versions. The set of documents should be presented as a single bound proposal to the directors of Masterspeak, with a contents list and consecutive page numbers. They will also wish to see the separate documentation in its finished form so each piece should be appropriately presented as it would look – with its own sequence of numbering, headers and footers etc. You should also prepare a publication that is exactly what the Japanese visitors will receive. Before receiving a final budget, you will have to present your proposals as a multimedia presentation in order to convince directors that it is worthwhile.

Index

accounting **76**
   balance sheets 74, **78**
   cash flow forecasts 74, 211–12, **214**
   cost 74, **76**
   management **76**
   profit and loss 74, 216–17, 218–19
   sole traders 128
administration departments
   activities 78–9
   job titles 79
   legal 79
   local councils 77
   multi-skills 79
   other departments 79
advertising
   agencies 43
   arguments against 47
   benefits 47
   cost-effectiveness 47
   media 44–5
   recruitment 52
   regulations 45
   targeting 43–4
appraisal 50, 55–6
Asda 6, 7

balance sheets 74, **76**
bankruptcy 130, **132**
batch production **85**
Boots the Chemists, Japan 22–3
brand image 47
break-even points 204, **208**
   calculation 207
   charts 204
   contribution 207, **208**
   cost changes 206
bulk buying 25
business mix 10–11
buying and selling
   business statements of account 229, **231**, 235–6, 238
   cheques 227–8, **232**, 236, 238
   credit notes 227, **231**
   delivery notes 223–4, **231**, 234, 236
   documentation 222, 230
   goods received notes 226, **231**
   order numbers 222–3, 234
   purchase orders 222–3, **231**, 234
   receipts 229, **232**, 237, 239
   remittance advice slips 227–9, **231**, 236–7, 238
   sales invoices 224–6, **231**, 234–5, 237

capital *see* finance
Capital Radio 10–12
careers
   changing 56
   promotion 54–5, 56
case studies
   Cookswell Garage 188–92
   garden centres 249–55
   Hardings Ltd 240–42
   ICI 120–23
   information technology 256–8
   Libran Group 117–19
   National Stadium 245–8
   Nugardens Ltd 243–4
   sole traders 185–7
cash flow
   forecasts 74, 211–12, **214**
   inflow 210, **214**
   net inflow 212, **214**
   net outflow 212, **214**
   outflow 210, **214**
   problems of 210
   regulating 211
chains of production 163, 164–5, 198
   primary 164, 165, **165**, 198
   secondary 164, 165, **165**, 198
   tertiary 164–5, **165**, 198
charities 17–18, 20, **21**
Charity Commissioners 17, 20
cheques 227–8, **232**, 236, 238
communications
   see also information technology
   channels 99, **103**, 105, **108**
   external 106–8, **108**
   formal oral 100
   formal written **018**, 102–3, 106
   growth 24–5, 171
   informal oral 99–100, 106
   informal written 101–2, **108**
   information technology 78
   internal 98–9, 102–3
   international 106, 107
   regulations 106–7
company secretaries 79, **80**
competition, objectives 14, 33
computers 111
   software 113, **116**

Confederation of British Industry [CBI] 64, **65**
consumer cooperatives 158, 161
Contracts of Employment 60–61, **65**
contribution 207, **208**
Cookswell Garage 188–92
Cooperative Retail Society [CRS] 158, 161
cooperatives 159, **162**
    consumer 161
    mutual societies 158–9, 161–2, **162**
    producer 160–61
    worker 159–60
corporate culture 7, **9**
cost accounting 74, **76**
costs 197, **202**
    break-even points 204–7, **208**
    changes 206
    depreciation 198
    direct 74
    fixed 199–200, **202**, 204, 206
    indirect 74
    running 199, **202**, 210
    sales 217, **220**
    start-up 199, **202**, 210
    total 201, 204
    unit 201, **202**
    variable 200, **202**, 204, 206
Crash Dummies 127, 133
credit notes 227, **231**
curriculum vitae [CV] 53, **58**
customer services
    distribution 87, **89**
    importance 87
    marketing 8
    moment of truth 88, **89**
    public relations 87, 88
customers
    loyalty 32–3, 46
    satisfaction 32
    as stakeholders 174, 176
cycle of objectives 30, **34**

debentures 142
debt finance 73, **75**
debts
    factoring 142
    liability 130, 131, **132**, 139
decentralisation 96, **96**
decision-making
    growth 24
    sole traders 130
Deeds of Partnership 134, 135, 136, **137**
delayering 96, **96**
delivery notes 223–4, **231**, 234, 236
demergers 27, 29–30

demutualisation **162**
depreciation 198
deregulation 150, **162**
direct sales 46
Disability Discrimination Act [1995] 69
discrimination **70**
    see also equal opportunities
    direct 67
    indirect 67
    positive 67–8, **70**
diseconomies of scale 24–5, **28**, 131
dismissal 56–7
distribution 87, **89**, 164–5
diversification 26, **28**
dividends 12–13, **14**, **162**
downsizing 95, **96**

e-commerce 42
e-mail, internal 110
economies of scale 24, 25, **28**
employees
    contracts 60–61
    health and safety 61–2
    innovation by 90–91
    leaving 56–7
    rights 59
    as stakeholders 175, 176
    trade unions 62–4
    working hours 64
employers' organisations 64
employment
    changes 167–9
    full-time 169–70
    part-time 169–70
Enterprise Zones 181–2
entrepreneurs 12, **14**
equal opportunities **70**
    disability 69
    gender 67–8
    race 66, 68–9
    work 69–70
Equal Opportunities Commission 67
Equal Pay Act [1970] 67
European Union [EU] 63, 64, 70, 181
expenses 13, **220**
external growth **28**
    mergers 25–6
    take-overs 26

finance
    accounts 73–4
    debentures 142
    franchises 154–5, 156
    grants 73, **75–6**, 129–30, 180–81

limited companies 73
loans 73, 106, 142
owners 72–3, **75**, 129
partnerships 73, 135, 136
retainied profits 73, **75**, 142, 219
shares 73, 140–41, 142
sole traders 72–3, 129–30
finance departments
   job titles 72
   marketing 43
   other departments 43, 72
   production 83
financial institutions 106
flow production **85**
Fox Saddlers 42
franchises 153, **157**
   advantages 156
   control 155, 156
   disadvantages 156
   finance 154–5, 156
   McDonalds 152, 155
   rail 152
   royalties 153, 154, **157**
   setting up 154
   television 153, 155

garden centres 249–55
Golden Wonder crisps 35
goods received notes 226, **231**
grants 73, **75–6**, 120–30
   relocation 180–81
Greenpeace 18
growth **28**
   communication 24–5
   decision–making 24
   external 25–6, **28**
   financial benefits 24
   internal 25, **28**
   management 24, 25
   marketing benefits 24
   objectives 23, 24
   overseas 22–3
   risk-taking 24
   technical benefits 24
   zero option 27

Hardings Ltd 240–42
health care 171
health and safety 61–2
Health and Safety at Work Act [1974] 61
Help the Aged 16–17
hierachies 91–2, 93
human resources **57**
   appraisal 50, 55–6

job analysis 52–3, **57**
job descriptions 52–3, **57**
job titles 51
marketing 47–8
recruitment 51–3
releasing staff 56–7
selection 53
staff retention 55, **58**
training 54–5

Imperial Chemical Industries [ICI] 27, 120–23
importation 105
Income Tax 128, 130, 218
industrial action 62–4, **65**
information technology [IT]
   case studies 256–8
   e-commerce 42, 110
   Internet marketing 5, 112, 113–15
   intranets 110, 111, 112
   market research 40
   mobile phones 36, 112
   security 112
   telecommunications 78
   video-conferencing 110, 112
innovation 33, 90–91
integration **28**
   conglomerate 26
   horizontal 26
   lateral 26
   vertical 26
internal [organic] growth 25, **28**
Internet 113–15
   ISPs 114, **116**
   marketing 5, 112, 167
   websites 115
intranets 110, 111, 112
invoices 224–6, **231**, 234–5, 237

job applications
   curriculum vitae 53, **58**
   forms 53
   letters 53
job descriptions 52–3, **57**
job production **84**
Jobseekers' Allowance 52
just-in-time production **85**

Kell & McGrane Ltd 203, 221, 233
Kent Clarke hairdressing 196
Kodak 173

Learning and Skills Councils [LSC] 130, 181
leases **157**
leisure and sport industry 171

liability
    limited 143, **144**
    shared 135
    unlimited 130, **132**, 135
Libran Group 117–19
limited liability companies [Ltd] 139, **144**
    see also public limited companies
    Articles of Association 140
    Certificate of Incorporation 140
    finance 73–4, 142
    liquidation 144
    Memorandum of Association 140
    ownership 143, **144**
    registration 140
location factors
    building costs 180, 181
    competition 183
    customers 183
    grant aid 180–81
    labour force 178, 180
    traditions 183
    training 181
    transport 182
London Underground 145

mail handling 78
management
    authority 92, **96**
    decentralisation 96, **96**
    delayering 96, **96**
    sole traders 95
management accounting **76**
management of change 56
manufacturing industry 171
market analysis 38, 39
market research
    information technology 40
    primary (field) 37, 38, **41**
    responses 35
    secondary (desk) 37–8, **41**
market segmentation 39–40, **41**
market share 5–6, 31
market-oriented firms 35, 38, **41**
marketing department
    communications 107
    customer services 8
    finance 43, 48
    human resources 47–8
    production 48, 83
    promotion 43–5
    public relations 45–6
    research 37–8
    roles in 36–7
markets

changing 35
    internal 150, **151**
    niche 27, **28**
    protection 14
maximising 7, 8, **9**, 12, 176, **177**
McDonalds 152, 155
media promotion 44–5, **48**
meetings, formal structure 100–1, **103**
merchandising 47, **48**
mergers 25–6
Micromagic 6
Microsoft Corporation 138–9
mission statements 8, **9**
mobile phones 36, 112
monopolies, natural 148
motivation **177**
mutual societies 158–9, 161–2, **162**

National Health Service 20
National Insurance Contributions 128, 130–31
National Stadium 245–8
nationalisation 149, **151**
niche marketing 27, **28**
Nissan [UK] 81, 178–9
non-profit organisations
    charities 17–18, 20, **21**
    public sector 20
    voluntary 19, 20, **21**
Nugardens Ltd 243–4

objectives **9**
    cycle of 30, **34**
    ethical 8
    growth 23, 24, 32
    long-term 6–7
    maximising 7, 8, 12, 176, **177**
    measuring 7, 30–32
    minimising 7
    profits 12, 31, 32
    qualitative 32–3
    quantitative 31–2
    reaching 7
    reviewing 30, **34**
    satisficing 7–8, **9**, 176, **177**
    short-term 7
    SMART 30–31
order numbers 222–3, 234
organisational structures **96**
    circular 93, 94
    divisions 94–5
    hierachies 91–3
    informal 95
    matrix charts 93–4
    sideways 93

overdrafts 211, **214**
overseas expansion 22

Partnership Act [1890] 136, **137**
partnerships 133, **137**
   advantages 134–5
   agreements 134, 135, 136, **137**
   control 136
   debt liability 135, 136
   finance 73, 135, 136
   sleeping 136
picketing 62, 63, **65**
point-of-sale material **48**
population groups 39–40
pressure groups 19, **21**, 33
pricing policies 6, 7, 46, **89**
private finance initiative [PFI] 150, **151**
privatisation 149, **151**
producer cooperatives 160–61
product-oriented firms 39, **41**
production
   batch **85**
   chains of 163, 164–5, 198
   flow **85**
   job **84**
   just-in-time **85**
production departments
   control 82
   finance 83
   job titles 82–3
   marketing 48, 83
   planning 82
   purchasing 83–4
   quality control 82, **85**
   resources 83–4
products
   image 46
   promotion 46
   quality 82, **85**, 88
profit and loss accounts 74, 216–17
   performance indicator 218–19
   taxation 218
profits **14**, 216
   calculating 11–12
   expenses 13
   fluctuating 215–16, 219
   gross 13, **14**, 217, **220**
   net 13, **14**, 217, 219, **220**
   objectives 31, 32
   retained 13, 73, **75**, 142, 219
   taxation 219
promotion **48**
   accounts department 43
   advertising 43–4

branding 47
creative department 43
expenditure 43
media 44–5, **48**
merchandising 47, **48**
production department 43
public limited companies [plc]
   accounts 73, 108
   annual reports 108
   finance 142
   flotation 140–41
   liquidation 144
   ownership 143, **144**
   shares 140–41, 142
public private partnerships [PPP] 150, **151**
public relations 45–6, **48**, 87, 88, **89**
public sector organisations **21**, 146, **151**
   corporations 147
   national government 146–7
   nationalisation 149, **151**
   natural monopolies 148
   non-profit 20
   privatisation 149, **151**
   QUANGOs 147, **151**
purchase orders 222, **231**, 234
purchasing departments 83–4

qualitative objectives
   competition 33
   customer loyalty 32–3
   customer satisfaction 32
   innovation 33
   reputation 33
   services 33
   social awareness 33
quality control 82, **85**
QUANGOs 147, **151**
quantitative objectives
   efficiency 31–2
   expansion 32
   market share 31
   profits 31, 32
   sales 31
   survival 31
quorum 101, **103**

Race Relations Act [1976] 68–9
Race Relations Commission 66
raw materials 164
receipts 229, **232**, 237, 239
reception 78
recruitment **57**
   advertising 52
   applications 52–3

person specification **58**
selection 53–4
redundancies 56, 95
relocation grants 180–81
remittance advice slips 227–9, **231**, 236–7, 238
reprographics 79
reputation 33
resignations 56
retailing 170–71
retirement 56
revenue
    changes to 198
    sales 11, 12, 198, **202**, 204, 217, **220**
risk-taking 12, 24
Rover/BMW 71
royalties 153, 154, **157**

Sainsbury's 5–6
sales
    costs 217, **220**
    direct 46, 167
    Internet 5, 112, 167
    invoices 224–6, **231**, 234–5, 237
    objectives 31
    pricing policies 6, 7, 46, **89**, 198
    promotions 46
    revenue 11, 12, **14**, 198, **202**, 204, 217, **220**
satisficing 7–8, **9**, 176, **177**
selling *see* buying and selling
shareholders 12, 73, 174
shares
    cooperatives 161
    dividends 12–13, **14**, 73
    issue 73, 140–41, 142
    trading 141
SMART objectives 30–31
social awareness 33
Social Chapter [EU] 70
sole traders 128, **132**
    accounts 128
    advantages 131
    aims 128–9
    case study 185–7
    debt liability 130, 131, **132**
    decision-making 130
    disadvantages 131
    finance 72–3, 129–30
    management 95
    profits 130–31

    restrictions 128
    satisficing 6, 7–8, 128–9
    starting up 128
    taxation 128, 130–31
    training 131
span of control **96**
stakeholders 174, **177**
    customers 174, 176
    employees 175, 176
    local community 175–6
    owners 174, 176
    responding to 176–7
    suppliers 175, 176
strategies 7, **9**
strikes 62–3
subordinates **96**
supermarkets 5, 86, 170
suppliers, as stakeholders 175

take-overs 26
target segments 44
Tesco 5, 7
3M Post-it notes 90–91
Total Quality Management [TQM] 82, **85**
trade unions 62–4
Trades Union Congress [TUC] 64, **65**
training
    induction 54, **58**
    off-the-job 55
    on-the-job 55
    sole traders 131
Training and Enterprise Councils *see* Learning and Skills Councils
transport industry 171
Treetops 98–9, 104, 110
turnover *see* revenue

unemployment 52, 69–70

value added **165**
Value Added Tax [VAT] 128, 218, 225, 235
video-conferencing 110, 112
Virgin Group 29–30, 215
voluntary organisations 19, 20, **21**
Voluntary Service Overseas [VSO] 19

wages, minimum 69
work study methods **85**
worker cooperatives 159–60